VOICE OF THE PIONEER

VOLUME TWO

More first-person accounts from
CBC's best-loved radio program

Bill McNeil

Macmillan of Canada
A Division of Gage Publishing Limited
Toronto, Canada

Canadian Cataloguing in Publication Data

McNeil, Bill, date.
    Voice of the Pioneer

"Pioneers of all sorts—prospectors, scientists, homesteaders, teachers, bush pilots, and many others—tell their fascinating stories here, as they have told them on Canada's best-loved radio program."

ISBN 0-7705-1730-7 (v. 1).—0-7715-9808-4 (v. 2).

1. Voice of the Pioneer (Radio program)
2. Pioneers—Canada—Interviews. 3. Canada—Biography. I. Title.

FC25.M333 1978   971.06'092'2   C78-001537-1
F1005.M32 1978

Design by: John Murtagh

Macmillan of Canada
A Division of Gage Publishing Limited
Toronto, Canada

Printed in Canada

Dedicated to
LIAM and BRONWYN
The New Generation

Contents

Introduction

Memories are very precious to people, especially when they reach that period of life commonly referred to as old age. Just when this mystical state is arrived at is anybody's guess, but it should certainly not be gauged by any calendar. I meet more "old" people than the average person because of the nature of my work, and I think of very few of them as "old".

Things like cars and furniture and shoes get old. Radios get old, as do TV sets and all of the latest electronic gizmos. Very quickly they wear out and join history's trash pile, having served the purpose for which man created them. Some of them gain a second life with a cleaning and restoration, and may even gain an honoured place as "antiques", curious reminders of a way of life now past. However, when they no longer perform a useful function, most things are discarded and replaced by other newer and more useful items.

People, on the other hand, are different. Although the physical machinery slows down with the passing years, the mind and the spirit generally continue to grow. If one believes that experience is the best teacher, then one can also reasonably expect that, the older one gets, the more knowledge of life one acquires. In other times and cultures, old age was equated with wisdom, with the knowledge that the elders would pass on to those disadvantaged by youth and inexperience. Elders were respected for the knowledge that only they possessed.

Isn't it strange that in our "enlightened" age, we seem to shun contact with those of greater years? Perhaps we are afraid of facing up to our own mortality. How else could we be satisfied to see our elders pushed aside into ghettos for the aged? How indeed! Especially as we ourselves are the ultimate losers. We need their knowledge of life, their experiences, their capacity to love; and we need their memories.

We need to know the past if we want to capture the future. The aged are living books, willing and anxious to turn the pages of their own lives if someone will listen. In my experience, listening is a fascinating adventure.

How better can you find out what it was like to live at a certain time, or to take part in a particular event? One can sit with these participants of history, hear their words, and watch their eyes brighten with the memories of days of triumph and sadness. The excitement and adventure of those days of our history come alive again.

You share the experience of guiding a covered wagon over the unbroken expanse of the prairies, searching for gold in the North, or building a sod or log hut on virgin land. You feel the joy and the heartache of those lives, emotions that no movie can ever hope to match because these memories are real.

And you learn so much. I believe I could build a sod house myself now. A lady on the prairies told me how hers was constructed. I watched her carefully in my mind's eye, and the undertaking was a lot of work. I also feel I could build a log house. A man in Northern Ontario told me that I could do it once I mastered the corners. A lady from British Columbia told me not to build too high because that makes the house hard to heat. She and her husband made that mistake. I know what I can safely eat if I'm ever lost in the woods, and I know why the grain elevators on the prairies are shaped the way they are. I know how far a horse and wagon can comfortably travel in a day, and I believe I could tell you how to recognize silver or gold in the rocks. With a little practice, I could jig cod, cure animal skins, bake bannock, fly a small airplane, and run a dog team in the North. I could also fell a tree, scatter seed, and determine the best place to find blueberries. I could fight a forest fire, a prairie fire, or a fire in a coal mine.

Oh, there are so many things I could do, and I know how because I've had the privilege of hearing how from people who did. I could fillet a fish, skin a beaver, or keep warm in a snowbank at sixty below zero. I know how it feels to be black, yellow, or red, to belong to a visible minority. I know how it feels to make a fortune, and to lose one. But I know these things only because older people told me. Through their voices and memories, I have experienced more of life's experiences than one life can offer.

All I had to do was listen—something I learned to do in the mining town of Glace Bay, Cape Breton, where I grew up. People talked a lot in Glace Bay, and they told stories rather than read. Many couldn't read very well, as they had to leave school to work in the mines when they were nine or ten years of age. They grew up with a thirst for knowledge that expressed itself in the oral tradition. When they weren't talking, they were listening. When their day's work was done, they gathered on street corners and traded stories long into the night. As a small boy, I was "a little pitcher with big ears": and those men were superb storytellers, practitioners of an art they didn't learn from books—and the best of them were always the oldest.

In that society, retirement villas hadn't been invented, so the aged were with us in every home, and, I might add, they were much respected. Like one's elders, birth and death were respected as well. In fact, when the dead were "waked" in the family parlour, neighbours came in to comfort the bereaved and tell stories about the deceased.

In my contacts with the elders of our country, I am constantly amazed by the retention of their memories. Events and happenings long forgotten in the history books are often stored nowhere else but in the minds of those individuals who were there. These important events, it seems, were generally not considered important enough to be otherwise recorded at the time. So much of our history is lost this way. Family and community history is often lost forever when an elder dies. And part of our country's birthright is buried with them.

Have you ever heard someone say, "I wish I had taken a tape recorder and sat down with Grandma for a long chat. I meant to, but somehow I never got around to it." One day it is too late, and the memories are gone. That is a tragedy. The minds of those still alive contain memories that go back to a time when few people could write, when family history was passed on orally from one generation to the next; so it's easy to see why family history rarely found its way into print. Today, however, there's no excuse; the time to record those memories is now. We will not have the opportunity to do so forever.

I have my own list of thousands of names of people I would like to talk with. Most of these names are sent to me by people across the country who listen to my CBC radio program, "Voice of the Pioneer". These are people who feel that an aunt, or an uncle, or a grandparent, or someone else they know, would be a fascinating guest for the program, and I agree. I wish I could talk with them all; but that's not possible, of course. About all I can do in most cases is add their names to my very long list, which grows at a rate of five or so a week. That's approximately 260 a year, and if you'll remember that "Voice of the Pioneer" is now in its eighteenth year, you'll see that I have a problem. I worry about the names I won't get around to, and I hope that someone else will turn a tape recorder on. These memories are invaluable, and until they are recorded, only one person has them.

I want to thank all of those who sat down with me and endured my questions, but I also want them to know how much I enjoyed their company. They continue to provide me with some of the great moments of my life.

My thanks also to the CBC, which makes these moments possible. Thanks to my producer, Art Crighton, who never complains when my wanderings cause him extra work. Thanks, too, to my broadcasting companion of many years, Cy Strange, who has to fill two chairs while I am away.

I couldn't do it without the help and support of Eileen either, who has helped me put it all together while finding time to do all the other things that wives and mothers do.

My thanks to the good people at Macmillan—publisher Doug Gibson is not just a good man at his craft; he's the best. He has encouraged and helped so many Canadian authors that he might be at least eighty years old, but he's not. He's just forty, and he has brought with him the same kind of wisdom, enthusiasm, and knowledge from his native Scotland that his fellow countrymen brought as pioneers so many years ago.

Kathleen Richards, the editor who worked closely with me on this book, is slightly more than half Doug's age, and just over a third of mine, which only proves that there is no generation gap. Her enthusiasm for the material and her skill in working with it have also contributed to the final book.

Thanks, too, to those many pioneers who have contributed their memories not only in this book, but in the form of written books and articles of their own which will be invaluable to future generations. They include John Charyk, Margaret Arkinstall, Peggy Holmes, Hartley Trussler, Daniel Hill, Magne Stortroen, Erwin MacDonald, "Dude" Lavington, Mabel Halbert, Joe Garner, "Tiny" Peet, and Lorne Smith Eady.

Finally, I would like to express my gratitude to the pioneer cheese-maker of Stratford, Ontario, whose picture appears on the jacket. Frank Leslie is what we all wish to be like in our eighties. He has boundless energy and imagination. He never stands still for longer than a minute, and his good humour is infectious.

BILL MCNEIL
Toronto, Ontario

Frank McDougall Just Another Means of Travel

Frank McDougall combined his training as a forester with that of civil-service bush pilot to become the first flying Deputy Minister of Lands and Forests in the province of Ontario. After the First World War, the Ontario government began experimenting with leased war-assets planes in forestry work, and this led to the establishment of the Ontario Provincial Air Service in 1924.

The pilots were mostly young men who had learned to fly those early craft in the First World War, and they wanted to keep on flying when the war was over. Some were able to buy old planes from war assets, and they were willing to go anywhere and do anything just to stay in the air. Flying was still very new, and everyone was excited by its development.

Now, in 1924, I was a young forester doing surveys and other chores on ground, and when I'd look up and see those planes, so free, and moving so fast, I made up my mind that I, too, was going to fly some day. You see, the planes were first used for sketching out what the forest reserves looked like from the air. I was part of the survey team on the ground, which established check-points that would be used in conjunction with their drawings. This was long before aerial photography came into being.

I knew that as a forester and a surveyor, I couldn't compete in the business I was in unless I could fly. The airplane gave you command. It was a choice of walking through the woods at a mile an hour, or flying over them at a hundred miles an hour, as simple as that. The H-boats were getting phased out, too, in the early twenties, and the Moths were coming in, which was the first big breakthrough in flying over the old war-assets stuff.

The old Curtis HS2L war-surplus planes were used for this work around 1922, but they also had a machine called the Vickers Viking, which was a nice plane; but it had a great big front cockpit, and Jenkens, the observer, sat in there. Well, one nice sunny day, he was out sketching, and they hit one of

1

these down drafts, and he was nearly chucked out of the machine. He barely managed to catch his hand under the edge of the dashboard and save himself. This became a joke with everyone afterwards—how Jenkens almost got chucked out—but it terrified him so much that he never again sat in that big open cockpit without tying himself in with a long piece of rope.

A few years later, he was in one of the H-boats, tied in as usual, when the pilot thought he was going to crash into a set of raised railway tracks, so he deliberately brought it down into the lake. With the plane upside-down in the water, the result was that Jenkens nearly drowned before he could get his rope untied. I suppose that was an example of an early seat belt—not a very good one, but a seat belt nevertheless.

Stories like this one might give some credence to the idea that early flying was a haywire and "make-do" operation, but this wasn't so at all. The pilots of those machines were ex-war pilots, highly experienced, and devoted, some of them still flying despite serious war wounds. Jack Leach, for example, was a terrific pilot, even though he had lost a leg in the war.

Also, the mechanics were the best in the land, and I think that accounts for the great air-service record back then. They were quite often British-trained mechanics who had been through the war, and they brought their skills to peacetime work. They were never given the credit they deserved. They knew everything there was to know about those machines. They knew how to keep them flying—and flying safely. The publicity always seemed to go to the pilots rather than the guy who did the housekeeping. In the early days, the pilot and the mechanic always flew together, so I suppose the very fact that the mechanic knew he was going to be up there himself made him that much more careful.

The pilots, too, made sure that those planes were in good shape. They put them through all kinds of tests on their own. I remember one time Jack Leach took out one of the new all-metal Hamilton planes, which were a great deal heavier than the ones we'd been using up to then. This was in Sault Ste. Marie. Well, he took that thing up, and put it through the toughest tests he could dream up. He loved pushing those planes to the limit, especially if there was an audience on the ground. He'd fly straight up in the air, and then come diving straight down over the city, that plane rattling like a bucket of nuts and bolts, and the watchers on the ground terrified. But Jack only wanted to be sure that that plane could take the worst that man or nature could throw at it. Anyway, while all of this was going on, the mayor of the Sault rushed over to the airfield and grabbed hold of Jack's supervisor. "Get that maniac down out of there. . . . Get him down!" The supervisor said: "You're the one who's worried; you get him down!" Jack didn't come down till he was satisfied that plane was okay.

Flying was new. Most people had never even seen aircraft, and the stories of planes stunting and zooming were fresh in their minds. It was very difficult to get it into them that the aircraft was just another means of travel. Most said, "They'll never get me up in one of those things." By 1929 I had a licence, and as part of my job with the Department of Lands and Forests—as the Department of Natural Resources was then called—I would fly up to Algonquin Park. I found that the parks people there were terrified of planes, so whenever possible, I would make it a policy to talk them out of their fears and take them up for a short run. Gradually they came to appreciate that the plane was simply a faster means of transportation in doing their jobs. They could take off in the morning, fly a hundred miles into the bush, and be back at their desks by afternoon. In one morning they could do a job that had previously taken them a week.

At that time we surveyed a block of timber which stretched from Cochrane, Ontario, to James Bay to see if there was enough timber there to warrant building the Ontario Northland Railway. At the end of the summer, the results showed that there wasn't. They built the railway anyway.

In 1924 the Ontario government decided to buy a fleet of Moths and formally begin its own air service. The sole fault I could see with these planes was that, although they were two-seaters, there was only one set of controls, which meant that if anything happened to the pilot, you were out of luck. I kept insisting that dual controls were needed, and eventually I won. I think my judgement was vindicated later because of an incident at the Lakehead.

The pilot of one of our single-control planes unfastened his belt, presumably to pass a note to the passenger in the front seat. The plane hit a down draft, and he was chucked out and killed. The observer went down to his death, too, as there wasn't another control. I was flying around as a passenger in these planes, and, of course, I was learning a lot because of the chance I had with dual controls; in 1929 I got to be a pilot myself.

We stationed planes in Algonquin Park from 1931 to 1941, and they proved invaluable in many ways. After I was made Deputy Minister of Natural Resources with my headquarters in Toronto, I insisted on having a plane at Toronto Island Airport, so that ten minutes after I left my office, I could be in that plane, heading off to the forests. I could travel all the province in a matter of three days—something that couldn't be done as well in three months before the airplane. Also, if there were any hot spots—any forest fires—I could jump in the plane and be there in no time at all without disturbing anyone else.

As I flew, I kept learning more and more about the province until I knew the whole place like the back of my hand. I always felt that the plane was the best possible way to get around. It kept me mentally and physically alert, and fully in touch with all I needed to know. For instance, if I saw something down below that I wanted to know more about, I'd simply drop down and land and have a look. There was always a great sense of discovery in this. You could be seeing something that nobody had seen before. When you landed, you could have been standing where nobody had stood before.

Up until 1947 there had been only patchwork surveys, never a complete aerial forest inventory. Because of that 1947 survey, Kenting Aircraft came into being. They had their first contract with the Ontario government. After that, they branched out all over Canada, and then all over the world, doing aerial surveys.

Safety is the big factor in flying. You see, up to a thousandth part of a second, you're perfectly safe, and then suddenly you must make a decision, and you must act on it. Once you go beyond a certain point, you're in danger. I always felt that each pilot should always be aware of what the other is thinking. If one of them feels they're getting into something dangerous, they should say so immediately and there should be no argument. The slightest doubt on the part of either is reason enough to turn back.

That's the way I operated myself, and the other pilots I

flew with understood that. I remember a couple of occasions where that policy kept us out of trouble. It was mostly weather that caused the difficulties. I only had one forced landing that was caused by engine failure in the thirty-eight years I flew. I had just taken off when the engine cut out completely, but I was able to swing right back and land in a lake. Another time at the Sault, in a Moth, I stalled out of a sideslip—my own fault—and I busted the undercarriage all to blazes, but I was able to patch it up on my own and fly it back.

The only other occasion when I had an engine fall out was when I was taking off at Sudbury. It was a DeHavilland 61, a very modern, powerful biplane which carried eight people in the cabin and the pilot sat behind. It was like a gigantic Puss-Moth. Bill Hicks was flying and he was about to pull off the water when it sounded like we hit a stone wall. Bill, a navy-trained pilot, yelled to us in the cabin, "Stand by to abandon ship!" We looked out, and there was no engine. Both top engine mounts had torn off and the engine had swung down under the fuselage and was facing backwards. One of the propeller blades had sheared off completely. It was later found in the trees back behind the lake. Parts of the floats were chopped off, and a couple of front struts were gone. It was mashed up pretty badly. However, we were only in the process of taking off when it happened. A few minutes later, we'd probably be goners.

When I crawled out of that, I tried to figure what we could do. I cut one of the extra wires off one of the rudders and used it to replace the cross-bracing wire, which was broken, and shored it up with a stick. The front strut I replaced with a birch tree from the bush, which I jammed against the broken one and tied in with a piece of rope. We fooled around with the engine and got it back in place somehow or other, and when we finished, it was pretty hillbilly-looking, but I said to Bill, "Let's taxi around the lake a bit and see if everything holds together." It did, so we took off, and flew that thing back to the Sault.

That wasn't such an unusual thing to do back then. All of the pilots had to contend with things like that. If you broke a float while running on a rock, you'd patch it up somehow. You always carried wire and rope and other things for emergency patch-up jobs.

We didn't have radio in those days, but we had message

bags tied to blocks of wood and long streamers, so when we managed to get that plane back, we circled the hangar for a while, diving down a few times to indicate there was trouble. I tossed the message bag out, asking them to have a motorboat ready, as we had a busted undercarriage. We landed all right and taxied right in. That was the end of that.

A fellow by the name of Al Lloyd set up a radio system for aircraft that was the best in the world at the time. That enabled us to do a great many things we couldn't do before— such as mercy flights. Most people don't know it, but Ontario had one of the biggest air-ambulance services in the world. If a local doctor anywhere in the province, no matter how remote, said something was an emergency, we would fly the patient out. If there was no doctor, the pilot could use his own judgement on what was or wasn't an emergency. Many, many lives were saved with this service, and it gave those who had to go into the bush for long periods confidence that they were never alone. They had their radios, and the planes were on standby. The federal government set up an air search-and-rescue system, which included calling in the help of the provinces whenever they were needed.

We had excellent pilots—men who were absolutely solid and dependable. Some of them did everything exactly by the book. For instance, Terry, an Englishman, operated on a schedule doing all of his runs in the early part of the day so that he could be home in time for tea. Then there were the real adventurers, always pushing themselves and their aircraft to the limits, testing how far they could go, and what they could do.

Jack Leach with his one leg was one of these. One Sunday morning, he was stunting around with a DeHavilland 61 over Port Arthur. A large crowd gathered on shore to watch, and Jack was really getting into it. He brought it down and climbed into one of the new all-metal Hamiltons and took that up. He climbed, dove, and looped, and did all sorts of tricks. The bigger the crowd became, the more daring he got, until finally the show came to an end with the plane crashing into the lake. That was the end of the Hamilton, and the end of Jack Leach.

Jack had been a daredevil. There's no doubt about that, and so were many of the pilots who came out of the First World War. They were accustomed to flying in the days before parachutes, and their minds were conditioned to the risks because they had see many of their buddies go down in flames. When they came back, they were heroes in a glamorous profession. Because of this, they felt that they had to show off and perform for an audience even though those aircraft weren't designed for it.

There was a very narrow margin between flying speed and stalling speed, and the good ones realized that. These were the ones who survived, and these were also the ones who fanned out across the country from the Ontario Provincial Service and brought their skills to other companies and other airlines. They shared their experience with younger men while they changed from glamour boys to businessmen. These men always had a respect for their machines and they always said "we" as Lindbergh did when referring to themselves and their planes. I felt that way too. I was just the brain that was privileged to guide this marvellous machine that must be given the lion's share of the credit for opening up this country. The bush pilots and their small planes were the ones who kept on steadily pushing back the frontiers, making it possible for people to live in remote areas. They have to be counted as some of Canada's greatest, and most courageous, pioneers.

Mabel L. Halbert Before the Coming of the Telephone

On the original homesteads as well as on the more settled farms of eastern and central Canada, life gradually developed its own rhythm. There were always things that had to be done, and every member of the family was part of a working team. Mabel L. Halbert, born in 1897, has lived and worked all her life on a farm in Dufferin County, Ontario. Certainly during her childhood, the work on a farm was never done.

There was plenty of work to be done all summer and we children had our chores. Hens had the run of the barnyard and buildings, and often laid their eggs in unexpected places. It was the job of the children to find these eggs, but in spite of much vigilance, a hen would sometimes show up with a flock of ten or more chicks. She would have to be caught and put into a coop—a little wooden house with slats across the front, through which the chicks could go and run outside. It was our job to see that she was fed and watered every day, and to move the coop to fresh grass whenever necessary.

Many farmers kept geese, and the eggs were laid in early spring. We would take them away from the nest to a safe place in the house and cover them with a piece of wool to keep them warm. We marked and dated each egg so that each goose could set on her own. When the goslings were hatched, it was a big task to see that they were safe in the goose-house—in the event that a thunderstorm blew up, and also to keep the gander away!

In the fall, the neighbour women got together for the plucking of the geese. That was a messy, miserable job which was speeded up in a sociable atmosphere. From the down and feathers they made comforters, feather ticks, and pillows. My mother-in-law made me a beautiful comforter covered with paisley-patterned sateen when I married.

The calves had to be fed skim milk from a pail, and after being permitted to nurse a few days from their mothers, they strongly resented having their heads pushed into that pail, and hands were often bitten. Also, if a lamb was orphaned, it would have to be fed cow's milk from a bottle. They could become a real nuisance, but they were very lovable pets.

It was always special to see a colt arrive. We had one who needed help getting on its feet to nurse. Maud, its mother, and her colt were pastured in the orchard, and I was picked to be the nursemaid. One day Maud turned and bit me on the shoulder and, although I suffered only minor injuries, the colt had to fend for himself after that. I wanted nothing more to do with that chore. Pumping water for the horses and cattle was another big job. Some farmers would have a windmill for this endless pumping, but we didn't, and we children were responsible.

In those days we wasted nothing. If the kitchen refuse had any nutrients at all, it went into the swill pail for the pigs. In the summer the cows were brought from the pasture morning and evening and milked by hand. Then the milk had to be separated. It was very hard to turn the separator handle. You couldn't do it too fast or too slow and it would usually be done by two people. The skim milk was given to the calves and pigs; and the cream was cooled in the cellar, and churned once a week or so.

That could be a tedious job sometimes. I remember one time I churned for hours and hours, and when the butter came, it was some of the finest I had ever churned. When my brother came in to supper, I told him what a time I had had with it, but I added, "It's so good, though, that I think I'll pack a crock of it for showing at the Shelburne Fair." I did show it and was rewarded by winning first prize.

On our farm we always had a few acres of potatoes, turnips and mangels. Hoeing weeds from the potato patch was a summer job that was always waiting. Potatoes had to be hilled up to prevent sunburn, and we sprayed the bugs with Paris green, or they were picked off by the youngsters and put into a can. My father made a gadget for dusting the plants with poison, and we would walk up and down the rows, holding one end of this broom handle and shaking the poison out through the loose cheesecloth bag. Each potato would be picked off the ground at harvest, and put into a pail, which we'd lug over and dump into the waiting bag. They'd be stored loose in the cellar, where they were graded by hand, one potato at a time, and packed in ninety-pound bags which were sold.

Turnip seeds are very small, so they were sown thickly. When the seedlings were up, we had to thin them out with a hoe, leaving several inches between each plant for space to grow. These were harvested in the fall, but first we cut off the tops because they were good to eat as greens too. After that, one of the men would drive the horse and harrow over the patch to loosen the turnips from the ground. Then we children would pick them up and throw them into the wagon and ride on the full load to the barn, where we would toss them into the root house.

We also picked apples in the fall. The very early pioneers had planted fruit trees, so every farmstead had a fine orchard in my day. Climbing trees was a welcome change from the back-breaking potato and turnip harvesting. Just the same, though, it wasn't easy work. Winter apples were stored in barrels, but the fall varieties had to be peeled, quartered, and dried, and were used to make pies in the winter.

I clipped a poem about these pies from a 1901 *Farmer Advocate* magazine:

I loathe, abhor, detest, despise,
Abominate, dried apple pies.
I like good bread, I like good meat,
Or anything that's fit to eat.
But of all poor grub beneath the skies
The poorest is dried apple pies.

Give me the toothache or sore eyes
But don't give me dried apple pies!
The farmer takes his gnarliest fruit
'Tis wormy, bitter, and hard to boot,
He leaves the hulls to make us cough,
And don't take half the peelings off!

Then on a dirty cord 'tis strung,
And in a garret window hung.
And there it serves as roost for flies,
Until it's made up into pies!
Tread on my corns, or tell me lies,
But don't feed me dried apple pies!

Later on, of course, conditions were more sanitary.

My father took a screen from the fanning mill and suspended it from the ceiling just above the stove. My mother would lay out the peeled, cored, and quartered apples. She was very particular that not a trace of hull or peeling was left on her apples. Then the screen was lowered to within a few inches of the stove at night. In the morning it was raised high enough so that it didn't interfere with normal use of the stove. Each morning, this screen would be replenished with fresh apples as the drying ones were pushed closer together. This procedure would be repeated in the evening. When the dried apples were mixed with prunes, raisins, or figs bought from a store, they made very good pies, and at a fraction of the cost of using all store-bought fruit. Pie was a staple in all farmhouses. It was served at least once a day and no housewife would be caught dead without a pie in her house! One woman I remember made twenty pies every Saturday.

All the vegetables and salads we ate were grown in our own garden, which kept us busy every spare moment, although working it was very satisfying. Harvesting, pickling, and preserving the produce took up a great deal of a housewife's time in addition to the garden. We turned berry-picking time into a fun time by packing a picnic lunch and going out with neighbours. Some took their small babies along in a clothes basket.

Fuel trees were cut down with an axe and a saw for our heating, and sawed into stove-length pieces with a cross-cut saw by two of the men, one at each end. The wood was split and piled in the bush to dry all summer, and then brought into the woodshed before the snowfall. We did the daily splitting and filled the wood box for the kitchen stove after school. The knotty blocks were used in the front-room box stoves where the fire burned all night. The only heat we had in the bedrooms was that given off by the stovepipes that snaked through the rooms to the chimney. These, too, had to be cleaned on a regular basis or else the soot in them would catch fire. It was always a job that was dreaded. When the men put these pipes together again after the cleaning, there were a lot of unmentionable words from men who at all other times wouldn't think of using that kind of language. The ashes had to be taken out every day, and the ashes from the hardwood put in a leach and watered to extract the lye. When combined with tallow rendered from the fat of home-killed animals, this made soap. People who burned coal sifted the ashes to recycle any burnable bits left over, as coal was expensive.

We had no indoor plumbing then and toilets were outside privies, cold in winter and seldom visited at night. There would be chamber pots under all the beds. The lamps and lanterns had to be filled with coal oil, their wicks trimmed and chimneys shined daily. The cream separator also had to be washed and scalded every day. We had all kinds of other chores, but this will give a fair idea of what life was like back then.

Getting the family photo taken was a "must". It was an ordeal but an exciting one. All appointments were made personally for these sessions. A time was chosen when all the family members could be together. When the big day arrived, we'd dress up in our Sunday best, and we'd need two horse-drawn vehicles to take us all into town. The photographer's studio was fascinating with a variety of scenic backdrops lining the walls, and chairs, settees, and stools to accommodate all ages and sizes. The camera was mounted on a tripod and covered by a large black drape. After getting everyone into their positions, the photographer would duck in under the drape to peer through the lens and see that all was right. Keeping a pose and a pleasant expression wasn't easy and it was a relief when the camera would click. Then we would wait with excitement for the proofs to arrive, when we'd make our decisions on what prints we wanted and what kinds of frames would be best. Even though there was very little money, everyone managed by hook or by crook to find enough to pay for these pictures. We saved our pennies, too, to buy the frames for them.

Money wasn't wasted as there was so little of it. Children's clothes were made from the good parts of worn-out clothing from the older members of the family. Sugar and flour bags were used to make all sorts of things, such as pillow cases, aprons, luncheon cloths, petticoats, lining for clothes, and also quilts. Some of these would be coloured with dye, but at one time flour was sold in bags of blue-and-white or red-and-white check material which made up into many attractive articles of clothing and things like that. We children went barefoot in summer then, so every night feet had to be washed, and usually the washcloth would be a piece from a man's worn-out shirt.

The centre of community life was the general store. It had a big box stove and all sorts of things displayed on the shelves: ironstone chinaware, lamps, smoothing irons, pots and pans, tea kettles, and so on. It was a real feast for the eyes and the nose, with the big round cheeses and boxes and barrels of food. In a back room were kept ropes, wire, axe handles, kegs of nails, and tools of all types. It was a great place for the men to gather in the evening where they would discuss the news of the day and what went on in the neighbourhood.

But the coming of the telephone really opened up communication among rural people. There'd be twenty or more subscribers on each line, and when it rang, people would rush to take down the receiver and listen to the news or gossip. The telephone itself was a large box fastened on the wall. When the crank was turned, the operator would take your number and ring the special ring of whoever it was you were calling. Each subscriber had special combinations of short and long rings. One long ring would call all subscribers to the phones because this meant an emergency. One stormy Sunday, a minister had the operator ring the emergency ring, and when everybody had picked up the phones, he delivered his sermon.

Next came radio, powered by batteries. It was such a thrill to hear real live voices talking or singing. My father would listen so attentively. He said, "The time will come when we will be able to see these people as they perform as well as hear them."

Angus McGowan Forerunners, They Called Them

The Highland Clearances in the years after the 1745 rebellion in Scotland resulted in the settling of much of eastern Canada, including Prince Edward Island. Like many other descendants of those early settlers, Angus McGowan, born in 1906, of Montague, Prince Edward Island, retains strong memories of his family's past and his life in Canada.

The cruelties inflicted on those people are hard to believe today. When they were driven off the land, they had no place to go, except the docks, where they were packed in these leaky old ships, with not enough food and water, and sent off to the wilds of North America and Australia. When they got to P.E.I., it was like starting from scratch, as they had only a few possessions that they were permitted to take along.

Most of the groups didn't have doctors with them, so whenever anyone became ill, they were looked after by someone who knew a little bit of folk medicine. Most often this would be a woman—a "granny", as she was called. My great-great-grandmother, Anne MacDonald, was a "granny", and she delivered five hundred babies in her time. People would come from miles around to see her. This would be in the Belfast district of Prince Edward Island where the ship the *Polly* landed. There was a leader, Dr. MacAulay, with that group of settlers, who was a clergyman and a medical doctor, but when he died in 1827, there was a period of fifteen years before they got another doctor—a man named Muir, who came from the Isle of Skye in 1842. There's no written record of what my great-great-grandmother and some of those early pioneers did. It's simply been passed down orally from one generation to the next.

The Indians who lived here at the time helped them a lot. Since there was no medicine, the Indians taught them how to get certain things from the bark of trees and from roots in the ground. Those were the Micmac tribe, and one would have to wonder what those early settlers would have done without them. They taught them many things, including how to build their log houses. They got along very well with the settlers, and there doesn't seem to be any record of trouble as there was in New Brunswick and Newfoundland.

Lord Selkirk was the man who led the first settlers to Prince Edward Island. You hear his name mostly in connection with the settlement in Manitoba, but he came here first, some years before his journeys to the West. Our family came in 1803 when Selkirk brought the settlers on three ships: the *Polly*, which took about three hundred from Skye; the *Dykes*, which loaded at the Isle of Mull; and the *Oughton*, which loaded at South Uist, with a bunch of Scottish Catholics, many of whom stayed on Prince Edward Island, but a lot of them eventually went to Cape Breton. Most of those settlers faced nothing but trees. The only exceptions were those who came on the *Polly*, which landed in a cove where the French had tried to establish forty or so years before, but finally gave up. The *Polly* settlers found some old homes still standing, along with a church and a ready-made cemetery. That whole area is now called Selkirk Park.

The other settlers had to make do with tents, which they learned to make with the help of the Indians. They stayed in those till they got log houses. Their first winter was the worst. One ship carrying supplies didn't arrive because it went down, and they had to survive until the spring on clams they dug from two or three feet under the ice. Most of them made it till the warm weather.

Those early pioneers were a very hardy lot. They had to be! They were the ones who had survived the sickness and the hunger on board the ships bringing them, and although they didn't realize it at the time, they were better off coming here, despite all the hardships they had to endure. Back in Scotland they had been little better than slaves, working for a landlord and barely scratching a living from the soil. However, they really loved that land, and they were literally torn away from it—burned out, in many cases.

They were scared of the forests, which they had never seen before. Everything was so unfamiliar. Naturally a lot of tears were shed, and they sang sad songs, and dwelt a lot on their unfortunate plight. But here they were free for the first time, and they owned their own land, also for the first time. They were free to speak their Gaelic language, wear their tartans, and play their bagpipes, all of these things forbidden in Scotland after the 1745 rebellion.

Then, when they got here, their beginnings were so hard, they didn't have time to realize that they were much better off. They persevered, though, and re-established a life that contained all the things they missed from back home—the *ceilidhs*, the singing and dancing, and above all, the language. When I was growing up, before and during World War One, and for a long time after, Prince Edward Island was more like Scotland than Scotland itself. The people were very close and there were always great parties. Anything and everything was an excuse for a get-together. The young people would have "fudge parties" where we'd get a pile of sugar and make fudge, and that would lead to dancing and singing and sessions of telling ghost stories.

Everyone told ghost stories back in those days. I had an old grand-aunt who looked after us for our mother at times, and she had a great collection of ghost stories. She would scare the life out of us so that we couldn't sleep, but we loved them. We'd constantly be on her to tell another and another. Now, some people think that ghosts are nonsense, but I'm not so sure. She told us, for example, about these two brothers, my grand-uncles, by the name of Murchison back in 1880. One was the captain of a ship and the other was the mate. One time they had to stop in New York on the way from Europe to P.E.I. One of the crew, a man called MacLean, came to them and said he had a vision that they would be shipwrecked on the way from New York, and he described just how it was supposed to happen. He was so convinced that this was true, he wouldn't go with them. When the ship left New York without him, sure enough, when they were passing the coast of Newfoundland, the ship went down exactly where he had said it would. That's not a story. That's a fact.

The Scots were great believers in the spiritual, and they were forever on the lookout for signs that things were going to happen. Forerunners, they called them. There was a man who lived around here who was always called on to make the caskets when someone died. Well, there was one period of months when nobody died, and his services weren't needed. He was a farmer, and he didn't get any money for making them. It was simply something that had to be done and he did it. Well, one day he woke up feeling very depressed, and after he had breakfast, the first thing he did was go outside where he kept some dried lumber, and he began building a casket. When his wife asked him why, he said he didn't know, but that he just felt it had to be done. Before he was finished, a wagon pulled up through his gate, and his neighbour came and told him that a member of his family had died during the night and he needed a casket. Now that, too, is a true story.

There is a story of the burning ship that's still seen around here, and every time it appears, a lot of people see it. I never saw it, but I know lots who did, including my own brother, James, who is a Presbyterian minister. He was at River John in Nova Scotia when he saw it. He said it was definitely a flaming ship and that he saw it plain as day. Another man on the other side of the river, Donald Campbell, confirmed that he saw it, too, and in the same place, at the same time. Another man I know, captain of the Wood Island ferry, once saw it in the Northumberland Strait. Some say it's just something that's caused by the setting sun hitting the water, but that's not true. Too many reputable people have confirmed that it was a burning ship, and what's more, it still appears from time to time.

The Scots seem to have more sensitivity to things such as that. It's a part of their early strong religious tradition, I guess. Over where my family came from, the Isle of Skye, the Presbyterian religion was a very strong influence in the lives of the people. My great-grandfather's brother, John McGowan, was living on Skye back in 1820, and he decided he wanted to join the Baptist Church. The Presbyterians ordered his landlord to kick him off his land, and the landlord did just that. Another man, a schoolteacher by the name of Sam MacLeod, ran into the same thing. When he joined the Baptists, he was fired from his job, and told to clear out of the schoolhouse as fast as he could. He asked if he could take his chair with him as he had bought it himself. When he was told that he could, he said, "I guess I'm luckier than kings and queens, because when they get tossed out, they can't keep their thrones." He came to P.E.I. in 1829, and he brought his chair with him. It's here in our museum, which tells the whole story of how the various Scottish families came here, why, and when. I have great respect for those ancestors of mine, because they sure made a great island out of this place.

Bob Bowman A Radio System for Canada

The great mass-communications systems we take for
granted today had their beginnings a mere sixty-five
years ago when radio was invented. Until that time most
people had lived in a state of isolation, depending chiefly
on newspapers to tell them what was happening in other
parts of their own country and the rest of the world. For
Canadians, a small population spread out across a vast
expanse of land, radio was a godsend; and it became more
important than the railroad in linking our country
together. For the first time, Canadians in one province
could hear what their neighbours were saying thousands
of miles away, and they could hear it the same day that it
was said. Today, with one electronic marvel after
another, it is hard to appreciate the miracle that radio was
when it first entered Canadian households in the 1920s.
Bob Bowman remembers the earliest days of the CBC and
its development.

I was a very young boy at the time, about ten years old,
and my family lived in Ottawa. One of my neighbours, Grant
McNeil—who later became one of the founders of the CCF—
was then a civil servant with the federal government. He had
built a crystal set which he was very proud of and he was
showing it to us children. This was around 1920 when the
Department of Marine and Fisheries was experimenting with
a small radio station called "OA". He let me listen on his
headset, and I could hear these voices coming out of the air—
just like magic. I was so excited by the whole thing that I got
Mr. McNeil to show me how to build a crystal set of my own.

The most expensive part was the Brandes headphone,
which cost eight dollars. The coil I made myself by winding
copper wire around and around on a circular oatmeal box.
This would then be shellacked, and fitted with a part called a
"slider", and, of course, the little crystal, which cost a quarter. That's about all there was to it, but I can tell you it worked
like a charm.

One night shortly after I built it, I brought in not only the
Ottawa station OA, but also a small station built by the son of

lumber baron J. R. Booth. It was his latest toy, but he would bring the orchestra from the Château Laurier out to his house to play. Well, I heard this on my little crystal set, and I also heard KDKA, in Pittsburgh, along with WGY, WJZ, and WBZ, which were other stations in the United States. The next day nobody would believe me, as crystal sets were only supposed to bring in local stations.

Another night, when I should have been asleep, my father caught me listening to my set, and he was furious, as he didn't have any use for this new-fangled thing called "radio". He was editor of the Ottawa *Citizen*, and as far as he was concerned, newspapers were the only thing. I said, "Dad, please come here, and listen. I've got Chicago!" Well, he didn't want to, but he finally put the earphones on and he heard it too. He was enthralled, and began to take an interest in radio for the first time.

He quickly realized that unless the government smartened up and nationalized radio, our radio would belong to the Americans. NBC and CBS already had an interest in stations in Montreal and Toronto. Dad could see that unless we did something soon, they'd have it all.

He began writing editorials about the need to nationalize radio in Canada, and he received support from a group called "The Canadian Radio League", Alan Plaunt, Graham Spry, and Margaret Southam. Gradually the movement to keep our radio Canadian spread right across Canada, and Mackenzie King appointed the Aird Commission to look into the subject. My father was one of the three members.

This led to the nationalization of radio and the establishment of the CRBC [Canadian Radio Broadcasting Commission]. The Conservatives under R. B. Bennett were responsible for doing that, because, although King appointed the original Royal Commission, they were defeated before radio was nationalized in 1932.

Now, I had become an avid radio listener, right from my first crystal set all through school and university, and felt I knew something about it, so when I became a reporter on the Ottawa *Citizen*, they had me do radio and the CRBC as part of my beat. I would go out and see the CRBC chairman, Hector Charlesworth, every day to find out what was happening, and it became apparent that the system wasn't working the way it should.

The Conservatives made the mistake of doing their own thing instead of following the Aird Report, which recommended a board of governors and a general manager. Instead, they opted for three controllers—Charlesworth, Steele, and Maher. This system didn't work from the start.

Then they brought over a Canadian named Gladstone Murray, who was working with the BBC in England, to study the system, ascertain what was wrong, and make recommendations. I got to know Murray very well in my role as reporter, and later I went to Britain and joined the BBC myself. I saw him a great deal over there, and together we drew up plans for what would happen should the day come when the CRBC would be dissolved and replaced by the CBC, with Murray as general manager. We felt sure this is what would happen—and it did, in 1936. He came to Canada, and shortly after, I returned too, and joined the staff of CBC in December of that year.

The CBC had inherited a few stations from the old CRBC, in Vancouver, Winnipeg, Toronto, Ottawa, and Moncton. These had originally belonged to the Canadian National Railways, but they gave them up when radio was nationalized. The mandate of the CBC was to bring national radio to all Canadians, so they had to seek the help of privately owned stations to broadcast national programs. These private stations were called "affiliates".

Now, without this system, those out in the small communities wouldn't have had good Canadian radio because most private stations wanted to make money, and they could do this only by concentrating their efforts in the big population centres. The smaller places would be left with what they could pick up in the air, which would be mostly American programs. Therefore, as early as 1936, the great percentage of the Canadian population had access to good, national Canadian programs through the CBC.

It was only night-time operation at first, beginning at 6 P.M. Eastern Time, so the West got kind of short-changed, as recording was difficult and we didn't have delayed broadcasts. Our facilities were meagre—very often just hotel rooms. If you were doing a drama, and needed the sound of a waterfall, oftentimes it would be simply the flush of the toilet. A forest fire would be simulated by one of the actors crunching a piece of cellophane from his cigarette package in front of the microphone. Maybe it was primitive, but it worked, and it was exciting and fun for all who were involved, and also for the listeners who knew how to use their imaginations.

One of my first jobs in 1936 was to do a Christmas broadcast in Callander, Ontario, of the Dionne quintuplets, who were then two years old. That's memorable for me, as Dr. Dafoe, who was always depicted as a kindly man, kept me and my technician waiting for hours outside in the freezing weather while he had his Christmas dinner.

It's also memorable because of the way these "live" remote radio broadcasts were done. Every word I said was written for me in Toronto, and every word Dafoe spoke was written in Toronto, too. All we were required to do was stand outside in the sub-zero temperatures and read it. I guess the broadcast executives of those days didn't figure on anyone except themselves having any brains.

I remember being sent down Hollinger Mine to do a broadcast, where everything was written for me by someone who had never been down a mine himself. It was utter drivel and had no relation whatsoever to what was going on around me. However, I had to do what I was told.

In 1937 we expanded to daytime radio, beginning at noon, and by this time I had been made Director of Special Events. The first thing I did was to abolish the practice of scripting those actuality broadcasts. It was also about this time that a group of studio musicians in Toronto were asked to fill an empty spot on a short-term basis for the network. That "short term" lasted for twenty-two years, because those musicians, Bert Pearl and his Happy Gang, became an immediate hit, and were the first real stars of the CBC. Besides Bert there was Bob Farnon, Blaine Mathe, Kay Stokes (at the organ), and announcer Herb May, and that group expanded as the years passed. They were great. Those were the experimentation days of the CBC. Everyone had ideas, and we were willing to try everything.

For the CBC, 1939 was a big year and a year of change. The war clouds were thickening over Europe, but a beloved King George VI and Queen Elizabeth nevertheless went ahead with a long-planned visit to Canada. It was the first Royal visit, an exhilarating event for all Canadians, and a real challenge for the CBC to cover as they crossed the country by train. We had to figure out how to do this, as it had never been done anywhere before. We had to cover a full thirty days of events over thousands of miles, in two languages, leapfrogging broadcast teams and constantly inventing ways of doing things that had never before been done.

When that was done with—and very successfully, too—we had to do something else that had never been done before. We had to broadcast a war! There was nobody to ask, "How do I do this?"

As Director of Special Events, I was the first to be sent overseas, along with my engineer, Art Holmes. We went on the first troopship with the First Canadian Division, and started sending reports back home immediately. Those were the days before tape recorders, so Art had to invent a mobile studio to carry the bulky disc-recording machines around to where the action was. We were in London all through the Blitz and we were even down at Dieppe when the Canadian forces were almost totally wiped out in a German trap.

We had Canadian reporters such as Matthew Halton, Bert Powley, and Peter Stursberg covering the action all over Europe, reporting directly to the listeners back home. From the beginning to the end of World War Two, the CBC was there, and I believe that that is really when our public broadcasting system came of age and became an integral part of Canadian life. That's when we gained acceptance and learned our true role as a medium—to provide information along with enter-tainment.

Magne Stortroen A Cheque for Ten Cents

One of the first obstacles an immigrant to Canada had to overcome was the unbelievable size of the country. For the prairie settler, a train journey of endless days and nights followed by more days by horse and wagon led to his final arrival at a spot in the middle of nowhere. For young men seeking adventure and fortunes in other parts of Canada, the disillusionment was even greater. Magne Stortroen of Pottsville, Ontario, remembers his first Canadian experience as a lumberman.

I was twenty years old when I left Norway for Canada with my friend Karl in 1923. There had been some publicity in the newspapers about the opportunities in Canada for work at high wages and chances to take a homestead of one hundred sixty acres for very little money. Farmland in Norway was expensive and hard to come by. One hundred sixty acres sounded very impressive. I did not know of anyone who had come back broke and disillusioned.

So this adventure was to be my opportunity. There were maybe two or three hundred going aboard this very boat. There were eleven hundred immigrants altogether on the ship which brought us over, men and women of all nationalities. Our first glimpse of Canada was Quebec City, where we passed through customs before boarding the train for a twenty-four-hour trip to Timmins in Northern Ontario.

In the old-style immigrant coaches the seats were wood, built to a contoured form with narrow wood slats. Above every two seats and above the windows along the length of the coach was a wide wooden shelf about three by six feet. It was hinged on the wall and kept up during the day by two chains, which supported it when it was let down for sleeping. There was enough room for two slim fellows to sleep on it, if they were good friends.

Soon after we arrived in Timmins, Karl got a job underground at the Hollinger Mine, while I was working on the surface with about fifteen other men, shovelling gravel into four-wheeled wagons for $3.76 a day. That did not seem such a great deal after all the "get-rich-quick" stories we had heard back in Norway. It was not long before Karl was complaining about his job underground. So after twelve days of working for the mine we both hired on at the employment office in Timmins to work in the bush for seventy dollars a month plus board in a lumber camp near Iroquois Falls. We had both worked in the bush at home, and Karl had worked in bush camps in the United States. We went to the Hollinger office and collected our pay.

The next morning we packed all our worldly goods into a suitcase and packsacks and boarded the early train for Iroquois Falls, about forty miles away. Since the railway was the only means of travel in Northern Ontario in 1923, that is how we got to our destination on a sunny day late in September.

After inquiring at the company's office and showing our slip for employment, we were told that the camp we were hired for was fifteen miles out in the bush, and that we had better wait for the "mail car" later that afternoon. The ride on the mail car was an unforgettable experience. Besides the driver's cab, there was only a platform or plank floor approximately eight feet by twelve feet with no railing or fence around it. After three cardboard boxes were loaded, the driver mumbled something and motioned us to get on. So we threw our packs and suitcases onto the car, climbed aboard, and sat on the packsacks. After we passed the big bridge over the river we were in the bush, but here it had been cut over and just some small trees were left.

Well, the rails ahead were really something to see. They looked more like crooked spruce poles laid down. As the car sped on over little gullies and curving around the bigger stumps, I fully expected it to jump off the rails at any time. It would have been so much better if there had been a post or a rope or something to hold onto. At last we got into bush that had not been cut, and not long after that we stopped at some rough log camps.

One of two long buildings was the sleeping camp, we could see, as the door was open. The other was the cookery and dining hall all in one. A man came out of a smaller building which proved to be the office, serving also as a storehouse for blankets, clothes, tobacco, and so on. He went over to talk with the driver and then they motioned us to get off the car.

After throwing our packs on the ground, we stopped and

took a closer look at the place. It was a rough-looking yard with many stumps between the buildings. A grindstone with a hand crank was sitting on an iron rod between two poles leaning against the sleeping camp, and two washtubs rested upside down against a stump. About fifteen yards behind the sleeping camp was a building with a large pile of hay bales beside it which was apparently the stable.

The man who had been talking to the driver was the clerk for the camp, and he came over and spoke to my partner. We walked with him into the office and gave him the slips of paper from the employment office which stated we were hired to work for seventy dollars a month with board; bed was not mentioned. After writing down our names, he gave us each two grey blankets and walked over to the sleeping camp with us. He showed us two empty bunks, one top and one bottom, then left us standing there. We were so appalled by the accommodation we did not say a word.

The building was about sixty feet long and made out of spruce logs with the bark left on. In some places the moss between the logs had fallen out, or maybe had been pushed out to provide ventilation as I found out later. There were only a couple of small windows in the whole camp, each about sixteen by twenty inches, one window at the far end of the building and the other near the door. Under it was a shallow sink or trough, three to four feet long, made of two-inch planks, and also two washbasins turned upside down in this larger sink. On a shelf there were two water pails with dippers in them for drinking.

The drain from the sink consisted of two planks nailed together in a V-shape passed through a hole in the wall. The water ran onto the ground about five or six feet from the entrance. Fortunately the ground was sloping away but it would be a mess later, especially come spring. The two wash-tubs against the stump outside were for washing clothes. Rather limited facilities to allow fifty or sixty men to keep clean, we thought, and September 23 was still early in the log-cutting season.

The sleeping quarters were something else. On one side of the building was a solid bunk along one wall with a piece of board as the only division between each man, all sleeping with their heads to the outside wall. On the other side the bunks were the same except for the eight-foot space allowed for washing in the sink. The floor space between the bunks was about seven feet. In the centre of the floor was a stove, much like a large oil drum on its side, supported by four short legs to kept it off the rough board floor. The stove took four-foot wood, and one man kept the fire going all night in every camp. The final touch was haywire strung from one end of the camp to the other for the men to hang their wet socks and shirts on when they came in from the bush.

As there was still lots of time until supper and no one was around yet, we spread the blankets on the empty bunks and put our packs on the bunks. Then we took a walk along one of the trails into the bush. For a forest that had never been touched or cut by man, it was not very impressive. There were a few spruce trees about eighteen inches in diameter, but most were only a foot thick or even less.

We watched two men working for a while, then turned back towards the camp again, wanting to be there to observe the men as they came in. Karl told me that except for the clerk talking to him he had heard nothing but French spoken. I still had difficulty in recognizing one language from the other. The only two words I was sure of when we landed in Quebec City were "yes" and "no". Since we had associated and lived only with other newcomers (or "greenhorns" as we were often called by other fellow Scandinavians who had been here longer and could speak some English), we had not learned much English.

We did not have long to wait until the men started to come in from the bush. We sat on our bunks and watched as they came in. Some men would wash their hands, but many could not be bothered standing in line since there were only two basins for them all. Karl said to me, "I think we came to a camp where everybody is lousy."

Some of the men were lining up outside the cookery waiting for the supper bell. The bell was a steel rod bent to a triangular shape and hung on a piece of haywire while another piece of steel was used to hit it. You could easily hear it half a mile away. When the bell sounded it was like the signal for a race and not just a meal. Half the fellows were running, dodging, or jumping over stumps—and no stump was less than two feet high—on the way to the cookery. I still don't know why, as there was room for everybody to sit at one time. When we got there we stopped just inside the door until the man in charge motioned us to take two empty seats at the farthest table. The tables were made of dressed lumber with oilcloth on top and long benches on each side. The food was steaming hot with more variety than I had ever seen before on one table. However, there were no fancy dishes. The plates and cups were tin. Jams, syrup, and molasses were served in three-pound tins.

At the table the men were not allowed to talk except to ask to have things passed to them. The cook and helpers all wore big white aprons and had shirt-sleeves rolled up to the elbows. A large man was walking up and down between the tables to see that empty dishes were filled up, and also to keep order and enforce the no-talking rule. He always had a big butcher knife in his hand, but I don't know why, except perhaps to lend weight to his authority to enforce the no-talking rule.

The only noise heard was fifty or sixty men cutting their meat and potatoes on tin plates, and men eating soup out of the small, deep tin plates, some in a very noisy, slurpy manner. There were louder noises from the kitchen, of big pots, pans, and kettles being emptied and moved about. Then, of course, there was the steady going back and forth with the empty and refilled dishes. So it was a long way from being a quiet dining room in spite of the no-talking rule.

From my place at the table I could easily observe the big fellow with the butcher knife in his hand, André, walking back and forth. Clearly here was a man who would not step off the road for anybody. He was not particularly tall but was solidly built with a short neck and a collar about size eighteen. His face was not easily forgotten either, with a nose sort of flattened and pushed to one side and a wide scar on one cheek. He had a generally weather-beaten appearance and forearms tattooed up to the elbows.

Two men near us started to talk and as soon as he noticed, the hand with the butcher knife came up high over his head, and he shouted loudly over the noise, "Shut up!" It became much quieter and I never forgot what "shut up" meant after that.

Karl and I went to see the foreman after supper. He wanted us to cut sixteen-foot logs on contract at four or five cents a piece depending on the size. He said all the monthly rated jobs were filled just now and he would show us a cutting area next morning.

After Karl explained this to me in Norwegian we looked at each other. This was something we had not thought about. We had already counted that if we could stick to the job for seven months at seventy dollars per month, we ought to have about four hundred dollars clear. That was a lot of money. This new proposal confused us, but the thought went through my head that maybe this way we could make even more money. Karl said, "We don't have a choice. We have to take his offer or just walk out." So we agreed, and the clerk issued us tools for the job. He pointed out that these tools would be charged against us, and when we returned them we would be charged rent for them. If we lost them we would pay full price, so Karl told him he had better keep them until morning.

Outside the camp there was a fellow carrying water with two pails from the small creek just behind the cookhouse and dumping it into one of the washtubs to wash some dirty socks and a shirt. The scene inside the camp that evening has stayed with me over all these years, and always will. It seemed most fellows smoked a pipe, and a good many of them were smoking "shag", a home-grown tobacco from southern Ontario sold in bundles of full-length leaves. The objectionable part was the strong smell and the way my eyes smarted from the smoke, even though I was used to smoking tobacco myself. Some of the men were playing cards, a few of them with their shirts off, but matches were the only things I saw changing hands, the big box variety that were in general use at that time.

There was a fire in the camp stove in spite of the fairly warm September evening, and the most obvious reason for the fire was the lines filled with dirty socks and underwear, and shirts wet with sweat. Some men were mending socks or patching pants and shirts. The lighting was provided by a coal-oil lamp which sat on a shelf above the sink and another at the far end of the camp. There was also a storm lantern that I later found out was used by the teamsters when they went out to feed their horses late in the evening and early in the morning between 4:30 and 5:00 A.M. Some of the men had candles at the heads of their bunks. Karl and I had a deck of cards and were playing too, but mostly we just observed what was happening.

Suddenly Karl said to me, "Look at those three fellows in the far end." The lighting was poor, of course, but there was no mistaking that two of the men had their shirts off and we observed that they were picking lice from their underwear and from under their armpits and throwing them on the floor. The third man was rubbing some salve on one of the other men's backs.

Karl said, "Well, if every man is not lousy yet, he will be before long. I'm going to talk to the foremen. No doubt they have some dynamite here that they use when they make roads: maybe he will let me have one stick."

I knew they used dynamite for blasting rocks or stumps, but I didn't have the slightest idea what Karl had in mind. In a short while he was back. He sat down on the bunk with a smile, pulled a stick of dynamite from his pocket, and proceeded to take the paper from it. What was inside was like oily, sticky sawdust. He sprinkled this along the boards that served as a division between his bunk and his neighbour's, and said that this would keep lice out of his bunk. Then he did the same to my upper bunk. The mattress was the same type as the type as the army used in their barracks, about two inches thick, and would roll up into a compact bundle. We had no pillows, but the packsack served nicely for that and Karl was liberal with the dynamite there. Having taken these precautions we felt better about lying on the bunk.

About nine-thirty the "bull cook" came into camp (the bull cook was the man who kept the fires going all night), put some more wood in the stove, and, after shouting something to the men, proceeded to turn out the lights. In about five or ten minutes all was quiet. Everybody slept in his underwear, which was mostly heavy wool. I had the upper bunk but the heat and smell up there was too much to let me sleep, so I pushed some moss out from between the logs near my head to let in some fresh air and at last I went to sleep.

We were wakened at five-forty-five the next morning by the same "bell" that called us to supper. I had a bad headache when I awoke, and I mentioned this to Karl. He said, "Yes, I have one too. It's from the dynamite, but it won't last long after we get out in the fresh air." He proved to be right. Shortly after six the bell sounded again, this time for breakfast. The breakfast table was just as lavish with food as the supper one had been. Piles of fried bacon on big plates, ham, eggs by the dozen, fried and boiled, porridge and other cereal, pies, cakes, jams, and plums. The tea, coffee, and milk were all served in big white enamel jugs. The milk, of course, was canned and some was diluted so it tasted like fresh milk. Everyone had a hearty appetite. One man ate six hard-boiled eggs, and a number of other things besides.

After breakfast we went back to camp, and prepared to go into the bush. A short time later the foreman came into camp, and told my partner that he had asked the cook to prepare a lunch for us, and as soon as we were ready we were to go to the office, get our tools, and then head out to the bush. We would not be back until suppertime. I went over to the cookery and a fellow there gave me a paper bag and two tin cups in a small pail that had once held three pounds of lard. This was to serve as our kettle for making tea or coffee.

I later learned that there was a camp every five miles of similar size to the one we had just left. Well, we walked along the track the mail car had gone on, and after about two miles or more we went into the bush and walked for five or ten minutes. The foreman stopped and talked to Karl, pointing to some trees that had slash marks. They formed some line or boundary. Then the foreman left us standing there, looking at each other and at the bush. A log cutter would call it rather poor bush but it was a nice clear morning and we were good and warm from carrying our tools and our fast walk; so we took our shirts off and put our clothes and lunch in a safe place near a big tree.

We cut as a team rather than individually, and we went at it with all the vigour and skill we could muster just to see how we would make out. We had to clear a skid road for the skidder's horse, and the logs had to be near enough to put the chain on when he came to pull them out. The skidder was on contract too.

After we noticed it was twelve o'clock, I made a fire while Karl went to look for a hole in the swamp where he could get some water. The lunch was very simple—a loaf of bread made by the camp cook, a chunk of salt pork, and a piece of bologna with some tea. We ate everything there was, but saved a little tea for later on. The afternoon went as fast as the morning, and as we did not want to be late for supper, we hid our tools and started back. We heard the supper bell ring before we reached camp but there were plenty of eats left for us.

After supper I decided to wash a pair of socks. I had stepped into a deep hole in the swamp, so I washed my socks and hung them outside to dry. Later we both went over to the clerk and Karl got a pair of bushman's pants, as he had torn his pretty badly during the day. I took out a heavy lumberjack shirt. It was more insurance against the weather, as we were about two and a half miles from camp and had no place to take shelter. Since it was getting dark, I went outside to bring in my clean socks but someone had already taken them.

The next morning before we started to cut, we counted what we had cut the first day; at 168 logs it was less than we thought we had cut. The way we had worked, we thought we should have done better. When we were having lunch Karl said, "I suppose the foreman had to come this far to find us the poorest piece of bush they have. It looks to me like they don't want us here at all." "Well," I said, "except for the meals I would not mind being out of here."

But we went back again, and late that afternoon were hard at it when the foreman came to see how we were doing. Karl talked with him, and Karl told me when he left that he had asked the foreman to count our logs, and that we would like to leave the next day. He had told Karl that that was not his job, but he would send the scaler (the man who counts wood in the bush camp), who, he said, was not far away. We were determined not to be late for supper again, so we cut a few more logs, tidied up our skid way, and counted our logs—358. We took our tools and headed back to camp.

Once there, we handed in our tools to the clerk and Karl asked him if there was any chance of transportation out the next day. He was told the mail car would be going out about suppertime. That evening as we played cards we looked at those men who worked so hard and lived in what we thought were miserable conditions. I had been in Canada less than three weeks and could not help thinking of the stories we had heard back in Norway and even more on our way over on the boat.

Well, here we were, facing life and conditions as they really were. The great opportunity to make a fortune looked pretty slim. We decided to walk out instead of waiting for the mail car. We could be back in town by noon, we thought, if we started shortly after breakfast. The next morning we packed our bags right after breakfast and when the men had gone into the bush, we went to see the clerk. He told us that the scalers counted our logs and there were nine less than we had said, but he had to go by the scalers' report. Well, we were not about to show him he was wrong, not for a five-mile walk and thirty-six cents, so Karl told him to keep the logs. After he had deducted for our meals, shirt and pants, and rent for tools, he handed us each a cheque. Karl's was for fifteen cents, and mine was for ten cents.

I have always regretted cashing that cheque; it would have been a memorable souvenir. We went back to camp, picked up our packs, and started walking down the railway. The optimism and ignorance of youth are not easily discouraged. We were off to seek our fortune again. Who knew what we might find? This was a big country, and we had only just started to explore its possibilities.

William Heeney Father of Frozen Food

Today's frozen-food industry is gigantic; and the fast-freezing of fresh food is still considered the best and easiest way of preserving food. The industry, however, is still a relatively young one, having been first introduced to the public in 1932. Much of the pioneering and development of frozen foods was done right here in Canada by young William Heeney of Ottawa, who had become acquainted with Dr. Clarence Birdseye, a young American scientist who was working on a problem.

I first met Dr. Birdseye while I was working in Philadelphia. He was then employed by the Port Authority of New York who wanted him to find a solution for the deplorable conditions at the Fulton Street Fish Market at the time. The smells around there were overpowering, due to decomposed fish and other things. In connection with that work he went to Labrador and set up a small laboratory right alongside the water where he could catch his own fish—in other words, get them as fresh as possible—through a hole in the ice. So, at forty degrees below zero, he would be pulling these fish out of the water and throwing them beside him on the ice. By the time he got them inside his lab they were usually frozen solid because of the low outside temperature.

Now the thing he noticed was that when the fish started to defrost in the warm areas, they actually wiggled a bit, which meant that they came back to life momentarily. From this observation he devised the concept that quick-freezing actually arrested life's processes. That conclusion was really the concept of quick-freezing. You see, when you take a fish out of the water, it starts to decompose almost immediately; once you freeze it right away, the life processes—including decomposition—stop. After defrosting, the fish were just as fresh as the moment they were taken from the water. He concluded that if it does that with fish, it can be done with other food products such as fruits and vegetables.

The idea of freezing food, of course, is probably as old as man. People in cold climates have probably been doing it always, but adapting that principle to a system where everybody could always have fresh frozen food was the big obstacle. Up to this time there were four common methods of preserving food that worked, up to a certain point. One was the old root house they had on farms, where root vegetables like potatoes were preserved by keeping them cool but not frozen. Another was by freezing some things naturally in below-zero temperatures outside and hoping it would be all right when taken in for consumption. The third was a method the farmer had of burying meat deep in the ground and letting it stay there as long as possible. Then there was the method of drying and salting meats and fish.

Birdseye's problem was how to arrest these life processes in such a way that when an item was defrosted, it would be just as good as when it was frozen. He had this idea of freezing in some kind of a wrapper—something like the "boil-in-the-bag" idea that we know today. He was looking for the right material when he came to see me in Philadelphia.

Our company did have a product but it wasn't suitable for what he wanted. Anyway, he stayed with me the whole day explaining and talking about his ideas. He wanted to devise a system where the nutrients and the flavour from the fresh product are saved by sealing them in. He talked about how he wanted the consumer to cook the products right in the bag so that there'd never be contact between the food and the water. He was very enthusiastic about his plans, and that enthusiasm rubbed off on me. He convinced me that I should go back to Canada and work on the idea there. Canadians, he said, produced most fruits and vegetables during a very limited growing season, and since they couldn't preserve adequately in large volume for future use, they had to bring in so-called "fresh" food from the United States.

He talked about how much of Canada's potential was being wasted. "You've got a natural situation there for freezing," he said. "You should freeze these products and sell them in the winter months and in this way you could help the farmers expand their markets from a matter of weeks to the whole fifty-two weeks of the year." The other thing which impressed me a great deal was when he said that most products grown in northern climes like Canada have better colour and flavour. "You've got much better food value out of what you produce in Canada," he said, "than what you get from the deep South. First of all, they harvest them at an early stage of ripeness when they are not really ready, hoping they will ripen on the way north and not spoil. But," he said, "you in Canada could take them just at the optimum moment of maturity, freeze them, and you'd have something fresher than you could bring from the South."

Well, this really intrigued me. This was a new idea that could expand the whole agricultural industry in Canada. If it worked well, it would give the public something better than they ever had before. I was fired with enthusiasm for the idea, so just as soon as I reasonably could, I packed my bags and headed home.

The first thing I did was enlist the help of my sister who was working as a scientist with the federal Department of Agriculture at the Experimental Farms. At that time she was trying to find a better method of preserving strawberries and raspberries for use in the making of ice cream. I explained the theory of fast-freezing to her and told her that, if she thought the idea had merit, I would take the idea to the Dominion Horticulturalist. She agreed that I should do that. So when I put my idea to the Dominion Horticulturalist, he was intrigued and said, "Why, certainly, we will work with you one hundred per cent." I was overjoyed.

Right from the beginning I would have this excellent scientific service of the Department of Agriculture available to help select the best varieties of strawberries and raspberries for quality and flavour, the ones with the best growing time, and so on. The science service went to work on selection of vegetables and fruit for experimentation and they figured out what some of my difficulties would be. For example, at that time about 120 different varieties of peas were being grown. Selection of the best ones for freezing and consumption was no small task. Because we were able to take their advice about varieties they were already working on, we were able to get an immediate start. Then we had to jointly decide what kind of package we would need to package these products, what kind of freezing we were going to do, and how we were going to do it.

There were no quick freezers anywhere in those days except the ones being used to make ice cream. However, the Experimental Farm had a below-zero-temperature freezer which they used for scientific testing of various things. We were able to use that for our first trial lot of six thousand pounds. That was all right for testing purposes but no good for commercial distribution of our products. Before establishing our own freezer plant, however, we had to devise some way of distributing the product to customers.

That's when I thought of the milk people. Since they were already distributing ice cream, I thought it would be a natural for them to take around our frozen fruits at the same time. So I went to the Ottawa Dairy and talked it over with the manager, who immediately saw the possibilities. He said, "You let us have them and we'll sell them right off our milk wagons." Another problem to be overcome, the most difficult of all, was the public fear of anything frozen being poisonous, that maybe these things were already contaminated before they were frozen. To overcome this natural prejudice, we went out giving demonstrations and proving to people that the poison concept was false. The public had to see for themselves.

While we were doing all these things on our own around the Ottawa area, Birdseye was developing his own ways of doing things and running test markets in the New England states. We weren't connected at all. He was working out the problems with the help of General Foods in the U.S., while I was developing my own system with the help of the Department of Agriculture here.

With the help of the Ottawa Dairy and their milk wagons, we got our first trial lot out to homes in the Ottawa area in 1932. From that modest start, the first real commercial frozen foods sold fast and well in Canada. All the dairies had ice-cream cold storage, so they could store our products safely for long periods. The products were so well-accepted the first year that in the second year we were faced with tremendous orders from all over eastern Ontario and western Quebec. The one problem was that they could only take them out on the milk wagons when the weather was cold, so we had to caution them to budget their sales according to that cold period of the year.

The berry products went so fast that we didn't have time for about three years to even think of adding vegetables to our line. But all the time our experimental work was continuing.

Soon the demand for vegetables came and that brought on another problem. The dairies said they couldn't consider handling them because vegetables didn't relate in any way to the sale of milk, cream, or ice cream. They said, "Just berries—that's all." We had to start looking for another way of getting these things to the public. Of course, you must remember, too, that the public didn't have home freezers in 1932, so they could buy only small amounts of frozen foods that they could use up in a relatively short time. Most homes had ice-boxes and that was all.

Once we got past the experimental stage, we started out in a big way in Simcoe, Ontario, where they had an excellent cold storage with sub-zero temperatures. They had their own berry growers' association and the different varieties of fruit that we needed. Ultimately we established additional plants to pack the fruits in Toronto, Quebec, and Prince Edward Island.

Home freezers didn't come along until the end of the thirties and the end of the Depression. In the intervening years, what was called a "locker plant" was developed. The lockers were bins the customer could rent, in which he would put his frozen foods in storage. But they were inconvenient because the consumer had to go there to get his stored food. Then the refrigeration people saw the prospects and they began to convert their ice-cream cabinets into holding cabinets for frozen food for homes and stores. As volume of usage by customers continued to increase, home freezers came on the market and almost everybody had a refrigerator with a freezing compartment in their homes. That made the locker plants redundant. So, as you can see, it was that sort of evolution that developed with acceptance and increased production from year to year.

The thing that I always emphasize is that Canada introduced frozen food not only to Canada, but to many parts of the world, even in advance of Dr. Birdseye. The reason for this is that the Birdseye people had a big job getting it going inside the vast United States market. They weren't particularly interested beyond their own borders. I'm not taking anything away from them; they did the pioneering in the United States. We did our own pioneering during that entire development period of twenty years right here in Canada.

Gwyneth Shirley War Bride

Many thousands of women came to Canada as a direct result of the two world wars. These were the young girls—mainly from the British Isles—who had met and married Canadian boys after brief wartime courtships. They knew little about their soldier husbands, or the new country where they would be spending the rest of their lives. At home they had to deal with family disapproval, as well as the resentment of their countrymen, who accused them of leaving a sinking ship. Similarly, in Canada they faced the resentment of those who accused them of "stealing our Canadian boys". In the passion of courtship some of these same boys had lied about, or greatly exaggerated, the living conditions to be expected in Canada.

When the wars ended, the brides were left by their new husbands for a long time in Britain, to eventually be gathered up like so much forgotten baggage and sent over by the hundreds in old vessels that had earlier served as troopships. One of them—Gwyneth Shirley, now of Cochrane, Ontario—remembers the sadness of leaving her homeland.

I met my husband at a dance. Pubs were also favourite spots for girls and boys to meet. Formal introductions were something that didn't enter the picture in wartime England. He says it was my red hair and WAAF uniform that first attracted him. I liked him because he was shy, quiet, and well behaved, while so many of the other Canadians were very wild. We made it a point to look for the quiet, shy, ones.

I was stationed in the RAF near Folkestone and he was at a nearby army camp, and I remember that our first actual date was interrupted by the zooming overhead of the first buzz bombs coming across the English Channel. We just stood there and gazed in wonder, not knowing what on earth was happening. And we heard and saw the first on our first date.

Things happen quickly in wartime. We met in May of 1944, and became engaged almost right away. We didn't have long together as D-Day was the next month, and John was being sent to Europe to join the fighting shortly after. So we decided to marry as soon as possible. I recall one form sent by the Canadian army to my parents which contained the question: "Do you realize that you may never see your daughter again?" What a chilling thought that must have been for them!

We were married at a church that was so old it was listed in the Domesday Book. The RAF padre performed the ceremony, and everything that could go wrong went wrong. Our whole honeymoon was a comedy of errors. Then, John was off very quickly to the fight in Europe, and I didn't see him again until the end of the war. We had a brief time together before he was sent back to Canada with his regiment, and I was left behind— pregnant, and living with my parents in London. It was to be a long time before I would see him again.

My son was born in England in 1946, and all I can say about that is that it was a rotten, lonely experience, in a very strict government nursing home, where no visitors except husbands were permitted. That left me with nobody, as my husband, of course, was in Canada. There was red tape galore, and I had a horrible woman doctor who told me I *had* to breastfeed my baby as there was a shortage of "real" milk. Despite the fact that I couldn't breastfeed, I was kept there and made to *try* and *try*. The result of all this was that I got a breast infection, and instead of my child's birth being a joyful experience, it was an awful one, that I'd like to forget, but cannot.

After an interminable amount of time, I finally received word that I'd be sailing in January of 1947 with a group of other war brides. In spite of all the waiting I had done, saying good-bye to my parents was the worst thing of all. We had to say our farewells in London, as that was where the hostel "clearing centre" was located, and no parents were allowed at dockside in Southampton, which was probably just as well.

The *Aquitania*, the old troopship that we were to sail on, had been a beautiful ship in her day, but her day was long past. The strange thing was that the mothers with babies were crowded below deck, forty to a cabin. Wives with no children got the better, smaller cabins, shared with just a few others. I will say, though, that the food was marvellous, after the years of rationing and shortages in Britain. The ironic thing is that we couldn't eat it, as shortly after we set sail, we were hit by Atlantic storms, and everyone was seasick. Then there was a terrible outbreak of gastroenteritis among the babies, including my three-month-old son. We knew that it was urgently necessary to get to a hospital as soon as the ship docked in Halifax, but a terrible fog held us up hour after precious hour, day after day, until finally, after two weeks at sea, we arrived.

My first sight of Canada was a string of ambulances lined up to take the sick babies to Stadacona hospital. That, too, was horrible. We mothers just sat waiting in the hospital, and nobody brought us news, or even spoke to us. The navy nurses were most unfriendly and cold, and looked at us as if we were dirt. No one offered anything—not even a cup of tea. We were all so miserable, and wondering if this was what our lives were to be like in Canada, when fortunately a Salvation Army captain arrived and took us to a "Sally Ann" hostel, where the atmosphere was altogether different. I've never stopped being grateful for that.

But oh, Halifax was so bitterly cold that winter night when we arrived. When I heard the *Aquitania*'s whistles blasting on her way back to England, I felt like running out in my nightie, and shouting, "Wait for me!" Actually, there were war brides in that hostel who already *were* on their way back home. They had arrived earlier, and discovered that their husbands had lied to them about life in Canada, or they discovered their men had other women, or that their in-laws didn't want them. There were many reasons brides left for England very soon after landing in Canada.

Those of us with sick babies were not allowed to visit our children at Stadacona, and we were forced to just wait around until they told us that our babies were well enough to be picked up for the long train journeys ahead.

Eventually this did come about, and after a train ride that never seemed to end, I arrived at a little place called Porquis Junction, in Ontario. It took days to get there from Halifax, and after all the misery I had suffered since my arrival in Canada, I really didn't know what to expect any more. However, my husband met me at the station. It was the first time that I had seen him in anything but a uniform. He was wearing one of those fur hats that northerners wear, and to me, he looked very Russian. "Who is this stranger?" I thought, "what have I done?" But then, when my in-laws met us, they seemed very nice, and we drove in their beautiful car to

Cochrane through what seemed like a long tunnel of snow piled so high on each side you couldn't see over the top of it. I'd never seen anything like it in England, but at least I was finding out that my husband hadn't lied to me, and that he did indeed come from a good family.

We lived with his parents in their large, lovely home, and every afternoon, when my mother-in-law would go to her room to rest, I would go to mine while the baby slept. I would hear the radio in another room, and the one thing I remember best is a man's deep voice extolling the virtues of a product called "Templeton's TRCs...Why suffer the misery of rheumatism..."followed by an old song or hymn. I'd be lying there with tears streaming down my face, wondering what I was doing in this white wilderness.

Homesickness was almost worse than seasickness. I hated hanging the baby wash outdoors when it was thirty degrees below zero. It was supposed to kill the germs, but it very nearly killed me. The diapers would be as stiff as boards when I brought them indoors, piled high in the basket and obscuring my view. Just going outside to get them meant I'd have to dress as if I were leaving on an Arctic expedition.

That first winter, aside from my trips to the clothes line, I guess I went out about once a week for a walk to the corner drug store. As I look back on it now, I wonder why I didn't assert myself more. Perhaps the cold had frozen my brain. I had somehow got the idea that going for walks was something that Canadians didn't do. Certainly my in-laws always seemed to drive wherever they went. No one suggested I get a sleigh for the baby, so, as a result, I never saw other babies outside, and I assumed that was something that was never done either. I had an awful lot to learn.

I had heard vaguely of bridal showers, but in my mind they were somehow akin to tribal customs. I had the idea that they were some sort of horrible initiation, where I would be thrown in a pool of water, and forced to swim naked, or something like that. When my mother-in-law announced that she was having one for me in the form of an open house, I was filled with dread, but very relieved when it actually occurred. It was quite a splendid affair, for which she had bought me an expensive and "exclusive" dress in Toronto. It was navy, with white beaded birds cascading down one shoulder—very, very dramatic. I was thrilled, and feeling quite grand, until the third or fourth guest walked through the door wearing one exactly like it. However, that made for a lot of laughs, and helped break down a lot of barriers.

The next three years brought many changes in our lives. We got our own little "wartime" house—and a second, and then a third baby. I was still terribly homesick, and somehow my husband managed for me to have a trip back home with our three small boys.

The trip turned out to be a terrible mistake. My mother somehow got the idea that I was coming home for good when she saw the amount of luggage I had. It had taken her those three years since I left to get over saying good-bye, and here I was back again. I tried to tell her something about how I missed the scenery and green fields of England, but she thought I'd gone crazy, and kept telling me that my place was back in Canada with my husband. I suppose she didn't really believe that I was only back for a visit. Anyway, the holiday wasn't what I thought it would be, and I sailed for Canada much earlier than I had planned. Maybe it was good that it turned out that way, because when I did return I settled down.

My last child was a girl, born in 1952, so the intervening years were spent bringing up my four children, and fitting in with the social life of Cochrane. The town has always had frequent changes of population. You'd get to know people, and make good friends; then they'd leave, and move on to other parts. After this happens a few times, you're almost afraid to make new friends and suffer the heartbreak of losing them again.

In the years since I came, the population has changed from majority English to something like sixty per cent French-speaking. They are such a kind and helpful people who have been wonderful to me in so many times of need. We've had some very humorous things happen in this respect too.

That first home of ours made us so very happy that we named it "Hawkinge" after the RAF base where I'd been stationed. We felt that was very romantic, and also it was a custom in England to put the name of the *house* on homes. The result was that people would come to our door with the greeting, "Bonjour, Madame 'Awkinge." After this happened a few times, we just quietly took the sign down.

When I first ordered groceries on the phone, I used my high-school French, and felt very proud of myself. The weirdest groceries I ever saw were delivered, including chocolate cherries, and pickled onions—or was it pickled cherries and chocolate onions? Anyway, I have never tried ordering in French again, although I value the friendships I have made with these wonderful people.

I'll always love the British Isles, but that 's all in the past. Canada is my country now. It's where my children and grandchildren live, and it's where a marriage that began in the madness of wartime survived, and provided a lot of happiness for forty years.

My WAAF uniform is now in a museum in a place called Ailsa Craig, Ontario, along with other relics of the RAF, the RCAF, and the war. I have many memories of my service days, of those mixed-up times which sometimes now seem more like a dream.

Frank Leslie That Eleven-Ton Cheese

While the pioneers of this century were clearing the land
and building sod huts and log cabins in the North and on
the western plains, many parts of eastern and central
Canada had settled into a pastoral farming life. Most dairy
farms produced more milk than they could use, so the
excess was sent off to the many cheese factories that dot-
ted the landscape of southern Ontario, Quebec, and the
Maritimes. Frank Leslie, now eighty-two, owned such a
factory in Stratford, Ontario, for many years.

I was born in 1902 to a cheese-making family. I can't
remember when I wasn't involved with cheese, and at the age
of eighty-two, I'm still at it.

Automation and machines have taken over from the hands
of man, and that's too bad because cheese-making is something that goes all the way back to biblical times, when a
goat's stomach was used for the transporting of milk for the
midday meal. Often when this stomach container was opened,
the milk had coagulated into curds and whey. Until recent
years, cheese-making was really a cottage industry, where
some families had better cooks who appreciated the necessity
of sanitation and who had their own little tricks and recipes.

Certain geographical factors also lent themselves to the
production of better cheese. A good plentiful supply of cool
fresh spring water was one thing. Having access to a nice cool
cave where you were assured of a properly maintained temperature between forty and sixty degrees was another. That
was important because proper storage temperatures before
the age of refrigeration were very hard to come by. Lush
pastures for cows were very important, too, to cheese-makers. All of these factors eventually led to better cheese, and
this evolved over the years into the cheese-factory system.

Of course, the most important thing of all was the quality
of the milk that was used. Holsteins were large-volume producers, whereas the old fashioned Durham, Shorthorn, and
Jersey produced milk mostly for butter and the carcass for
beef. The types of herds often determined where the factories
were located. As it came from many different farms with

various types of pastures and fodder, the milk wouldn't be the same at all times, even in the same district. Some areas had certain elements in the soil that produced very fine cheese milk, with the result that these areas became famous for their product. A lot of luck was involved, but there was also a lot of skill and pride on the part of the cheese-makers.

The factory system began in the Ingersoll–Norwich area of Ontario in the 1870s and 1880s, and it spread very rapidly up until the 1920s. These factories were all over the place, never very far from the farms which supplied them with milk. My uncle, Dr. J. A. Ruddick, grew up beside a cheese factory, and therefore had a great deal of knowledge of the making of cheese. He introduced a lot of quality-control measures so that a uniformity of methods came to Canada's cheese-making industry. He was supervisor of twenty-five factories at a time when there was no refrigeration, and the problems he had to solve were immense.

Although they had ice chambers to maintain lower temperatures in the curing rooms, they were not very efficient, as they depended on a large and plentiful supply of ice. If we had a long, hot summer, the ice could easily be exhausted. Ice was cut from local rivers and ponds in the winter and covered with sawdust and stored until it was needed. It was hard, though, to estimate just how much would be needed.

Canada began to become famous for its cheese around the turn of the century when a substantial market developed in Great Britain. Cheese was a big part of the diet of miners. Their lunches would consist of a block of cheese and a loaf of bread. For agricultural workers, too, it was their noon meal with bread and some ale. Cheese was cheap and plentiful. The demand for good cheese meant a continuing outlet for surplus farm products. It was a very competitive business, which meant that quality was always uppermost in the minds of the cheese-makers.

At one point, Canada shipped well over two hundred million pounds of cheese to Britain, our main market outlet, in one year, most of it from eastern and western Ontario and Quebec. Some of the other provinces developed cheese industries, but unfortunately they never amounted to very much.

Milk was delivered by horse and wagon, so transportation played a major role in where the factories and creameries were located, along with the availability of raw product and good drainage and sewerage. This resulted in a great multitude of factories located only two or three miles from each other. The milk had to be delivered daily, and it had to be made into cheese on the day that it was produced. There were two milkings, both delivered to the factory separately, but this changed when the night's milking would be held over, and mixed at the same time with the morning's milk for delivery.

The cheese-making process takes from seven to eight hours. This meant that there was a limit on the time when milk could be brought in if it was to become cheese that day. The process couldn't be started if the milk was sour, as it would coagulate due to the excess of lactic acid. If the milk was over-ripe or had gone sour, the farmer would take it back home, where he made old-fashioned "crowdie", which was a form of cottage cheese. Crowdie was made by adding a bit of salt, a bit of heat, and then draining out the whey. It was a good product which they ate at home, so the milk wasn't wasted.

A pork industry usually developed at the same time. Some factories sold the whey wholesale to someone who owned a yard where there was a large number of hogs, but, generally speaking, the whey was returned to the farmer in his empty milk cans and he would feed his own hogs with it. Perth and Oxford became very large producers of pork as a result of the whey and buttermilk they used for feeding hogs. In that way, pork was a by-product of the cheese business.

Then there were the creameries. Whether they were creameries or cheese factories depended on the type of cattle in the area: Holsteins, the high-volume milk producers for cheese, or cows that produced high-fat-content milk for cream. These farmers would separate their cream and deliver it to the creameries around the countryside.

Ontario became very famous for its Cheddar cheese, not only in Canada, but in the United States, Britain, and other parts of the world. Cheddar is a highly concentrated, low-emulsion cheese that can be carried with a minimum amount of refrigeration without spoiling. This was a big selling point. It had an extended life because of the low moisture and high acid, which is a natural preservative. Production was relatively simple, and it could easily be stored in cool cellars.

Towards the end of the nineteenth century, in an effort to publicize Ontario Cheddar, makers began making giant cheeses which drew a lot of worldwide attention. These huge cheeses became quite a factor in the development of export trade. Cheese was one of the main sources of income for farmers in areas where cheese was produced. One of these cheeses weighed 22,000 pounds—eleven tons! Pictures of it appeared in newspapers around the world. It was exhibited in Chicago and New York, and eventually ended up in England. It was a big drawing card at the Chicago World's Fair of 1893. My uncle, Dr. Ruddick, who was later dairy commissioner for Canada, was the man who supervised the making of that big cheese, and he was also responsible for the transportation of it from place to place. They had to have a custom-made flatcar to transport it on the railway.

It takes ten to eleven pounds of milk to make one pound of cheese, so they were handling in the area of three hundred and fifty thousand pounds of milk on the day that that eleven-ton cheese was made. In the big factories today, that would be no problem; but back in 1893 it was nothing short of a miracle. The mould for it had to be especially made from boiler-plate steel because of the tremendous pressure involved in the process.

The biggest problem in the making of that eleven-ton cheese was assembling the curd. No one factory had nearly enough at one time, so they had teams of horses and wagons racing in with curd from different factories to a central point where the mould was. It was then transferred from the wagons to the big mould, with everyone hoping that the salting had been properly done at those various factories and that the temperature of each load was pretty much the same. It was a huge task and took a great deal of planning, and the fact that it worked at all says a lot about the skills of those men who were working with such primitive equipment.

It was all worth it, though. That cheese helped to establish the Canadian industry in many markets, including the United States and Britain. Also, in Canada, that cheese and the men who made it became the stuff of legends for many, many years. I was very proud of the part my uncle played.

In 1924 I started in the business myself as an apprentice in a neighbourhood factory. Keeping everything sparkling clean was my first job, and from that I learned all the other little jobs, one at a time, until everything became second nature by the time my five-year apprenticeship was up.

Milk wasn't delivered on Sundays, which made for very long Saturdays at the factory. By the time the evening's milk came in, it was two o'clock in the morning. Sunday was a strict day of rest, but on Monday it was another very hard day again. Everything had to be speeded up on Mondays as the Sunday milk was beginning to get ripe, and the process had to be started before it spoiled. Working hours never entered the picture at all. Each man's job was to continue working until all of the milk was safely put into production.

In those days, a lot of the personality of the cheese-maker was put into the product. He used all of his senses. He was constantly testing and smelling and squeezing the mixture, making sure that everything was progressing the way he wanted it. He looked on it as something alive, and, of course, living things act in certain ways. He knew how it should taste and smell at every step along the way. The end product was very much an extension of the skills and personality of the man or woman in charge of making it.

Today that kind of devotion has largely disappeared in the huge factory operations, but you can still find it in some of the smaller family businesses. I've always looked on cheese as a living product that keeps on changing until the day it's consumed. Like any other living thing, it responds to the love and care you give it.

Before the new settlers came, it was the task of government survey teams to map the land and mark out the lots. Here a team pauses for a lunch of moose meat at one of their caches along the Finlay River, British Columbia, in 1914. The coming of the airplane revolutionized surveying.

Not until 1924 did the Ontario government purchase thirteen flying boats to patrol the province's forests on the lookout for fires. Frank McDougall (middle foreground) was a surveyor-turned-pilot with the early Ontario Provincial Air Service. "When I'd look up and see those planes, so free, and moving so fast, I made up my mind that I, too, was going to fly some day." 2

3

First settlers, first land, first home. "The Indians who lived here at the time helped them a lot. They taught them many things, including how to build their log houses." (Angus McGowan)

4

Scottish settlers arriving in Canada in 1911. Their crossing was easier than that of the first settlers to Prince Edward Island a century before. "The cruelties inflicted on those people are hard to believe today. When they were driven off the land, they had no place to go except for the docks, where they were packed into these leaky old ships with not enough food and water, and sent off to the wilds of North America and Australia." (Angus McGowan)

5

Although most of the English war brides like Gwyneth Shirley and Peggy Holmes looked forward to being reunited with their Canadian soldier husbands, they were wholly unprepared for the very different living conditions here. Gwyneth Shirley remembers that one of the many forms sent to her parents by the Canadian Army asked, "Do you realize that you may never see your daughter again?"

*The famous eleven-ton cheese made in Perth, Ontario, was
exhibited at the Chicago World Fair in 1893.*

7

A drama broadcast from the CNR-owned radio station in Ottawa in the 1920s. Canadian National Railways established the first network of radio stations in Canada to entertain passengers on board their trains. "It was such a thrill to hear real live voices talking or singing. My father said, 'The time will come when we will be able to see these people as they perform as well as hear them.'" (Mabel L. Halbert)

8

Bob Bowman, the first CBC reporter overseas in 1939, talks with a wounded soldier hospitalized after the Dieppe Raid.

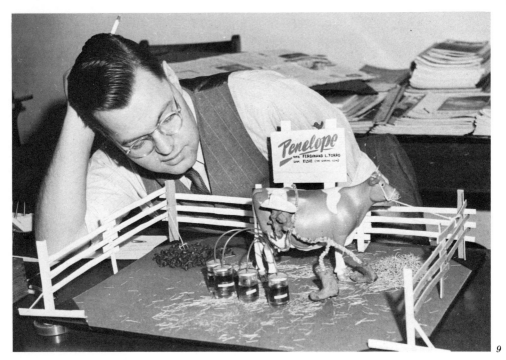

H. Gordon Green, fiction editor of the Family Herald *from 1948 to 1968, discovered one day that his desk top had become a farmyard for his prized desk ornament, a Guernsey cow model. "The* Herald *was a real national newspaper and, although basically rural, it was much more than that."*

A mixed team shares the load as these settlers arrive in "sunny Saskatchewan" in 1909. "We went first by train as far as we could to the end of steel. We bought a wagon there—just a grain box on wheels, really—with no spring in the seat. We had to bounce over rutted corduroy and mud roads for thirty miles." (Peggy Holmes)

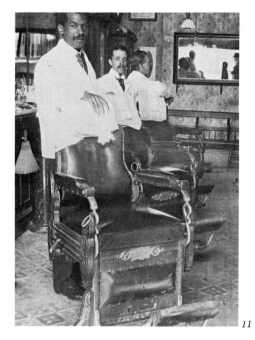

Barber Charles Duval in his Collingwood, Ontario, shop at the turn of the century, and, on the right, with his wife, Chestina, and family. The Reverend William King (below) founded the community of Buxton, Ontario, in 1847. "He brought with him fourteen slaves that he had inherited from a Louisiana plantation family he had married into. He freed them and brought them to Canada, and started the Buxton settlement. It grew to about a thousand blacks, and it was an extremely well-organized community." (Dr. Daniel Hill)

14

"They had to clear the trees and grub those roots out of the ground, and that was back-breaking, soul-destroying work." (Fred "Tiny" Peet)

1

A "Ward" aeroplane ready to take off, to the horrified delight of the spectators. "The chief engineer at the Club had worked with the famous Colonel Coady in England in 1909. Coady at that time was experimenting with a biplane braced with wires. Every time he landed, the wires would break and have to be restrung all over again—each time with stronger wire." (Jack Hardman)

Erwin MacDonald On the Road to Cariboo

Most of the fortune hunters who joined the Yukon gold
rush came out with even less than they had had going in.
The fortunes were limited to very few, and many of those
who struggled over the Chilkoot Pass expecting to find
lumps of gold to be picked up off the ground found themselves working for miners' wages which were quickly
squandered in the bars and saloons of centres like Daw-
son City. When the fever died down, many wandered
south to the developing West, where the CPR was opening
up vast stretches of land for homesteading. That was as
far as some ever got on their return journeys. Erwin Mac-
Donald, born in 1893, says that his father was one of those
who found new opportunities in Canada's Cariboo Country.

My dad was the son of one of those Glengarry Scotsmen
who were kicked off their land in the old country in favour of
sheep. When they came to Canada in the last century, a good
many of them settled in the Ottawa Valley, where there was
plenty of free land and lots of trees; so they naturally got into
lumbering—not because they knew anything about the lumber
business, but because the trees were there and there was a
market for them. Dad became a pretty good lumberjack, but
when stories of gold in the Yukon began to spread, he decided
that was the place for him.

He headed west with his partner, and he did manage to get
in on the tail end of the gold rush, but he never hit anything
big. When that started to die down, he and his buddy figured
they could make some money buying cattle and selling the
meat to the construction camps that were building the Canadian Pacific Railway at the time. The men were always hungry for meat; and for a while, this worked out well until Dad
got hurt very badly. He was tangled up in a rope attached to a
wild steer they were trying to get across a stream. Dad was
knocked down, and the rope got caught around his legs. The
frightened animal took off through the rocks with Dad bouncing and dragging behind. By the time his partner managed to
rope the steer and stop him, nearly every bone in Dad's body

was broken, and he was almost dead. His partner did the only thing he could do, building a raft, loading Dad onto it; and he headed through the Arrow Lakes to the Columbia River.

A week later, they got to the first spot where there was a settlement large enough to have a doctor, which was Fort Colville in the state of Washington. Dad was pretty far gone, but between the doctor and the nurse—Melinda Prouty—they saved his life. Melinda was just eighteen years old and Dad was forty, but they fell in love, and when he was well enough, they were married, and settled down in Washington, where they raised cattle, and eventually five children. However, Dad was more of a prospector than anything else. He always had this gold thing on his mind and his prospecting gear never was away from him, even on the small ranch. He was panning in every little stream he came across.

But then my mother died in childbirth one winter. The baby died also, and she was buried with it in her arms. We were all badly broken up—especially Dad, who just went to pieces. The five of us children had to go live in an orphanage for a few years, as Dad's poor health prevented him from being able to look after us. He'd come to see us frequently, assuring us that we'd all be back together soon.

Then one day he came to tell us that we were all going to Canada soon. I was thirteen, the youngest of the boys, and I just couldn't wait! When we crossed the border into southern Alberta the winter was already on. The North West Mounted Police suggested we stay with them, and we did, and that was a good thing, as that winter of 1906–7 was one of the worst winters Alberta had ever experienced.

When spring arrived, we were making plans to move west again, so we three boys went into Edmonton in May for some pack horses, and the family was on the move once more. We rested for about a week in the Yellowhead Pass, and then moved south, where we picked up the headwaters of the Thompson River, and followed that until we were within eighty miles of Kamloops, British Columbia, to a place called Little Fort, which was an old outpost of the Hudson's Bay Company. From there we followed an old gold-rush trail to Hundred Mile House, on the road to Cariboo.

On our second day out, we came across the most beautiful field we'd ever seen. It was about three miles of open sidehill sloping up from Lake Daroche, with grass as high as a horse's back. Dad said, "Boys, this is the place I saw in my dreams, and this is where we'll stop." And that part of the Cariboo was the place we finally put our roots. It was as if we had reached heaven after that long trip and the months of constantly moving.

On the travel out west, we hardly saw anybody. It was a wide-open west in those days, with empty space as far as the eye could see. We did see one or two outfits packing in supplies for fur buyers, and a few survey teams getting ready for the building of the railroad, but I don't remember running across more than a dozen white people the whole summer. One fellow we did meet was a half-breed, whose name also was MacDonald. He was packing in supplies and opening up little stores along the trail to the west where the settlers would be able to get provisions. We wanted to buy supplies from him but he said he would only deal if we helped him build his store. We agreed, and set out cutting the timber for it. The logs were about eight or ten inches across and forty feet long, so it was quite a sizeable building. It was about nine feet high, and after we put the roof up, we built rough counters made out of hand-hewn poles on the inside, and made shelves for his merchandise. While we were doing this, the half-breed, Donald MacDonald, a real smart, industrious guy, went into Edmonton and Lake St. Anne and bought the supplies with thirty pack horses from a store thirty miles down from the headwater of the Fraser River. It was wild, unbroken country then, and outside of a few trappers, we were about the first white people in there.

Once in a while, we'd meet a small band of Indians, consisting of two or three families on the move and living on the moose, deer, and fishing. These Indian bands spread out over the country. They were always small groups, because if their party got too big, there wouldn't be enough food. They were always very friendly, and they would trade things that they had for something we had. They liked the white man's food, which was very different from what they were accustomed to eating. They wouldn't ask for it though. They'd simply sit there, watching you take every bite until you couldn't stand it any more, and Dad would say, "For God's sake, give them some!" That's the reason we ran out of supplies and had to help this other fellow build his store. By the time these store owners packed it three hundred miles out into the bush, a sack of flour that cost two dollars in Edmonton would cost twenty-five or thirty dollars. That's the main reason we were so willing to trade labour for food.

We were miles into the bush, and everything had to be packed in on horses, which was difficult, especially in winter when it got down to thirty or forty below zero and there might be three feet of snow to contend with. Even with that though, nobody went hungry, as there was plenty of game, and one of the first things a homesteader would do when his land was cleared was to plant a vegetable garden. We also had plenty of fish and geese and ducks.

Dad would do anything if he thought it would get him out to the mountain country of British Columbia. He didn't like the prairies at all. He was a mountain man and a sharpshooter who never missed bringing down a running deer, and he always had this dream of his own piece of land where he could raise cattle, and maybe make another big gold find. Although he never stopped looking for it, he never did find it, despite the fact that he was almost ninety-eight years old when he died.

When we got there at first, there was only one white man, who made his living by trading booze to the Indians for furs, which wasn't good for the Indians, or for the country. But when we came and other settlers followed, that all stopped. Your closest neighbour might have been three or four miles away. It was a bit lonely at times, but there was always so much to do that you didn't have time to sit around and brood about it. It was as if we were all together in this thing.

We were expected to donate our time, too, to building the roads, which was a good thing in two ways. We needed roads, and it was a way to meet and get to know your neighbours. That road in was so very important. We wanted more settlers, and the surest way to get them into the bush was to have a road. Once in, they could claim one hundred and sixty acres of land for only ten dollars to file the claim, and another ten dollars to prove it up. The second ten dollars meant they had to live on it three years, which was proof to the government that you were seriously trying to make a home. Within two or three years we had enough people at Bridge Lake to form a community.

It started with one man opening up a store, Then, another fellow would open a blacksmith shop, and so on. When there were enough children, we got together and built the school. The first thing was a schoolhouse, and I remember the one we built at Bridge Lake. It was twenty-four feet wide, forty feet long, and two storeys high. The classroom was downstairs, and upstairs was for community affairs and dancing. It was built of logs and the labour was free as everybody pitched in. At that time my brother and I had a little sawmill, and we cut the rough lumber for the floors, which made it easier than the usual way of hewing it out with a broadaxe. I guess we had it finished in about six months, as everybody gave a day or two here and there whenever they could.

The first church didn't come along until we were there almost five years; however, once a month, a travelling minister would come and visit people in their homes. As more settlers came, the schoolhouse was used for religious services, but it wasn't long before we all wanted a real church, which was also built with free labour. The only money spent on it was for windows, and nails, mostly.

The West was filling up with homesteaders during those first years after we reached the Cariboo, good, hard-working people who'd work from sun-up to sundown. There was always so very much to do: building the homes, clearing the land for crops, and building up a community. I suppose it was a hard life, but we didn't think so then. You were accomplishing something, and you had the feeling of opening up new country.

It was a good life. For entertainment in wintertime we'd skate and ski. We made a lot of our own skis then, and we'd have square-dancing winter and summer in the school hall. The big event, though, was rodeos. I suppose we all fancied ourselves cowboys because of all the riding we had to do just to take care of our cattle. On Sundays a gang of us would get together and break horses so they could be ridden. We had a public corral for this, and it was lots of fun, besides being useful, as these horses had to be broken, and knowing how to ride well was a necessity. We raised our own horses. We'd buy a good stallion or two, and all of the homesteaders would use them with their mares in order to breed new colts. It was cheaper to raise our own than to buy them.

My father got one good horse from a band of Indians simply by riding him. He was wild, and wouldn't allow anyone to stay on his back. The chief let it be known that anyone who could ride him would get to keep him. Many tried, and the Indians would get quite a kick when this horse would buck them off in no time at all. My father decided to have a go at it one day, so he rode out to their camp. The Indians were all set for another big laugh, at his expense, but Dad stayed on. When he went to claim the horse, the chief said that there was one more condition—the winner had to marry the chief's daughter too. Well, Father had been a widower for a long time, and aside from any other reasons, he had no intention of changing his status. However, he did want that horse. The chief said that the marriage would take place the next day.

That night, when everyone else had gone to sleep, Dad sneaked over and got his own horse, plus the one he had won, and very quietly took them a long distance from the camp. Then he jumped on his own horse and with the other tied behind went galloping away, never stopping till he got home. He reasoned that if the chief could break his promise, then he could break one too. He never heard from them again, and that stallion proved to be a dandy. It sired a long line of fine horses in the Bridge Lake area of the Cariboo, where I came in order to establish my own property after I left my father's house.

Dad may have been restless and adventurous, and always on the go in the early years, but he knew what he wanted. When he found what he was looking for, he settled right in for the rest of his life.

George Learning The Slaughter of the Newfoundland Regiment

While other parts of the country were filling up with new people from many lands, the more settled eastern coast carried on with life as usual. For the young people on farms, in mines and manufacturing industries, or following in the footsteps of their fathers in the fishing industry, life was predictable and boring.

The outbreak of the First World War was a call to adventure and a chance to see the world. Canada's youth fell all over each other in their eagerness to be sent overseas. As George Learning of Newfoundland discovered, this was not a difficult proposition—"If you were big enough, you were old enough."

When the First World War started in 1914, I was only fifteen years old; but I was a big boy and I guess I looked older, having worked on the fishing boats since I was barely old enough to walk. All the boys were joining up for the Newfoundland Regiment and they couldn't wait to get over there before the war ended. Everybody felt if you didn't get over fast, you'd miss all the fun! So one day I made myself look as old as I could—which was kind of hard as I hadn't even begun shaving—and I went down to the recruiting office to join up. I had no trouble getting in at all, which didn't surprise me because I thought I was quite the man anyway.

Boy, was I excited when I got into that uniform and started strutting around St. John's. Those khakis were the proof that I was every bit the man I thought I was. Instead of shuffling along in rubber boots and overalls, I was marching down the streets clicking my heels on the sidewalk in time with an unheard drummer. George the fisherman was someone who had lived in my past. I was now George, the soldier. When I'd see a young girl coming my way, my back would get even straighter, my step more purposeful, and I would imagine that she'd be admiring this brave young man who was going off to save the country for her. All of this before I had even one day's training on the parade square. I joined for the fun, and it seemed like a nice way to get away from home for a while and see Europe. We also thought it would be over before the blink of an eye. I certainly never dreamed that any of us would be killed. That was something that never occurred to me.

I couldn't wait to get over and save my country. What fun it was going to be—what adventure—and the sooner the better. Well, as it turned out, it wasn't going to be that soon. First they had to make a soldier out of me. The drills and the training seemed to go on forever, although I suppose it was only a couple of months.

After I enlisted, I suffered one of the great disappointments of my life. They were sending a detachment over and I was supposed to go with them. I was just dancing in the streets, I was so happy. I went around saying good-bye to all my relatives and friends and counting the minutes till it was time to sail. Just before it was time to go, they had one of those last-minute medical inspections and, would you believe it, my name was taken off the list of those who'd be sailing, because I had a couple of boils on my neck, of all things! I couldn't figure what boils had to do with soldiering, but there it was. I was turned down! When they told me, I stood there with my mouth quivering, shaking and trying to keep them from seeing that I was crying. The bands were playing down on the docks, and the crowds were there to say good-bye to the brave boys, and there was I, fighting my way through them to get home where I could cry without being seen. I thought my life was over.

When I got home, there was a message that Captain Reeves wanted to see me immediately. I roared out the door like a deer, running top-speed through the streets, knocking into people and tripping all over myself in my anxiety to get back to the docks. When I arrived, the boat was already out in the stream, and when I found the captain's clerk he told me that they had changed their minds about the boils, and that if I had been there only ten minutes earlier, I could have gone. I looked out at that ship going farther and farther from shore and this time I didn't care how many people saw me crying. It was the very worst day of my life—up to that time. I didn't know it then, but the only way to describe what was in store would be "hell on earth".

My turn to sail came up again not long after that, and I

finally realized my dream of being a soldier on active duty. Some dream! After many different tours of duty we finally found ourselves in the Dardanelles, where it was very, very hot. Our military planners had us equipped with the heaviest clothing they could muster. We had heavy Stanfields underwear, thick khaki uniforms, heavy boots, and even puttees which wrapped our pant legs at our ankles, making sure that the heat couldn't escape. It was so hot that in the evening everyone was dismissed; but that didn't stop them from having regular route marches across the desert, Stanfields and all. The Red Cross was behind us all the time to tend to the boys who were fainting all over the place. An officer would be there for the examination too, because if it were found that you were shamming, they'd put you up on the crime sheet.

We were to get ready to go down to France. Well, that was the only thing that kept us going. We knew that France was cooler, and our Stanfields wouldn't drive us crazy with the itch. Also, to tell the truth, we were looking forward to meeting some of those "Mademoiselles from Armentières" that we'd been hearing about. However, when we finally did get to France, we were sent directly to the front lines.

There were seven hundred of us in the Newfoundland Regiment, the end of June 1916. We were sent into what was to become known as the Battle of Beaumont Hamel to relieve an English battalion. The first night, quite a number of our boys were killed and wounded, so we knew we were in for it. Our groups arrived at this fork in the road. One way was the "dump" where all of our equipment and supplies were, and the other road led to "White City", which was the Red Cross camps. It was full of the dead and dying. We kept on going past the "dump" and we got trapped by the flying shells and the constant bombardment.

It was as close as anything on earth to what hell must be. The boys were dying all around us, and there was no way that we could go forward or back. We couldn't show our heads over the holes we were in without getting shot at. The second night there, I reached into my knapsack and found half a sandwich and a little medicine bottle with about three ounces of whiskey that I'd forgotten I had. My buddy and I had that, and it was the only thing that passed our lips in forty-eight hours. The shelling kept up, and with all the explosions it was almost like midday at midnight. We were resigned to dying by this time, as it seemed to us that everyone else was dead. We just sat there, keeping our heads down, waiting for the shell that would end it for us.

Then, along about two in the morning, we heard something stirring above us, and a Scottish voice asked us who we were, and if we knew where we were. We identified ourselves, and he told us that almost everyone else was dead, and that we had better start crawling in the direction he pointed out. "Don't fall in any more shell holes," he said, "or you may never get out. Watch out for the enemy flares and take your time."

We followed his instructions, and when we finally crawled what seemed to be miles back to safety, we were told that most of the seven hundred men of the Newfoundland Regiment were dead, and we were part of a small handful of survivors. It was the worst slaughter you could imagine.

I hated the war by this time, everything about it, the dirt, the disease, and the killing. I was just seventeen years old, and I couldn't help thinking of that day two years before when I thought my life was finished because they had sailed away without me.

Peggy Holmes Luckier Than a Lot of Women Out There

The homestead years were the greenhorn years as the
country filled up with first-time farmers, many of whom
came from the cities of Europe, and didn't know a rake
from a hoe. People who had never hammered a nail suddenly found themselves required to construct their own
houses and grow their own food. The young Peggy
Holmes, born in 1898, and her husband were two of these
pioneers in the earliest days of Alberta's settlement.

I came from Hull in Yorkshire, England, as did my husband, but I didn't meet him until he came back from Canada
with the Canadian Forces in World War One. He had gone to
Canada in 1911 to take up homestead land, and his sister, who
was a schoolmate of mine, would talk about this cowboy
brother of hers in Canada.

She would say, "When he comes home, he'll fall in love
with you." I'd say, "That's ridiculous;" but in fact that's
exactly what happened. He and three of his friends who had
also filed on homesteads in Canada nailed their shacks up
when the war broke out in 1914, and came back over to
England with the 31st Battalion from Calgary. I suppose it
was love at first sight for both of us. I was sixteen and he was
twenty-six when we were introduced on one of his leaves
before he headed off to the trenches in France.

On another leave, three years later, we were married, but
of course, we had very little time together until he was sent
back to recuperate from wounds in 1918. Just before he was
to return to the trenches our friends had a birthday party for
me and going-away party for him. It was funny, because that
night a friend of mine sang "O Merrie England, Peaceful
England", a song she had refused to sing all through the war.
It was a time of very heavy casualties and hearing her beautiful contralto voice singing that song again gave us all a very
strange feeling.

Anyway, the following morning I was with Harry on the
train speeding down from the north of England to the south
before he embarked for the front lines again. We were both

very sad when suddenly the news spread all through the train that the Armistice was signed, and the war was over. No question about it—that was the most marvellous day of our lives.

By the time we were ready to sail for Canada, it was 1919, and Harry never gave me any clues of what to expect. Good thing that he hadn't. I probably wouldn't have come. All he said was that we would go out for two years to "prove up" the homestead. I didn't have much of an idea of what this meant, or even where it was. I remember that when I was asked by the people in Yorkshire where it was, I'd say, "I think it's at the foot of the Rockies." They'd say, "Which foot?" and laugh.

When we got to Calgary on the train, there were some of Harry's army friends waiting for us. We went to their home in Calgary, which seemed very nice, and then Harry decided that before we went on to the homestead, it would be a good idea if we spent six months or so working on this millionaire's ranch outside the city. It had ten square miles of land and masses of cattle. I thought that this was what Canada was going to be like for us.

I soon discovered, though, that we war brides weren't very popular. These seemed to be a feeling that war brides had stolen Canadian men. Of course, for somebody who was supposed to be employed at the ranch, I didn't know much. I couldn't bake bread or make butter, or anything, and they thought I was really dumb, and I guess maybe I was. Most of these other people up around there were American immigrants, and I'd overhear them say, "She don't know nothing. She's stupid," and they really resented me a lot. The manager of the ranch put us to work on the cook car when the regular cook had left in something of a hurry. Well, in England we had nothing to cook in wartime, so I had never learned to cook— and here we were getting meals for very large numbers of men at harvest time.

I told him I could do it, and he told me to get at it then, and that I would find the meat under the cook car. When I went to get it, what did I find but a whole carcass of a cow! I had no idea what to do, but in the end I got a saw and hacked off a big chunk that proved to be too big for the oven. I just hacked off some more, until finally it was fit into the oven and cooked. It must have been all right, as nobody complained.

Making bread was worse still. I didn't know about keeping yeast warm, or keeping the dough covered and punched down till it was ready for the oven. The first time I tried to milk a cow, nothing came out, and someone explained to me that I wasn't supposed to push up on the handles, I was supposed to pull down. I had to learn even the simplest of things. There were some disasters, I can tell you, but eventually I learned quite a bit, including some strange words in strange languages. In some way I managed and I stayed the whole six months as cook and then it came time to move to our homestead.

We went first by train as far as we could, about thirty miles north of St. Paul. That was where the tracks ended— "the end of steel", it was called. We bought a wagon there— just a grain box on wheels, really—with no spring on the seat. I especially remember that, as we had to bounce over rutted corduroy and mud roads for thirty miles. That took two full days, as there was no way the horses could go more than fifteen miles in one day.

When we finally arrived at the homestead site, there was nothing there. This little shack that Harry had built was burned down, and we had no roof to cover our heads, or any place to put our supplies. We found a little hut that some other homesteader had abandoned, and we lived in that until we got something built on our own land. By now, I was feeling dreadful and I remember having a nightmare that the end of the world had come. I awoke from it to discover it was an old horse scratching himself against the side of our hut.

The coyotes would frighten the life out of me too. When they'd be howling at the moon, I'd be howling with fear. It was all completely foreign to me, but I did get used to it. It was beautiful country, with spruce and poplar trees everywhere, and of course we were young and we made the best of it. We drew some plans for our log shack, and decided it would be something more than a little log dwelling—it would be a log house, with two storeys. That turned out to be a foolish decision, as we didn't realize that a place that size would be impossible to heat.

The wise homesteaders who were already there a while built log shacks that were low, but I had the idea that I could never live in one of those. So the two of us and our team of horses set out to extract the logs from the woods for our two-storey foolish fancy. Harry cut the trees and I peeled the bark from them. Then we'd hook the horses on and drag them back to the site, where Harry would cut the notches, and then the two of us would lay them in place—one on top of the other. When it got too high to lift them up, we bought some ropes, which we tied to the horses on one side of the building, and had them pulled up on these slanting poles. One had to be very ingenious on the homestead. If you didn't have something, you'd just have to go ahead and invent something else.

I was luckier than a lot of women out there, as Harry never left me alone while he went off to work. Where he went, I went. I didn't have children to worry over, so when he went to cut wood, I went with him and cut too. When he was clearing land, so was I. I loved peeling the bark from the logs with a drawknife, and Harry preferred working with an axe. He learned to use it after we got there, and he got to be very good at notching logs and squaring timber.

Even in the house, we worked together, as he was just as good as I had become at preparing food. Getting supplies wasn't easy. There was a little store five miles away, and that ten-mile round trip was about all the horses could do—but we did get some extra horses after we were there for a while. Some of these young fellows would get tired of trying to make a go of homesteading, would come and say they were leaving, and they'd trade their horses for something from us. Harry at one time got a horse for a suit of his clothes.

After several of these people had left, we had acquired a few horses and some cattle. That's how we built our stock up, plus the little bit of money we had. Besides the clothes we'd give these young men in trade for livestock, I'd usually give them a haircut. I got to be pretty good by practising on Harry's head, but he would say, "It's a good thing they can't see the backs of their necks, or they'd never let you cut their hair again."

A great many of the homesteaders gave up. It was just too hard for them. At one point, there were more going out than coming in, especially the ones who didn't have wives. They'd get so lonely that they would simply give up the "unequal struggle", they called it.

It took us a long time to build our house. When our first winter arrived, we still had no roof, so we pitched a tent inside the four walls, and lived in there. When my folks in England asked what our place was like, I wrote and said: "It's something like Selfridge's Roof Garden." I don't think they realized how primitive it was, and of course I wasn't going to tell them.

I don't believe I realized myself how hard life was, because it seemed something like a game. It was just the two of us, and we loved to ride our horses, and we'd sing together as we made our way along the trail. When we were clearing the land, we'd make huge bonfires, and we would dance around them. We did have a lot of fun.

But that first winter of 1919 was really terrible. It turned out to be the worst on record, and hundreds of head of cattle were lost in the blizzards all over Alberta. It began storming in October that year, and it never let up until May of 1920. Sometimes the temperature would drop to more than sixty below zero—so low down, the thermometer couldn't measure it. We'd see one or two neighbours during the winter, but mostly we'd be alone.

One of our neighbours claimed he was a cousin of Jesse James, and I believe it, because he was quite a wild man, and he was very proud of the relationship. There were a good many French in the area, too, and they were very nice; but we couldn't speak the language, and they couldn't speak ours, so except for trading a little with them, we couldn't have much of a relationship. They had a nice little community, with a church and a priest, and as much as we might have liked to be with them, or they with us, the language was too much of a barrier. Of course, they were about five miles from us and in those days, with a horse and a wagon, that was a very long distance—a day's trip.

When spring finally did come, we were able to plant a vegetable garden and it grew like mad. Our biggest job was clearing the land, because you had to clear so many acres in order to get your patent of ownership. After we got all the bush and trees off, we had to break the land with a team of horses and a walking plough.

We made a game of that too. We'd stick an alarm clock away up at the end of the furrow and call it the "town hall". Then we'd head for the "town hall" with the horses and plough, and gradually get it done. When it was time to seed it, Harry would get a basket and walk along, scattering seed in all directions. He looked very funny, and I'd almost collapse with laughter. He reminded me of someone from out of the Bible.

We did have one break on that land. There weren't many rocks to remove. It was gumbo, but not so many rocks as a lot of homesteaders had to contend with. We were able to get a bit of a crop of late oats in that second year, while at the same time clearing some of the land needed to satisfy the government requirements. You see, we had 320 acres altogether. There was Harry's original homestead grant of 160 acres, plus another 160 that the government gave to those who had been in the army.

That second grant was a hay section three miles away from our homestead which was an added problem in that we had to go all that distance to get the hay to feed the cattle. That meant six miles back and forth on an old hay rack with no trail to follow. Every time the rack hit a tree, we'd have to get off and make the trail wider with an axe. In the end, we got a rack for each of us, and brought two back at a time. Harry would break the trail, while I followed in his tracks. The hardest part of all, I think, was the "survival of the fittest" aspect of it all—having to destroy animals when food for them ran short.

One homesteader not far from us was left with seven children to look after when his wife died, and the same thing happened with another family. There were fourteen motherless children altogether. Things like that were pathetic. There was a lot of loneliness too. Many of the men would send for mail-order brides. We wrote the advertisement for one man, and sent it to the *Family Herald*. A lot of settlers could not read or write. This man was left with four children, so we wrote and said what a wonderful guy he was, and all the rest of it. He got a couple of answers with pictures, and finally one did come out. We saw then that the picture she sent had been taken many years before. But that didn't matter. That marriage and a lot of the others worked out because the women knew what was ahead of them, and they were prepared for a hard life. Usually, too, they were good to the children.

I never suffered loneliness at all, as I never left Harry. Whatever he did, I did, and wherever he went, I went, and we did everything together. I actually enjoyed the hard work of chopping trees, clearing land, and making hay, and Harry was happy to have me there with him. It was exciting to be building for the future, and, of course, we always had these goals we were working towards: you had to fence your 160 acres, plough so many acres, and build a home. When that was done you got title to the land, and all it cost in actual money was ten dollars. After that, you could keep it or sell it, or do whatever you wanted, because it was all yours.

The chances of selling it were nil, as nobody else wanted it in most cases. It was hard, there's no doubt about it, but I was happy, as it was almost like an extended honeymoon—not being tied to the shack all of the time, worried about what was going to happen to my man. I knew what was happening to him, because I was always there.

That big log house we built was a mistake, as I've said before. We just couldn't keep it warm, although it wasn't for want of trying. I spent endless hours looking for cracks that let air in from outside, and I devised my own recipe for filling them. I'd get hot manure from the cow before it froze, and mix it up with little bits of chopped hay, and things like that, and I'd shove it in those cracks like mortar. It didn't smell too good, but it kept the wind out. However, we never did devise a system of keeping the place warm. It was just too big.

The strange thing about that part of Alberta was that we never managed to form together into a community as they did in other places such as Peace River. We never got the churches or the stores or places like that. People kept going to other areas for supplies and their other needs, and no central community ever formed. We kept slogging away at it though, till we got our patent, and then my father came out from England for his health.

His doctor though it would be a wonderful idea for him to join his daughter in Canada and get all of that marvellous fresh air. Of course, he had no idea what it was like on the homestead. When he arrived, sick and ailing, he was horrified by the way we were living. "My God," was the first thing he said, "where is the bathroom?" Then it was, "Where is this?", "Where is that?" He wasn't so much horrified for himself. He simply couldn't understand why we had chosen to live our lives this way.

Anyway, as we had accomplished what we had set out to do, and obtained title to the land, we felt it was time to move on. We counted what little money we had, and found we didn't have enough to get to Calgary where we wanted to be, but we could afford tickets to Edmonton. We closed that chapter of our lives around 1923, and took up the next chapter in Edmonton, which was still in some sections a frontier town of mud streets and wooden sidewalks when we arrived. There were only two buildings of any note—the Parliament Buildings and the Macdonald Hotel—but there was more mud than anything else. We called Eighteenth Avenue "The Grand Canal" because it was so full of mud.

The people there came from everywhere. There were a lot of Ukrainians, French, and Germans in the north part of the city, and Anglo-Saxons down in the central part. It didn't seem to be conscious segregation—simply a case of people wanting to be with their own people. The Chinese had a section which they liked, and so on. I think they just wanted to be some place where they could understand the language that everyone else was speaking.

It was a good place for us to make a new start. With no money, and only our youth and our health, it was back to pioneering of a different sort all over again, and we enjoyed that too. I must have. I'm eighty-six now—still here, and still loving it.

Dr. Daniel Hill Slavery—That Monstrous Iniquity

Black people have played a significant role in the development of Canada, although slavery was practised here in the very early days just as it was in the United States. This ended in 1793 when John Graves Simcoe, the governor of Upper Canada, made the keeping of slaves illegal. His action encouraged runaway slaves from the United States to seek the asylum offered by Canada, and they crossed the border in great numbers. During the War of 1812, many blacks fought on the British side against their former masters, and by 1820 thousands were crossing into Canada via the "underground railroad". Dr. Daniel Hill was appointed Ombudsman for the province of Ontario in 1984 and is the author of *The Freedom Seekers*.

The first blacks in Canada came with the United Empire Loyalists, who were fleeing the country themselves in the 1780s. They came and brought their slaves—about seven hundred slaves altogether—who remained slaves until Simcoe's legislation. They were the very first, along with a few freedmen who just drifted in. It's interesting to note that about six of the sixteen members of Simcoe's government owned slaves.

I have spent a great deal of my life looking into the roots of my people, and of course this so-called underground railroad plays an important part. It wasn't a railway; railroad terms such as "station" and "terminal" were a means of confounding slave owners and other enemies. These "stations" and "terminals" were generally haylofts on the farms and cellars in the homes of Quakers and Congregationalists, or Presbyterians, usually religious leaders or others who were sympathetic towards them. An abolitionist on the American end would get word to a number of slaves on a plantation that if they could meet in a certain place at night, they would be spirited out by someone who could pilot them to the North. They would travel ten or twelve miles a night through Ohio, Kentucky, and some other states on their way north. The slaves came with their guide, sometimes in twos or threes, but rarely in large groups as it was so dangerous. Fives and tens were about the largest.

There was a network of way-stations where they could hide out all along the way. Mostly it was travel by night and sleep by day in designated basements or barns. They wouldn't have been able to survive without the assistance they received from white people and black freedmen on their journey.

Once they got to the northern states, they were free, but then the notorious Fugitive Slave Act was passed in 1850. This act said that any slave master could move north to find his "slave property" and the master could take his slaves back south with him. This caused a lot of consternation, and it sped up the work of the underground railroad, as blacks were no longer safe in the northern states.

Long before this, the Canadian government had proclaimed that any slave who reached British soil would be forever free. This Canadian law was passed in 1819, and was really an enlargement of what Governor Simcoe had done in 1793. Before that there was a system of slavery in Quebec and Ontario, although, of course, it wasn't as large as it was in the United States. After Simcoe outlawed it, the administrators of Upper Canada actually welcomed the slaves.

Although Canada was a haven for blacks where many whites did all they could for them, they also ran into a lot of discrimination. A great many people objected to this policy that if they got here, the slaves were free. What usually happened was that the slave would be set free and the hunters would be booted out of the country. If their owners had been rich men they would hire men to go after them, and sometimes pursue them even into Canada, where they'd try by subterfuge to kidnap them to get them back into the United States. They'd tie them up and cover them, and attempt to sneak them over the border. These slave hunters were breaking our laws, and if they were caught, the courts didn't take kindly to their activities.

About fifty thousand black slaves came into Canada during this period and settled in Chatham, Ontario, along the Niagara Peninsula, and in Toronto and Hamilton. However, after the American Civil War, most of them returned to their former homes in the States, as they wanted to be reunited with whatever family members they could find back there. They had emotional attachments to the small churches they had belonged to there. All through the years of slavery, these churches and the clergy were symbols of hope and the freedom they longed for. In addition, they had been promised the benefits of "reconstruction"—"forty acres and a mule", freedom, opportunity, jobs, and land, most of which they never did get. There were many false promises made by the government of the time, but the reason most of them went back was to seek out the kith and kin they had lost.

A small number, however, stayed in each of the Canadian centres where they had established themselves. Those who did stay constituted the core of today's black communities in Toronto, Hamilton, and those other places. It's easy to understand those who returned to the States.

Those who stayed were not given grants of free land, except in the case of those blacks who participated in the War of 1812. They were given lots of land in Oro Township in Simcoe County, Ontario. That's about the only case where the government sponsored or assisted black refugees. However, they did give them freedom and gave them the protection of the courts and the police.

They received a lot of voluntary help from the churches. The Anglicans, Methodists, and Wesleyans brought blacks and whites together to form anti-slavery societies and liberation groups. A whole proliferation of volunteer agencies assisted the slaves when they hit Canadian soil. Toronto's St. Lawrence Hall became a gathering place for fugitive slaves in the 1850s. They were given food and clothing and jobs by these volunteer people. The same type of thing took place in centres such as Windsor, Amherstburg, Hamilton, St. Catharines, and other Ontario towns and cities. The whole abolitionist movement had its roots in Ontario.

Some blacks moved to the Maritimes in an earlier period, but the major migration of them into Canada took place in Ontario after the Fugitive Slave Act of 1850, as it was much easier to get to.

There was a minister by the name of King who established a community called Buxton near Chatham, Ontario. The Reverend Mr. King was an aggressive and tough-minded Presbyterian who came to Canada West, as Ontario was then called, in 1847. He brought with him fourteen slaves that he had inherited from a Louisiana plantation family he married into. He freed them, and brought them to Canada, and started the settlement. It grew to about a thousand blacks, and was an extremely well-organized community. There was an excellent mission school which gave blacks a classical education. It was so good that many white people clamoured to get into it. It turned out a number of doctors, lawyers, and teachers who went all over the North. Reverend King insisted on excellence in Buxton, and he got it.

They had a grist mill, a sawmill, and a brick factory, which was one of the first in the country. Their farming methods were excellent, and it was, all in all, a first-class colony. What Buxton did was show that with co-operation and good educational opportunities, blacks could organize and take care of their own needs. This was a model community that flourished until after the Civil War, when it too died down, because most of these people had the same desires to get back to their roots.

Many of their descendants are still living in that general area today where they are farmers, teachers, businessmen, and so on. Today Buxton is a living museum of the part Canada played in freeing the black man.

One of the men who came out of Buxton was Dr. Alfred Shadd, one of the early doctors who went to Saskatchewan in the 1890s before Saskatchewan became a province of Canada. Another Buxton man was Dr. Abbott, who became the coroner of Kent County, and later the general resident physician at Toronto General Hospital. During the Civil War he was one of the few black doctors in the Union Army.

Now, all wasn't sweetness and light for blacks in Canada. In the 1850s and '60s, blacks were not permitted in the public schools. They were put in segregated schools and given a segregated education. Toronto was one of the few exceptions where they were integrated into the schools from the very earliest. For the most part, though, the only way they could get a proper education was to establish their own schools and mission schools, as in Buxton. In many cases, but not all, these schools were far superior to the schools they weren't permitted to enter.

An interesting point about the early days is that there was a split in thinking among black people. Some thought the ideal way to settle was in communities such as Buxton but others felt differently. They saw Buxton as a form of ghetto, and they preferred total integration into white communities. Places like Buxton, Wilberforce, and the Refugee Home Society near Dresden, formed by Josiah Henso, were all formed by black people who wanted to live apart from white people. It was their choice. Those who chose to integrate in the cities found themselves pushed into ghetto situations by white realtors.

On the steamers, for example, they weren't allowed to purchase first-class tickets. In restaurants, taverns, and public accommodations, they frequently encountered discrimination. They ran into it, too, in where they could buy property or lots. They suffered the humiliation of seeing American minstrel shows brought in with their so-called black acts which denigrated their race. They mounted many petitions to the government to stop this practice, but they rarely succeeded. Many things made the early black people unhappy, but on balance, they were much better off here than they had been as slaves.

We can be very proud of the part blacks have played in Canadian history, but it is disturbing to see so little mention of it in our history books. Blacks have played a major part in any wars which involved Canada. They were greatly involved in the settling of the West, and during the building of the Welland Canal they played a peace-keeping role, controlling the riots which broke out between the Irish Catholics and the Orangemen. In the War of 1812, they fought with John Brant, the son of the Mohawk leader, Joseph Brant. They were in the Battle of Queenston Heights, and Stoney Creek, and all over, but it seems popular historians have ignored black people, either through thoughtlessness or through racism.

Through the Black History Society we have formed, we now hope to make up for these omissions. We're searching for the records of early black pioneers. We've obtained proper recognition, for example, of W. P. Hubbard, who was a black alderman in the City of Toronto between 1896 and 1913. He was also the acting mayor and top controller for many years, and made a major contribution. His people had been refugee slaves from Virginia. With Sir Adam Beck he played a big part in establishing the hydro system. He was Canada's first major black politician, and his portrait is now hung in the City Hall due to the efforts of our society.

We're also having similar things done with Canada's first black physician, Dr. Abbott, and our first black King's Counsel, a lawyer named Davis, who came out of Amherstburg in the 1880s, and wasn't even permitted to article because no firm would take him. He had to sit special examinations for the government before he was allowed to practise. He became a brilliant courtroom lawyer and King's Counsel before the turn of the century. It's important that the public and the schools in Canada are aware of these people and the contributions blacks have made—for blacks and whites too.

The hardest part of life for those early people was simply getting adjusted to a new way of life. As slaves, someone else ordered how they would live their lives. Suddenly they had to cope with getting jobs, finding housing, and even getting clothing. Don't forget that when they came they were destitute and weren't able to bring anything with them. If it hadn't been for the volunteers and the churches, it's doubtful that they would have survived.

In spite of all these hardships, they knew that they were better off than they had been before. There were many, many white people who opened their hearts to those early blacks. George Brown of the Toronto *Globe* was one who helped greatly through the Abolitionist Society. He wrote blistering editorials in his newspaper about "that monstrous iniquity— American Slavery", and he and his family did a great deal with their own wealth and influence to help settle blacks in Upper Canada. He was the man who set Hubbard on the road to being the first major black politician. Brown encouraged and helped Hubbard when he was working for a livery stable as George Brown's driver. The blacks had many strong allies in the white community.

The Honourable Dr. Pauline McGibbon "It's Mr. Trudeau"

Despite the obvious fact that the West could never have been conquered without the support of the women who went along with their men, Canadian woman didn't have the right to vote until well into this century; they were not even officially recognized as persons until a landmark court decision in Alberta in 1929.

Another important milestone was the 1974 appointment of the first woman lieutenant-governor of a province in the British Commonwealth. In a term of office that lasted six years, Pauline McGibbon, born in 1910, became the best-loved and most approachable person ever to hold that office up to that time. As the provincial representative of the Queen in Canada, she worked seven-day weeks and crisscrossed the province so often that it was said that there wasn't a citizen of Ontario who hadn't seen her in person at least once. Her trademark was informality, and even children called her "Pauline".

In many ways, it was even more difficult for my husband, Don, than it was for me. After all, although I was the first woman in the job, he was the first husband of a lieutenant-governor. He had to explore the ground of how to act and what to do in many situations. He was accustomed to being a leader in the business world, and suddenly he was a companion to somebody who held an important office. There were many times at functions where people forgot to introduce him, or even forgot that he was there, because he insisted on remaining in the background. He always said it didn't bother him, but it sure did bother me. Whenever something like that happened, I'd make sure I introduced him myself.

We were both born and brought up in Sarnia, Ontario, went through school and university together, and were, you might say, childhood sweethearts. We were married during the Depression, and since our union produced no children and women didn't enter the work force as they do today, I did a lot of volunteer work, which gave me a great deal of satisfaction.

It also created opportunities: one volunteer job led to another, and although I didn't seek, or want, publicity, I was getting to be very well known—first locally, then provincially, and finally nationally, when I became national president of the IODE.

I was enjoying myself and getting to see parts of Canada I had never before seen, but I was also finding that the higher up you moved in these volunteer organizations, the more money it cost from your own purse. This worried me, as it was, after all, a drain on Don's finances. However, he never complained and he was proud and supportive of everything I did. I mention all of this because it has a bearing on the lieutenant-governor's appointment, which comes from the federal government. I was bowled over when it happened.

It was simply a case of being in the right place at the right time, I guess. Remembering back, there was a story in a newspaper on the Saturday which speculated on the next person who would hold the office, and suggesting that it might be a woman. As the Liberals were in power in Ottawa, and I never had been a Liberal, it never occurred to Don or me that I might be in the running. We were talking about it in the kitchen at breakfast, and trying to predict which of the prominent women we knew could fill the job. We didn't think for a second that it could be me. That was too far-fetched.

Our thoughts were about women who had been active in the Liberal party, and after breakfast we just forgot it for the rest of the weekend. On the following Monday I was in Ottawa for the installation of Mr. Léger as governor general, and several people asked me if I would be the next lieutenant-governor. It was natural, I suppose, that they should ask, as I was then in the spotlight quite a bit as the first woman chancellor of the University of Toronto. I would answer, "No way," and I was being totally honest, because I thought it was a political appointment.

Two days later, I was preparing dinner when the phone rang. The operator said, "Dr. Pauline McGibbon?" I answered that I was. She said, "The Prime Minister of Canada, the Honourable Pierre Elliott Trudeau, wishes to speak with you." That's when I knew. Don happened to walk into the kitchen at that time, so I put my hand over the telephone mouthpiece and said, "It's Mr. Trudeau." I had that awful "gone" feeling in the pit of my stomach when Mr. Trudeau came on the line, but I asked him some questions about the financing of the position because I was really concerned about how this might become a financial drain on my husband's resources. Mr. Trudeau said he knew how much would be coming from the federal treasury, but he wasn't quite sure of the provincial contribution.

I told him that I would call back with my answer. He told me that that would be fine, and he could be reached later that evening at Government House, where he would be having dinner with the Governor General, or that I would find him at his office at eight-thirty the following morning. I called some people who knew about these things, and I tried to call Mr. Trudeau back.

By then, however, the regular operator at Government House had gone home, and the security staff was on. The result was that I couldn't get through to tell the Prime Minister I would accept. It was terribly frustrating—especially as the telephone at my home began ringing. Radio stations were calling, saying, "Our Ottawa man says that you are the new lieutenant-governor." As I am no good at lying, and as I couldn't say yes because I hadn't formally accepted yet, it made a very difficult situation for me. Without answering the reporters' questions, I'd say, "Where did you hear that?" That way, I didn't answer yes or no.

When I got through to Mr. Trudeau the next morning, he told me that he would then take it into the Cabinet and call me back later. Well, that day I was chairing the honorary-degrees committee at the University of Toronto when the president, John Evans, was called from the room. That often happens, so I thought nothing at all of it, but when he came back he said that Canadian Press had just announced my appointment. The rest of that day was simply a confusion of radio, television, and newspaper reporters, and it wasn't until midnight that Don and I were able to sit down and have some of the turkey I had cooked for him. It was his birthday.

Joe Garner A Pretty Strange Story

Most of the immigrants who came to Canada in the early
part of this century were from the British Isles and
Europe. But there were others who just moved north
from the United States. Some came for the free land, and
others, like Joe Garner's father, were simply looking for
sanctuary.

My parents more or less fled to Canada from the Carolinas right after the turn of the century. Dad was a bit of a
paradox as a young man. Many of his best friends were
Negroes, but he was a member of the Ku Klux Klan at the same
time, if you can imagine that.

One night after a Klan meeting there was a rooster fight,
and Dad put his rooster up against one owned by the son of the
Klan leader. Dad's bird won and when the other fellow
wouldn't pay up, they got into a fight, and the result was that
Dad shot this fellow in the knee and someone else fired a shot
from the crowd and hit the guy in the shoulder. He was pretty
badly injured and was rushed off to a hospital. Dad never did
find out whether he lived or died because he didn't stay
around long enough to find out. He knew that some of the Klan
members would have killed him. So what he did was ride over
to my mother's house—she was only sixteen at the time—and
he got this priest to marry them at five o'clock in the morning.
Then they jumped into a democrat with a team of horses, and,
with some local policeman riding alongside till they reached a
safe distance, they caught the train to San Francisco and up
the coast to Vancouver, where he figured he'd be safe. He
knew he'd be a dead man if he lingered at all.

It's a pretty strange story, but that's how the Garners
came to Canada. My father was a scared man, and he never
once crossed that border into the United States after that. The
first night in Vancouver they stayed in a tent where Stanley
Park is now, and the following day they crossed over to
Victoria on Vancouver Island. He wanted to put as much
distance as possible between him and the Klan. The rest of his
family came too, because I suppose they figured they were all
in danger. They worked around Victoria that fall and winter.

Emily Carr's father had an outfitting business for miners going to the Klondike gold rush, and Dad worked for him. He got to know Emily Carr real well at that time, and they were friends for the rest of his life. I never figured out his relationship with Emily Carr. He spent a lot of time with her. He helped build her "House of All Sorts", and they were certainly very good friends. She was a struggling artist then, and a five-dollar bill would buy any one of her paintings. It seemed that wherever she was living at the time, that's where Father would go to find a job. When she was in Victoria, he'd get work there; and when she lived in Vancouver, he'd be found working at something in Vancouver.

But after that spell in Victoria—about eight or nine months in all—Dad and Mother put their possessions in a flat-bottomed skiff and rowed to what was then the wilderness end of Saltspring Island. They had to backpack their first baby, Ethel, and all their other things up to an old deserted log cabin about two miles from the beach.

That was their first home on Saltspring Island, although they had many more after. I think he felt safer if he kept on the move. He never got over the feeling that they were coming to get him, and it became his practice to always have a loaded revolver under his pillow and a loaded gun over every door in all the houses he lived in. He never lit a lamp at night without first covering the windows. His fears weren't exactly groundless, as I knew there was a Ku Klux Klan in Vancouver in those years.

One of the original pioneers of Saltspring, a black man by the name of Stark, was killed by an arrow shot through a window one night. The Stark family is a very old family on Saltspring. When they first came here, their cattle, sheep, and hogs were simply dropped off the boat that brought them and they had to swim ashore. Mr. Stark and his family were challenged that first night by a group of Indians who didn't want them there, but he managed to stand them off. He had bought his freedom in the South, and with a lot of other black people he and his family settled on Saltspring. We grew up with many of the children of freed slaves. As far as I can remember there was no prejudice against them at all. Two of our chums were the Woods boys, whose father was a Scot and their mother Negro. Theirs was a huge family of twenty-two children, and they were wonderful people who got along well on a mixture of agriculture and fishing.

There was a big Indian population on Saltspring at that time. There was absolutely no racial discrimination of any kind there. About forty per cent of the people had Indian blood, and there were many families of white and black blood, or even Hawaiian. The original Hawaiians had come there with Captain Cook. There were a huge lot of them, and it was difficult to distinguish between them and the Indians.

I was born in 1909, and during my young years there were plenty of deer in the forest, and the streams were full of trout. Apple and cherry trees were plentiful, and you could grow anything in the garden. Everybody was almost self-sufficient. There was a general store there since the last century and you could barter for anything else you needed such as baking powder, sugar, and staples like that. In the winter, when the chickens weren't laying, we'd barter potatoes for eggs, or a young lamb for baking powder and sugar, a mutton and beef for flour. Even in 1920, Woodward's store in Vancouver was doing barter business. For example, we'd send over a lamb and they'd send back the same value in what we ordered.

Some people had small boats, so there was a certain amount of trading between Saltspring and Victoria. They'd take sheep and pigs, apples, potatoes, and other vegetables to Victoria, and bring back tea and sugar and other supplies. As our family got established, we had a few farm animals: a milk cow and chickens, sheep and pigs that ran wild, a horse, and three acres of cleared land. That kept us going, as Dad often worked away from home.

It was very tough going for us just getting enough to stay alive in that wild country, and it really was wild! There were a lot of cougar on Saltspring then, and everyone considered them a nuisance more than anything else. They'd be after the sheep and cattle. I was chased by a cougar when I was eight years old. Any time I even mention it now, every moment comes back to haunt me. That thing stalked me all the way home, and I just managed to make it without him getting me.

That's the way we lived on Saltspring Island from early in the century right up to the time we left in 1926. It was pioneering in the truest sense of the word. There were no handouts, and you either succeeded or failed depending on your own resources. Growing up there was like an adventure every day, you might say, but your childhood was short.

I worked from the time I was nine years old. Dad got a wood-cutting contract for me and my brother Tom. We had to saw and buck two thousand feet of lumber a day. We'd fell the trees together. I'd do the bucking, and he'd do the teamster work. Tom was two years older than me. We got twenty-five cents an hour, and the way we kept track of our time was this. Each night, going home, we'd put two rocks on a different stump. Each rock meant four hours, or one dollar. On pay day, when we got our money in cash, we'd immediately go to the stumps and check the cash against the rocks. If they didn't match, we'd go right back and have it straightened out. Our employer, Captain Justice, was so impressed with our time-keeping that he just took our word for it from then on.

Father was hardly ever at home. He did a lot of work in other places, especially in Vancouver. He worked in warehouses or almost anywhere, as there was practically nothing he couldn't do. He was very handy, although he didn't do much around the house. He figured that Mother and the kids could do that. I was milking three cows when I was eight years old, before school and after. We had to learn to live without Father most of the time, as he was never there in the summer, and only half the time in winter.

When I was around eight years old, Dad had to take me to the city to see a dentist. Well, it was at Emily Carr's that we stayed the night. I remember I was very sick, and she was very nice to me. However, she had this little monkey that took an immediate dislike to me, and it kept trying to attack me. I suppose it was jealous or something. Emily Carr finally took it and locked it up in another room until we left.

We had a blacksmith on the Island, a man of amazing strength, by the name of Jim Maxwell. I saw him lift a big wagon, the weight of a small car today, that would ordinarily take three strong men to lift. He lifted it up and rested it on his knee while he took the wheel off and greased the axle. Then he put the wheel back and set the wagon back on the ground. Another time he broke his leg, and the doctor had to go to his place to set it. The doctor told us Jim was in terrible pain without chloroform or drugs of any kind, but he never uttered a sound while he was being worked on. He did have a big bottle of rum, though. The doctor said he made some pretty horrible faces, but he didn't complain or pass out as you might expect.

Jim Maxwell wasn't the only person like that. There were plenty of others like him. People just had to be strong to meet with the demands that nature put on them. The total population was only about three hundred, so they helped each other, and never allowed themselves to get soft. I remember coming home from church with Father one Sunday when he stopped in at the store to pick up a hundred-pound bag of flour. He just put that bag under one arm, and away we went for a three-mile uphill walk back to our place. On the way he stopped to talk with someone for about a half-hour. Not once did he put that bag down to rest, yet he wasn't more than one hundred and fifty pounds himself. Those people walked wherever they went.

There were no cars, no telephones, no newspapers, no hospital. There was a doctor, but you had to catch him at home. They made their own entertainment. Of course there was no radio as they didn't come till the late twenties, and the first gramophone I saw was in 1923. Everyone played some sort of instrument—banjo, fiddle, or something. They'd sing and dance, and with a big fire in the fireplace, they'd have a great time in somebody's house.

I don't think about that life as hard at all, but it certainly was different than it is today. A lot different. We had everything we needed. There was plenty of wildlife. We had fresh meat most of the time, and Mother would can what we couldn't eat in the summer, and we'd eat that in winter. The streams were bulging with trout, which we sometimes had three times a day during the season. There was no such thing as refrigeration, but nothing was wasted. Pork and beef would be salted or smoked.

As far as money was concerned, I didn't see any until I was seven years old, when Father put Tom and me to work for two months cutting slash at the north end of the farm. That was hard work! At the end of the summer, he gave me five cents and Tom a dime. We weren't exactly delighted, but we figured it was better than nothing, which was what we'd got before.

Dad wasn't what you'd call a generous man. Even when he had money, he kept it salted away and spent very little on his family. He was a hard taskmaster, and he made life hard for all of us, including Mother. She had ten children, and without her constant working, and caring, and making something out of nothing, I don't know how we could have survived. On the other hand, he seemed to look on his family as a work force. Even when he became comparatively wealthy, he held on to all of his money himself.

When the doctor told Mother after she'd had her last baby that she'd probably die if she had another, she decided to call it quits with Father. She packed up a few things—this was in 1927—and with eight of the children, she started a new life on the mainland in Vancouver. Three of those children she took with her were under six years. The only money she had was thirty-five dollars, and she sent us over to Vancouver with the instruction to "buy a lot, and build a house". The amazing thing is that we did that, and we did it in only three weeks. We paid $7.50 down on the lot. We went to a lumberyard and ordered a hundred and fifty dollars' worth of lumber with a five-dollar down payment, and agreed to pay the rest at five dollars a month. When Mother arrived, we had constructed a house twenty-two feet long by thirty feet with an upstairs. That night Mother and eight of her children slept in it. What a woman she was! Without her, we would never have made it through the tough years of the Depression ahead of us.

H. Gordon Green The Grand Old Lady with the Petticoats

The *Family Herald and Weekly Star* was one of the most popular newspapers ever published in Canada. It started in 1869 and published its final edition in 1968. H. Gordon Green of Ormstown, Quebec, was the paper's magazine editor from 1948 until the time of its demise.

The *Family Herald* was started by Hugh Graham, the publisher of the *Montreal Star*, and was really an offshoot of the newspaper. Graham, by the way, later became Lord Atholstan, his title from the name of his hometown, Atholstan, Quebec. He was born in very humble circumstances and never forgot where he came from after he made his fortune.

Now, for some reason or other, he hated the editor of the *Gleaner* in the nearby town of Huntington. The two towns were only six miles apart. Anyway, he started the *Montreal Star*, and six months later he came out with this weekly *Family Herald*, supposedly dedicated to the country people of Quebec. In reality what he wanted to do was put out a weekly that would put his hated rival, the *Huntington Gleaner*, out of business. It was begun as a grudge and this grudge was so great that at one time Hugh Graham sued Sellars, the *Gleaner* editor, for libel. He must have had something solid on him because Sellars went over the border to the States only ten miles away, and he stayed there until Sunday, when he galloped back to Huntington to publish his paper. The bailiff wasn't allowed to deliver a summons on Sundays, you see. After getting his paper out, Sellars would jump on his horse and gallop back over the border before midnight and he'd stay there until the following Sunday and do the same thing all over again.

It went on that way for a long time. But that's the genesis of the *Family Herald*. There was no noble purpose behind its beginning. Canada was only two years old then, and certainly in need of a national newspaper, but that wasn't the original purpose of the *Family Herald* at all. It was originally a very local publication. Gradually it grew to take in the English population of Quebec and those of the French population who had always read English-language newspapers in addition to their own. It surprised Hugh Graham when this paper began to have readers in Ontario and the Maritimes, and eventually all over the Dominion.

One of the things that made it so popular was that right from the very first it published Canadian fiction. When I came there in 1948 as their fiction editor, this policy was still in effect and the editor said to me, "Your first job here is to encourage Canadian writing. Buy what we can afford of it, but always be on the lookout for new writers." Going back over those old *Family Herald*s, you'll find names that later became quite famous; Charles G. D. Roberts had some of his first work published there, and so did Lucy Maud Montgomery, who gained her fame with *Anne of Green Gables*.

There was also a man from the States who lived in Canada at the time. His name was James Oliver Curwood. He came here so that he could absorb some of the feelings of "the wilds". His fiction always reflected that, set in the Canadian backwoods. His very first work was published in the *Family Herald*. Years afterwards when he was world-famous and so rich that he even built a castle in Michigan, he wrote the *Family Herald* to say that he had written his last novel, and he would like to give it to us—in other words, he would let us publish it first as a gesture of gratitude. This will give you an idea of how people came to feel about this newspaper.

It had become very important to the country as a whole all through its history, and even at the time of its demise, it had a paid circulation of over four hundred thousand. The readership, of course, was infinitely greater than that. Every member of the family became devoted to different parts of the paper. In the province of Nova Scotia, every post-office-box holder was a subscriber. At one point, when a member of the Nova Scotia legislature was attempting to get money for travelling libraries to go around Cape Breton, another MLA got up to oppose the idea. He said, "I know those people, and all they need is the Bible and the *Family Herald*." Of course, you could say that of almost anywhere in Canada at the time.

The paper had an association with the readers that no other paper or periodical had, or even aspired to. Subscribers could write in with almost any question and be assured of an answer. Maybe they'd find an old coin when they ripped up the linoleum, and they'd want to know whether or not it was worth anything. We had a lawyer on staff who would answer legal questions; the same with a veterinarian. One morning I came in and there was a box on my desk oozing something from it. I opened it, and there was a mess inside, with a badly soiled note on top that said, "This was taken from the inside of my horse. I think he died of worms. Would you please tell me what was wrong." Well, we had the mess analyzed, and we gave him an answer. I can't recall if it was worms or not.

Sometimes we'd be called upon to settle arguments between farmers fighting over some little thing that wasn't worth a legal fee, or even sending to our own lawyer. They would say, "We've decided to let the *Family Herald* settle our dispute." So we'd consider the points of their quarrel among ourselves and give them an answer, which they always accepted.

It was mainly a rural and small-town publication, and we went to great trouble to publish the pictures of prize-winning animals at the various fairs across the country. For years, when the pictures of the bulls came in, our staff artist had to air brush out the testicles. This kept up until one of the bulls' owners, a woman, threatened to sue the paper for defacing her bull. So that put an end to that very pious practice.

It was a very Victorian newspaper in manner and morals, which is why I dubbed her "The Grand Old Lady with the Petticoats". We couldn't, for instance, publish a short story which might have divorce as a solution. There was a very strict policy on advertisements, too. If anything smacked of cheating or exploiting the reader, they were very quick to rule that sort of advertising out.

I'm not sure if the policies of the paper grew out of Hugh Graham's own philosophy, or whether it was something that grew in spite of him. It certainly was at variance with some of the aspects of the early *Montreal Star*, its mother paper. The *Family Herald* was very high-principled, while the *Star* was, at times, the very opposite in those early days. The *Montreal Star* played a very large part in the defeat of Prime Minister Arthur Meighen because Hugh Graham published what is called a "roar-back". In other words, on the day before the election, he headlined a story that was absolutely false; namely, that if the vote didn't go Liberal, the Canadian Pacific

Railway would move their head office immediately from Montreal to Winnipeg. Meighen afterwards attributed his defeat largely to that writeup. Hugh Graham was not at all a saint, but the *Family Herald* was altogether different from the character of the man as it showed in the *Star*.

My own involvement with the *Herald* came about after I had written a few short stories for them while I was in the army during World War Two. Immediately after the war, my alma mater, the University of Michigan, offered me a fellowship, so I went back there to work on my master's degree while teaching. I was in the creative-writing class, which included Arthur Miller, who wrote *Death of a Salesman*, and Betty Smith, author of *A Tree Grows in Brooklyn*. At the end of that year I wrote a novel, which won a rather prestigious scholastic prize, The Hopewood Award. The news got back to Canada, as I was the first Canadian to win it. So, right away, I got a letter from the *Family Herald* congratulating me and asking if I'd be interested in accepting the post of fiction editor. I had already been offered a job by the university, and I felt comfortable there. A second letter came, followed by a rather indignant phone call from R. S. Kennedy, the editor, a hard-bitten man who had been in World War One and wounded seven times, including the loss of an eye. He was very gruff in this call, demanding to know why I wasn't answering his letters. I said I needed some time to think it over.

I called J. B. St. John, the former fiction editor of the *Herald*, and asked his advice, because he had worked for Kennedy. He said, "Look, stay where you are. I happen to know you're a fighter. R. S. is a fighter too, and you'll never get along, and besides he won't pay you properly." With this information I thought the easiest and most polite way to get out of it was to put a price on myself that he couldn't accept, which I did. It surprised me to have him come back with a letter of acceptance of my terms in which he added, "We will pay for the cost of moving you here." Well, that was it. I had no choice but to make the move, but I must say I never regretted it. That was 1948, and I stayed with the *Herald* till she died in 1968.

The *Family Herald and Weekly Star*, although they were combined as one paper, was really one publication. The *Her-*

ald was printed on cheap newsprint that ended up in the backhouse on most farms. It would run to about fifty-six pages. It was more news than feature articles. The news of the fairs was meticulously recorded and there was technical advice on various types of farming. In addition, there was the women's section, and the magazine section, which was mine. There was a section on old favourite songs, which later became, I think, the largest collection in the world, now preserved by McGill University.

In 1955 there came a dramatic change in the newspaper, because the *Weekly Star* portion was dropped and it became the *Family Herald* only. It was a magazine printed on slick paper and in full, beautiful colour. The kind of journalism also changed. It was believed that we were appealing to an audience that was increasingly urban and a decreasing number of our subscribers were really farmers. So we held on to those readers, and in addition, every article, no matter how technical, had to be written in such an interesting way that it would catch the attention of even a city reader who didn't know what end of a cow got up first.

Now that was quite a challenge to some of our farmer editors, and some of them fell by the wayside. We had writers all over Canada, of course, who had been sending in stories regularly to the *Family Herald*, including a man in Calgary who had, every year, sent a story on the results of the Calgary horse sale. It was simply an account of whose horses went to sale, what prices they sold for, and who bought them. Now we warned that fellow and all the others that this kind of reporting would no longer be accepted. From now on, we said, we want stories that would be interesting to anyone in Canada. Anyway, along came the sale of 1955, a time when horses were out of fashion and being sold for dogmeat. Well, this fellow's report came in exactly the same as it always had been—whose horses had been sold and so on. Under the new format we couldn't use that report so it never got printed.

Later on in Calgary I heard the story of one old man who had attended that sale and had bought fourteen of the most beautiful big draught horses that had entered the ring. He kept bidding, until finally somebody went up to the auctioneer and said, "That old man is a pensioner with no money at all." There was a conference and the auctioneer announced that the fourteen horses would have to be sold over again. This poor old man, it turned out, was a horse lover and he just couldn't bear the thought of those beautiful horses going for dogmeat. Now that was the kind of story we wanted from our correspondent out there, but he had been reporting the sale for so many years, he simply couldn't change his ways.

In spite of everything, the *Family Herald* died without warning in 1968. The editor was in Washington, D.C., when it happened, and he read it in the newspaper there. The staff was angry about the closure, as we all felt it was unnecessary. The paper never lost much money, and even that could have been made up. The publishers just felt it was on the way out, so why prolong the agony. It's a shame, too, because the *Family Herald* back in the Depression days was so successful that it carried the *Montreal Star* on its back. It was the one paper bringing in money. The subscribers were angry and they said, "If it was money you needed, why didn't you tell us?" The subscription price of three dollars hadn't been raised, even though it could and should have been.

The owners didn't even try to sell it. The feeling seemed to be that the family farm is dying out, and the whole emphasis was on "agribusiness", and the advertisements that used to come to us from the implement dealers were now being published in their own brochures. The owners never made any serious effort to make inroads into the cities. If it was being sold there at all, it was by subscription only.

In the Maritimes, for instance, our circulation man was told to do what he could to cut circulation, as the implement companies were objecting to our circulation figures being based on people who weren't going to buy any implements. I recall on one occasion a lovely full-colour cover of a team of horses drinking at a stream with the farmer standing beside them. One implement company objected, saying, "This isn't modern agriculture. This isn't selling tractors." So the word came down from our head office that we could have no more covers like that one. That was one instance of the advertiser controlling the quality and content of a newspaper.

It was rather an ignominious end for this paper that had helped hold Canada together through the early years— through days of immigration when the West was being settled, and through two great wars. It was a real national newspaper, and, although basically rural, it was much more than that. In 1968, on the day that it closed its doors for the last time, the staff gathered to say farewell to the "Grand Old Lady with the Petticoats". They tell me there were many tears shed, but I can't report that as a first-hand observer. I couldn't bring myself to attend.

Fred "Tiny" Peet "Sorry, No More Work, Boys"

Not all the homesteaders who came to Canada in the early years of western settlement stayed on their first farms. Some found the land too rocky to make a living. Others found their homesteads too remote and lonely. For one reason or another, many couldn't cope; so they would simply pull up stakes and move on, ever north and westward. Fred "Tiny" Peet saw most of the country by rail during the Depression and he, too, found himself gradually drawn to the North by rumours of work.

My parents settled in Manitoba at first, but the homestead land they had chosen proved so alkaline that they couldn't get a decent crop to grow no matter how they tried, so they moved on to Saskatchewan in 1912. Father bought two lots in the town of Prince Albert, which was booming. It was called "The Niagara of the North" because of the Le Colley Falls Power Dam which was being built at the time. It was supposed to become as great as Niagara and everyone was investing in it. Father put what little money he had in it, and one year later, the whole thing went bust and it broke the town completely for almost fifty years. Father lost everything. Even his two lots were worth nothing.

You could buy a homestead lot for ten dollars then, so we headed about eighteen miles northwest of the town, back to the land again. Times were desperately hard. The main reason I quit school at the age of thirteen was that to continue on into high school, I'd have to attend the one in Prince Albert as there was none in our district. I simply didn't have the clothes, and my parents couldn't afford to get them. Up to that time I had never had shoes, and as I was the youngest in the family, I was on the tail end of the hand-me-downs. I didn't want to go to school any more anyway, as I was anxious to become a man. I thought that thirteen years was long enough to have waited for that.

The first five years on that homestead were rough. To give an idea of just how little we had: there was one roll of toilet paper that Mom would put in the outhouse only when we had company. When they left, the roll was taken away, and the Eaton's catalogue went back in. The only money I ever saw was the cent we'd get paid for every gopher's tail we turned in.

Mother would get ten cents for a dozen eggs, and fifteen cents for every pound of butter she churned. My job was to deliver them, and I can remember that the only fruit I ever got was when one of the customers would sometimes give me a peach or a banana.

We never went hungry though, as there were always rabbits and potatoes, and something we called "pigweed". It's something like lambsquarter, a weed something like spinach, and it wasn't too bad at all.

I think that life was harder on the women than on the men because they suffered more for the children than themselves. They'd be with the children all the time, knowing they didn't have the food or clothing they should have.

The men who were off working on the land most of the time didn't see this, but they had it hard in a different way. They had to clear the trees and grub those roots out of the ground, and that was back-breaking, soul-destroying work. They'd work from morning till night, and through the night at times if a cow was about to calve or something like that happened. My parents took out a six-hundred-dollar mortgage in 1916, and they scrimped and saved wherever they could to pay it off, but even with all that, it wasn't paid off until 1926, two years after my father died.

When the mortgage was out of the way, things got a bit better, and I decided that the homestead could get along without me. This was in 1928. I was twenty, and I got a job in Prince Albert delivering coal for fifteen cents a ton. That meant shovelling it out of the wagon and into customers' bins. Well, as I was a big fellow, over six feet, that didn't bother me at all. When the man I worked for discovered that I was able to do forty tons and earn six dollars a day, he decided I was earning too much, so he cut me to ten cents a ton. That's when I quit and left Prince Albert behind. I got a lift with a bush pilot to a place called Rotten Stone Lake, three hundred miles to the north, and got a job there, the first of the many jobs that would keep me in the North for a big part of my life. When the

Depression hit, we were put in planes, and told, "Sorry, no more work, boys."

In 1930 I became a hobo, as many did, and I rode the rods from one end of the country to the other. It wasn't such a bad life after you knew what you were doing. I could jump aboard a train as fast as anyone, and I could jump off one too when I had to. There were "hobo jungles" all the way along the line, and I tried them all.

When the brakeman came along with this big steel bar, swinging it back and forth to clear off the train, I jumped off and ploughed into the cinders, getting scars on my face and arms, but I didn't break any bones. We were in the middle of nowhere, so there was nothing to do but keep walking along the tracks.

After dark, we crawled into a farmer's field and got something to eat from his garden before continuing on. Much later, we got to this hobo jungle at Sheep Creek, in the Turner Valley, the best of them all, and it was raining. I tell you, it was like coming to a palace. They had this big old tarpaulin slung up between trees, and a big fire going with a large pot of stew bubbling away. We were welcomed and fed, and pretty soon we began feeling not too bad. These so-called hoboes and bums were just a bunch of ordinary guys who wanted nothing more than a job, and were willing to go anywhere to find one. As we all lay around there talking of where there might be jobs, I remember that the general impression was that this "slump", as it was called, wouldn't last long, and pretty soon we'd all be working again. Certainly nobody ever thought it would last as long as the ten years it did, and that it would take a war to end it.

Someone mentioned the Turner Valley oil field and said there might be some work there, but someone else said that all those jobs had been filled with workers from the Petrolia field which closed down in Ontario. Despite this, I was so anxious to find something that I headed out there the next day and got a job thawing out oil wells that had been frozen solid by the terrible frost of that winter. I was hired the day I arrived, and had the first decent meal I'd had in months. The Royalite Company that hired me had good warm bunkhouses, good grub, and they paid us on time every two weeks, so I was in heaven. I was able to save money too, mainly because I didn't smoke or drink, and I had great ambitions.

But the following fall, as the Depression worsened, the company laid off all single men and gave the jobs to married ones with families, so it was back to riding the rods once again. Back and forth across the country. You were chasing rumours of work. When you got to the place, you'd find that there was nothing. A lot of the fellows would go to houses and ask for something to eat but I found I couldn't do that. As I had been very saving, I was never totally broke, and I'd keep some bologna and bread in my packsack all the time.

I went to soup kitchens, though, and was often shot at by angry farmers when I raided their gardens, but I couldn't beg for a meal at somebody's door. One day I was in the public library reading the want ads, when I saw a story about Gilbert LaBine making a big strike at Great Bear Lake in the Northwest Territories—gold, silver, uranium, everything! This would be around September of 1931. I made up my mind that after the fall harvesting—where I'd been promised a job—I'd make my way up to Great Bear Lake.

The government had a free course in prospecting which I took, and when that two-week course was over, I thought I knew everything there was to know about prospecting, and I was raring to go. About all I did know was how to tell coal from quartz, but that didn't matter. I had something to spur me on. When I read in the *Northern Miner* newspaper that the work at Great Bear was going to commence again in February of 1932, I grabbed a train for Edmonton and landed there just as LaBine's first crew were ready to leave for Great Bear.

I went to see Gilbert, and he said they wouldn't be hiring anyone to go there until early in May, which meant I had two months to hang around Edmonton. I picked up a newspaper on the corner to see if there were any jobs, and I can still remember what was on the front-page headlines. One story was about the thirty-eight-below-zero weather. Another headline said Lindbergh's baby had been kidnapped, and another said that they tracked down the Mad Trapper and were attempting to discover his identity. Those were the three big stories that day, and as it turned out, every day after, for a long time.

When I got myself settled in a boarding house I met a chap,

a Dominion land surveyor, by the name of Alex Stewart, who asked me if I'd be interested in going north as a prospector for a mining syndicate they were forming. I said, indeed, I was interested, so, with a friend named Olaf Slotten, I took off for the North for no pay—just a grubstake and a canoe.

We went across Athabasca Lake, down the Slave River, across Slave Lake, and overland to Fort Rae. At that time Yellowknife didn't even exist except for a few vacant Indian cabins. The first thing that happened was that we lost a lot of our supplies when the canoe overturned in some rapids. We salvaged our two sacks of flour, our raisins, and rice but we lost a lot. However, we shot some muskrats on the way across Great Slave and we were able to trade the pelts for some supplies at Rae, where a chap who ran Pinsky's Trading Post bootlegged them for us as we didn't have a licence. He got them for about half their worth. Anyway, we were the first ones to make it into Great Bear that year, and we started prospecting right away. This was early in May.

We were also the first white men to go north overland between Great Slave and Great Bear without Indian guides. We had to make fifty-four portages with two hundred and fifty pounds each on our backs, including an outboard motor. That was the most laborious part, but the worst part by far was the blackflies and the mosquitoes. They chewed you to pieces. We had no protection against them at all except for smudge pots that we'd light when we were making a meal.

When we finally got to Cameron Bay on Great Bear, we met Fred Watt and some other fellows there who were astounded when told them we'd come overland. They said, "It just isn't possible!" "Well," I said, "that may be so, but we did it anyway."

That summer we started in prospecting, and were going along fine until a fire came along and burnt everything we owned except for our canoe. Our tent was gone, our food, everything! Luckily our dynamite was stored at Cameron Bay. As we were down to three dollars and thought we were finished, a fellow offered us a hundred dollars for the dynamite, and the mining syndicate wired us another four hundred dollars, with a message: "Don't give up, boys. We're with you all the way." So we got back to prospecting again for the rest of the summer and we staked some very good claims and headed back to Edmonton, where we sold some of the shares for enough money to keep us going through the winter, until we could go back north in the spring.

In 1933 things got even worse. Mines were closing down, and the price of silver was down to thirty-two cents an ounce. The syndicate we worked for couldn't raise any more money and they were compelled to strike us from the pay roll. We found work whip-sawing lumber, doing carpenter work, broadaxing timber, and anything else we found. The next year we went to work again for the White Eagle Mine, but we weren't there long before it shut down.

We heard that there was work at Eldorado, so we walked sixty-five miles overland to Cameron Bay. It was thirty degrees below zero, January 1935, when we began walking. It took a few days, but there was work when we arrived, and that's what we wanted. During those "hungry thirties", you'd go anywhere and do anything—as long as it was legal.

I was fortunate in that I liked the North. I stayed there until 1938 and helped start up the mine at Yellowknife, and have been back and forth over the years ever since. The people up there made it all worthwhile. You couldn't find better anywhere on earth.

Jack Hardman The Astronauts of Their Day

The credit, the glory, and the glamour of pioneer flight in Canada goes to the bush pilots, and deservedly so. But there was another group of men, largely ignored in the historical accounts, who merit equal acclaim. These were the mechanics who kept the planes flying, who accompanied the pilots on their daredevil missions into unknown places, and who were often called upon to get the aircraft aloft again with nothing but haywire and on-the-spot ingenuity. Jack Hardman, now of Moncton, New Brunswick, flew with many of Canada's greatest flying pioneers and was responsible for keeping many of them safely airborne.

I came over from England after the First World War in 1919. I was fourteen years old at the time, and my parents decided to make their home in the area around Montreal. We all had to work, of course, and I found jobs as delivery boy and office boy, or anything else I could do, until finally I found one where I could learn my trade as an apprentice electrician. I really liked this, learning all there was to know about electricity, arc welding, machinery, and all that goes with it.

When I was around twenty years old, a friend in the peacetime air force took me out to see some planes he was working on at a hangar in Montreal. It was love at first sight for me, and I knew then and there that this was the type of work I wanted. The only planes I'd ever seen before were war planes in the skies over England, and, like any small boy, I was excited by them. Now, though, when I had actually touched a plane on the ground, and looked inside the engine and cockpit, I was simply enthralled, and determined to become a part of the flying game. I was working in Kingston, Ontario, then, and the first thing I did was to go back there and quit my job, pack my things, and head back to Montreal.

I went out to the flying club immediately and asked the chief instructor if he had a job for me. His answer was, "Well, not at the moment, but we have a young fellow who has joined the RCAF and his job will be vacant in a few weeks." I made up my mind to be on hand when that job came up.

I could think of nothing else but airplanes by this time. I found some work there, digging ditches and laying drainage tile, as they were building the St. Hubert Airport where the Montreal Flying Club had its headquarters. Every morning I'd keep watch from my ditch for the instructor who had told me of the up-coming job. When I'd see him approach, I'd hop out of the ditch and ask him, "Is that other fellow gone yet?" He'd say, "No, not yet." I went through this routine every morning until the day he said, "Yes, he's gone, and the job is yours if you want it." Well, I sure did want it.

The chief engineer at the club, Art Adams, had worked with the famous Colonel Coady in England in 1909 during the early flying days, and he knew what planes were all about. Coady at that time was experimenting with a biplane braced with wires. While the plane was in the air, everything would be fine, but every time he landed the wires would break and have to be restrung all over again—each time with stronger wire. But that's the way it was then. Everything was experiment. Try this, and try that, and try again. Coady, by the way, was the first man in the world to take off from the deck of a ship and land back on the deck again. He was a true aviation pioneer, and it excited me to work with Art Adams, who had worked with Coady.

Art taught me how to take engines apart, grind the valves, and put them together again. He also taught me how to replace and repair the fabric the wings were covered with. In fact I was learning everything about the working of planes, and by the time he was finished teaching me, I could take a plane apart, right down to the nuts and bolts, and put it back together. Art, however, had a booze problem, and he preferred spending time in the pub rather than the airfield; and what he was doing, really, was preparing me to be his replacement on the field while he was off drinking. I didn't mind that at all though, as I loved those planes so much.

We had six planes and two instructors, and everything would go along fine until one of the students would ground-loop a plane and bust a wing, and then I would have to go to the pub for Adams to help me take the wing off and replace it. He'd always come, but he would bawl the student out for interfering with his drinking.

One of our instructors, a Captain Sparks, made a business

for himself building airplanes for some Montreal millionaires who began a club at Dorval. On my days off, I would go to their club and do repairs. They were forever damaging the floats or things of that nature. When one of them damaged their plane in a crash, they would bring an engineer over from England to fix them up. They never worried about cost, these millionaires.

One time Captain Sparks took a plane with folding wings for a test flight. The wings were folded while it was on ground, you see; but when it was readied for the air, the wings would be brought forward, and a pin put through the hinges to hold the wings in place while aloft. Well, whatever happened, whether someone didn't put the pin in properly, or whatever, one of the wings folded while Sparks was in the air. The plane crashed, and he was killed.

Although I learned to fly while I was there, I never bothered getting a licence, as it was the mechanical part that I was interested in, not flying them myself. I was content to look after the machines. In some of the planes I would sit in a two-seater alongside the pilot. The crank for starting the engine was down below the instrument panel on the inside. It was like a crank on an old Model-T car, but the cranking would have to be done in the cramped quarters of the cockpit.

There were some great pilots. Captain Spooner and Captain Golds are two I remember. Then, of course, there was "Punch" Dickins. I didn't fly with Punch, but he was my superintendent when I worked in the Mackenzie District. "Wop" May was another, and I often flew with him as flying mechanic, going down the Mackenzie, delivering mail and passengers with float-equipped craft in summer and skis in winter.

My first trip with skis was with Archie McMullen, and when we got to the place on the Mackenzie somewhere, we couldn't land as it was all open water, and he had to go on until he found a frozen lake. By this time it was dark, so my first job on landing was to drain the oil from the plane and cover up the engine. In the meantime, Arch was making up our beds with sleeping bags and spruce boughs.

After we cooked some beans and turned in for the night, I kept waking up, feeling as though something was crawling all over my body. When I told Archie about it in the morning, we investigated, and found that my bed had been made right over a squirrel hole, and they were indeed coming in and out and crawling over me all night long. I suppose I provided a little unexpected warmth for them in the middle of an Arctic winter. Well, we had a great laugh over it, and set about getting some breakfast.

Then, as always, we put the oil from the plane on the stove to thaw it. We put the stove under the engine to warm it up, piled in our gear, and took off again. It was a constant battle in the North to keep the machine from seizing up in those very cold temperatures. Sometimes we used blowtorches to thaw the oil, which turned solid in a very few minutes up there. And then after every ten hours of flying, we would have to take out the push rods which worked the valves, and lubricate them. At thirty degrees below zero Fahrenheit, that can be quite a job. I would heat my wrenches and tools before I tackled that chore to keep my hands warm, as we could only use cotton gloves for it. I'd wear out about four pairs of gloves during just one job. One time, on a trip to Aklavik, I had to lubricate those valves twice.

Aklavik is on the Arctic Ocean, and we stayed there overnight while the people we brought the mail to would answer it right away, so we could fly it out with us on our return trip in the morning. We made the trip up there every two weeks and we'd stay overnight at places such as the Mission House in Cranberry Portage, the Hudson's Bay post, or the Signals barracks at Aklavik. We'd sleep on the floor in eiderdown sleeping bags. It took a few days to make a trip like that from our base at Fort McMurray. Everything and everybody for that part of the North was brought in by plane from Edmonton to Fort McMurray, and taken out by bush plane.

As there was no radio then, if a pilot had trouble he knew he'd be there for three days before help came. If a plane didn't show up where it was expected, the people back at base would wait three days before sending out a rescue plane equipped with various spare parts to fix the problem, whatever it was.

One of the mechanic's duties before the beginning of a trip was to sneak into the storeroom at McMurray and steal some parts to replace the ones he thought might break down. We were never issued with spares at all, things such as spark plugs or points, or other odds and ends. One mechanic I knew sneaked an extra cylinder aboard before they took off on a week-long trip up in the barren lands. When they got there, they had engine failure, and when they landed and examined it, they found one of the cylinders was shot.

The disgusted pilot said, "It'll take three days for them to get that part in here." "Oh no, it won't," replied the mechanic. He went back to where he had hidden the spare cylinder in the plane. The pilot, of course, was delighted. In a few hours they were back in the air once more. When they got back to base and told the story, the poor mechanic got a terrible bawling out from the boss for taking that cylinder without permission!

We were taking all kinds of passengers in there—prospectors, miners, and even nuns for the convent school at Cranberry Portage. We often flew in trappers and their dog teams. When the dogs got howling all together, that would make a noisy cargo, I'll tell you.

One time we had this big, husky chap who went crazy up at Great Bear Lake and was smashing up everything at the camp. We were pretty nervous about taking him out, but when he was aboard the plane he was as quiet as a mouse. However, the mechanic never let go of the crank for a second in case he started acting up. The Mounties met him at Fort McMurray and took him the rest of the way to Edmonton. We later found out that the fellow wasn't crazy at all. He simply wanted to get out of the North, and he didn't want to pay the fare; and he figured that if he acted crazy, he'd be taken out for nothing. His scheme didn't work, however, because the Mounties were on to him and before they let him go, they presented him with a bill for two hundred and sixty dollars.

It was a very empty northland back then. Yellowknife hadn't even come into being. Great Slave Lake Post was there, Fort Simpson, and Norman Wells. Arctic Red River and Aklavik were some of the other places that we'd stay overnight, but generally speaking there weren't many people up north. Punch Dickins was the first man to fly into Aklavik, and his plane was the first the natives there had ever seen. When he flew back there the following month, one of the Eskimos came over shyly and presented him with a soapstone model of his plane. Now, this Eskimo had only seen that one plane, but the replica he made from memory was perfect.

Everyone was excited about the changes the plane was making in life in the North. We would fly off into the wilderness for ten days at a time and, although it could be dangerous and the terrain was unknown, I can't recall that we were ever afraid. We were young, of course, and we were filled with the excitement of exploration. If we had to land because of trouble, we'd just make ourselves at home on the ice until we could take off again.

In those days, the pilots were looked on as heroes by everybody. People would gather around them when they'd walk down a street with their helmets and goggles, and they'd follow them everywhere they went. The mechanics who flew along with them didn't receive the same kind of treatment, though.

I remember one time at the airfield in Moncton, there were two pilots and me in a plane that crashed after take-off. We all suffered cuts and fractures and were pretty badly shaken up. So they rushed us to the hospital, and put the two pilots in private rooms with every doctor and nurse in the place fussing over them. I was taken to a bed in the public ward where I think they forgot all about me. A few hours later, one of the doctors came by and examined the cuts on my face. He said that the best medicine for me would be the fresh air, and that I could leave. When I got to the door, they told me that I couldn't go until I paid my bill. In the meantime the pilots were the centre of everybody's attention upstairs. After settling my bill, I walked down the street, and everyone is talking about the crash, and of how the pilots almost lost their lives. Nobody even asked me how I got the cuts on my face, but, you know, that didn't bother me one little bit.

Those fellows were all heroes of the times. They were the astronauts of their day, and as far as I was concerned I was lucky just to be working and flying with them.

Russell McNeil "Don't Let the Fire Go Out"

Although the greatest influx of people to Eastern Canada
came more than a century before the West was settled,
the immigrants at both times came for many of the same
reasons. They were looking for better lives, and often
were escaping persecution at home.

In the late eighteenth century, as a result of the infa-
mous Highland Clearances in Scotland, the first major
wave of Scottish settlers arrived, destitute, disillusioned,
and unhappy, on the shores of Nova Scotia. One of their
descendants, Russell McNeil, lived all his life on the island
of Cape Breton; and he found little changed on the island
since those earliest days of settlement.

Our people came over from Scotland at the time of the
Clearances when the landowners felt they could make more
money from sheep than people. They cleared the people off
the land and turned it into sheep pasture, so these families
had no choice but to leave altogether. This took place all over
the Highlands and the islands around the coast.

Most of the McNeils, or MacNeils, came from the Isle of
Barra in the Outer Hebrides, which is really a rocky, hard
island where the people lived very close to the land, scratching out a living between farming and fishing. It was a survival
existence, but they had been that way for hundreds of years,
and they loved their island. The chief of the McNeils lived
there, and they looked to him somewhat like a child looks to
its father. They felt secure.

However, when the Clearances came, it was obvious that
their chief was just another landlord, and he joined the others
in displacing people for sheep. They weren't asked to leave:
they were driven off by sheriffs and their deputies, who set
fire to the homes so that the people couldn't drift back to
them. They were a confused and heartbroken lot who left
Barra in the early part of the nineteenth century. They didn't
know what to do, or where to go, so when these ship owners
were advertising for people to go to the colonies—to Canada,
Australia, and New Zealand—the only thing they could do was

to take what little money they had and book passage on those leaky old boats.

They were crowded on board with not enough food and water, and it took them more than a month to get to Nova Scotia. It must have been terrible for them when they got here, as there was practically no sign of any civilization. The land was full of trees, which they didn't have on Barra, and there was nobody there to welcome them. They were very strong, though, and somehow they managed to survive, learning how to cut down trees and build log cabins, which enabled them to get through that first winter. In the spring they planted crops between the stumps, and gradually they established themselves.

The amazing thing was that the society they built was very much like the one they left behind, with the exception that they now owned the land they lived on. They did some farming, some fishing, spoke their Gaelic language, sang their Gaelic songs, played bagpipes and fiddles, built their little churches, and looked to the priest or the minister for guidance. They tried to forget the past, but the song makers and the storytellers wouldn't allow them to do that. You'll find those bleak and bitter memories enshrined forever in their folklore. The society that evolved from all of this survived for more than a century on Cape Breton Island, and indeed, there's still a lot of it here today.

I was born in 1896, and although I grew up in the early part of the twentieth century, life had not changed from what it must have been like two hundred years before. My father had a small farm at Ingonish on the northern part of the island, right on what is called the Cabot Trail today. In those days it was remote backwoods country, and the farm was so marginal that it couldn't even support our small family of father, mother, and four children. But we, as everybody else, had a small fishing boat, and we managed to have enough to eat— most of the time.

I can remember one time that we didn't, though. It was in the middle of one very bad winter. The only road over Cape Smokey was blocked by twenty feet of snow, and, as it is every winter, of course, the coast was surrounded by drift ice as far as the eye could see. The general store had run out of supplies, and the people were hungry. Now my father, who was a big, strong man known as "Captain John", just couldn't stand it any longer. Aside from a few potatoes in the cellar, and a bit of salted meat and fish, we had nothing to eat, and little prospects of getting any in the immediate future. I was about ten years old, and I recall him sitting there by the big stove in the kitchen, staring at the floor. Then, suddenly, he stood up and said to Mother, "I'm going." Mother didn't answer, but I remember that she looked awfully distressed. Father put on two pairs of woollen socks, pulled on a second pair of trousers, a second sweater, a big pair of boots, his heavy mackinaw, and his cap. Then he wrapped a large woollen scarf around his face, pulled on his mitts, and said to Mother as he went out the door into the storm, "Don't let the fire go out." When I asked Mother where he was going, she would only say that he was going for food.

Three days later he came back. He had a seventy-five-pound bag of flour on one shoulder, and a huge sack of other groceries slung over the other. He walked over and put both bags on the table, made his way to the kitchen couch, and immediately fell asleep—and stayed asleep for the next twenty-four hours.

Father had walked to Sydney thirty miles away through the woods to get that food, and then, with a load that must have weighed one hundred and fifty pounds, he walked back again, without once stopping to sleep. But that was the kind of people those early Scottish were. To him, that wasn't a remarkable feat. It was simply something that had to be done, and if he didn't do it, who else could?

Ernest Monteith Christmas Concerts and Chilblains

The old one-room country schools were often crudely built, cold, drafty, and lacking luxuries of any kind; but they were built from the dreams of people who wanted their children to get more from life than they had had themselves. These little buildings eventually produced the men and women who forged our Canada of today and they produced some of our fondest memories. The memories are all that is left because most of these schools have been pushed aside by an educational system that no longer needs them. Ernest Monteith of Cottam, Ontario, a teacher for forty-five years, treasures his memories of one-room schools.

When I first started to teach, the Depression was on. It was in a two-room school, with me as the principal and one other teacher, but after that I was in one-room schools where one had about forty pupils on average, divided between all the grades.

In the centre of the room was one of these old-fashioned pot-bellied stoves with a screen around it. How warm you were depended on how close you could get to that stove, but the thing I remember best is having cold feet. I don't think I ever took my overshoes off in class in the winter. Chilblains were common in those days—something you hardly ever hear of now. They came from getting your feet wet and cold, and it seems that once you got chilblains, your feet would forever after be susceptible to cold. In those days every second person had them. Anyway, I had them, and my feet were always cold, burning, and itching at the same time.

Once the children got back to school after the summer holidays, and we got into the routine of the new year, the next big thing, and the most enjoyable, was making plans for the Christmas concert. The school inspector always came around to the various schools, and warned the teachers that they weren't to spend too much time at this, but that seemed to be just a standard rule that was meant to be broken. The parents all expected a decent presentation at least two hours long, and to have their children in that concert, or connected to it in some way. The wise teacher made sure that they weren't disappointed.

Sometimes we had to stretch our ingenuity and the children's talents to do this, because we had no money to do much, and it was most often a case of making something out of nothing. One school that I taught in had no electricity, so we had as many children as possible bring coal-oil lamps which were placed on hooks on the walls of the room to form a bright stage. It looked wonderful too.

The only musical instrument we had was an old organ so full of dust and mice nests that the sound it made was anything but music. I decided that I'd better try to do something about that if we were to have any music at all, so I began going over to the school in the nights, and I took that organ completely apart. There were hundreds of parts lying around, and I cleaned and dusted them. I practically shovelled out the grime and never having done anything of that nature before, I felt pretty nervous when I started putting it all back together. But you know, despite the fact that I had a few pieces left over, that old organ sounded beautiful.

It was one of the really big events of the year. It would take months to get ready for those concerts—before, during, and after school hours. One lady from the area who had musical training came in and trained the children with their songs, and even though it always seemed that most of them had colds, she'd have them sounding like a choir of angels. There'd be a play to rehearse, new songs and recitations to be learned, sets to build, and other chores, but the closer it got to Christmas, the more excitement there was, not only in the school, but in the community as well. When the big night arrived, it was always wonderful. No matter what the quality of the performances, the applause would be deafening, and every year audiences would say the same thing: "This was the best one yet."

It was rather a lonely life. The schoolteacher in these small communities was almost always the only stranger there. Everyone knew everyone else, but the teacher knew no one, despite the efforts made by the people to make him or her feel at home. When you were invited out in the evening, it was very often to someone's house, where there would be a young girl whose parents were husband-hunting for her, and, of course, that made a young fellow pretty uncomfortable. I went through quite a few such evenings at various homes, and managed to survive it. The girl that I eventually married, I met on my own, and we were happily married for forty-eight years.

The teacher was not only the loneliest man in town, but he, or she, was also the most watched. No matter what one did, where one went, and with whom, the teacher's every action was noted and reported. People knew more about you than you knew about yourself; and because of this, you automatically became the most careful person in town, a model of good behaviour. You had no choice.

There was, however, a great satisfaction in teaching then, due to the tremendous chance it gave to help mould a child. You had them all day long for every subject; and in the one-room schools, you had them every year. You could follow their progress all the way along, and you had a great impact on their lives—in the manner they dressed, and on their social behaviour.

There was a great bond of respect at that time between the teacher and the students, and it was understood that there was a line that couldn't be crossed. The teacher was a figure of authority. He knew it, and the children knew it.

In those days, the teacher felt a great pride in the success of his students, and by the same token, much disappointment in those who failed. It got to be a very personal thing, and all of those children became your family, in a manner of speaking. You never forget them and it seems that a lot of them never forget you. I still get letters from men and women I taught forty-five or fifty years ago. Some of them simply want to stay in touch, or maybe they'll say that they just want to thank me for some advice I gave them so long ago.

There were many crosses to bear—low pay, difficult parents and school boards, lonely times in poor boarding houses, and some children who simply couldn't be helped—but the satisfactions more than made up for all of that. If I could have my time over, I'd gladly do it all again.

Oliver Charon The Town Was Just a Pile of Coal

One of the worst forest fires in Canadian history swept
across Northern Ontario in 1911. More than two hundred
people died—the exact number was never determined—in
what has come to be known as "the South Porcupine
Fire". The 1911 fire destroyed the rapidly growing communities of Cochrane, South Porcupine, parts of Timmins, Porquis Junction, and Goldlands. Homes, towns,
and whole communities were wiped out. Oliver Charon of
Cochrane was a schoolboy at the time.

I was born in Minnesota in 1901 and lived there till I was
ten; but at that time there was a big mine strike that lasted for
months and months, so my parents packed up and came up to
Northern Ontario in 1911. The town of Cochrane was just
getting started, and my father and some others came here
looking for work. My dad was a carpenter, and all the houses
were being built for the men who were constructing the
Ontario Northland Railroad. There were just a few houses in
town—maybe five or six, no more. We got here in May, and
from then until July new buildings were going up every day.
Everything was new. Then in July the fire came, and I tell you,
I'd never want to see anything like that again.

When the fire came we lived on Second Avenue, right on
the corner. They had started to dig a ditch in front for the
water line and sewers, and Dad and I took all we could from
the house and threw it in that ditch when we saw the fire
coming. We started to bury it, but there was no time. I remember my mother's sewing machine. She needed that, so we
threw it in the ditch along with some furniture and a lot of
small personal possessions. When we came back even those
things in the ditch were burned. We saved nothing at all!

At three o'clock in the afternoon it was as dark as it would
be at eleven or twelve at night, because of the black smoke
rolling over the town. It came from the southwest where the
forest was all spruce, balsam, and that kind of thing. You can
imagine what fire does in that!

We got the word: "Run to the station! Run to the station!"

The railroad put on all their equipment—boxcars, flatcars, whatever they had—to take people out. Train after train.

I recall when we left for the train, Dad had a small trunk on his back, and we were all running, but he couldn't go as fast as we could. After a little while he had to throw the trunk on the ground and run for his own life. He didn't even get on the same train as us, and Mother was nearly crazy all night worrying if he got caught in the fire. She didn't find out till the next day when we got back that he was all right. We all survived—my brother, my sister, my parents, and me.

We got in a boxcar at three o'clock, and I don't know how far they took us out, but it was night by the time we stopped. We stayed there overnight, and came back the next day to find that the town was just a pile of coal. Black stuff all over the place. Just about everything was gone! A few buildings were left, but very few. I remember one of them was the King George Hotel, a cement building, and there was one little house on Twelfth Avenue, the house of an Indian family. Their name was Commando. That's where Lake Commando got its name.

The railroad station was saved because it was all cement. That's where we all had to line up to get the provisions coming in from the government. They also sent in tents all pitched on a hill near town. That place at night was something to see! It looked just like an Indian village with all these little camp-fires, and the lights inside the tents shining through the canvas. It was really something!

The town began to rebuild almost immediately because the government sent in lumber. I remember the house we built was very small, but that didn't matter. It was something to go into away from the cold, and winter was coming fast. We were in the house by the time fall came around.

The reason Cochrane burned so fast was that the forest was too close to the town. The trees came right up to the edge of where we all lived. The thick forest was right across the road from our house; so when the fire came, there was nothing else for the town to do but burn. We were scared, of course, when the fire got close; but when we were running for our lives, we were really scared! Scared right out of our minds!

Five years later, in 1916, during another big fire, only half the town burned. My wife's sister and her two children were burned to death in that one. Fire was always the dread of people up here, but it didn't drive us out of the North, because where else could you go? Work was scarce all over the country. Anyway, people were strong, and it took more than fire to defeat them. We were used to the hard life, and fire was just one more thing!

John Enns Mennonites Were Masters of Their Own Time

Between the years 1923 and 1930, approximately twenty thousand Mennonites left Russia for Canada, as they found life in their homeland intolerable after the revolution of 1917. Under the new Communist régime they lost all their possessions and their freedom. When the government granted them permission to emigrate in 1923, an arrangement was made with CPR to transport them here on a "come-now-pay-later" basis to new homes in Ontario, Manitoba, Saskatchewan, and Alberta, where they sought to live as they had on the steppes of Russia, specializing in the production of wheat. Today John Enns is a retired schoolteacher and the last Mennonite living in the area of Reesor, Ontario.

The group of Mennonites that came to Ontario found themselves faced with conditions strange to them. They were dispersed to the homes of other Mennonites who were indeed farmers, but the farms were different from those they had known. Instead of wheat, the produce was mixed, aimed at serving the industrial market of southern Ontario. Most of the farmers could employ only one farmhand, so families were forced to split up in order to find jobs on various farms. The only day they could come together as a family was on Sunday. Most families began drifting into towns after a year or two, when factory jobs offered better pay, where they could enjoy a measure of independence, and, above all, where families could stay together. For some families this was the final solution to the problem of finding a permanent home and of adjusting to their new homeland.

But to others, working by the hour and punching time clocks in a factory were obnoxious. They tolerated all this for a while because there was a debt to pay to the CPR, and a nest egg to be provided for a new home, but this goal of again establishing their own independent holdings—where they and their children could be masters of their own time—was never allowed out of sight. They heard of their friends buying wheat farms out west, but they were afraid of the possible consequences of contracting unmanageable debts. With some of them, the idea gained ground more and more that the best way to make a new beginning would be to settle on cheap virgin land that would offer possibilities for the establishment of closed communities after the pattern of their colonies in Russia.

At this stage their attention was drawn to the possibility of homesteading in Northern Ontario. A Jacob Siemens of Winnipeg, probably a land agent, offered free tickets to a delegation to go north to look at homesteads available in the District of Cochrane. During the month of January 1925, Siemens went north accompanied by two men, and looked over the proposed area. They could not make a proper appraisal of the land because of the heavy cover of snow on it, but they noted the thick stands of spruce, and could estimate that in this, the prospective settlers would have a reliable source of income for a considerable period during which they would be able to clear land for farming.

When the delegates returned and reported their findings to a meeting, the majority of those present decided against settling in the northern forest. Neither they nor their forefathers had ever tackled the prospect of having to pull stumps. They judged it to be more advantageous to make a new beginning on the western prairie lands.

However, Thomas Reesor, a minister and leader in an old Mennonite congregation in the vicinity of Pickering, Ontario, had great faith in the possibilities that wooded homesteads offered, and he suggested that those who did not want to go west should give it a try. He offered to obtain the free settlers' tickets from the CNR for another inspection tour in the spring. This offer was accepted by a group of interested people, and at the beginning of May of the same year, four men went north for another look. Walking through the beautiful spring forest, with trees just breaking into leaf, and the swarms of mosquitoes and blackflies as yet unhatched, the four men came to a tentative decision to give it a try, provided they could obtain a good number of other interested people to join them.

When they returned from this trip, a call for volunteers was published in a German Mennonite weekly, and applications were received. All these people were summoned to a meeting in Waterloo for the purpose of consolidating plans.

John Enns

About thirty prospective settlers showed up and the meeting decided that all those who wanted to settle in the proposed area were to be in Toronto on the fifteenth of June, 1925, whence they would jointly depart to the North.

On the appointed day, a group assembled at the Toronto station, but only nine heads of families had shown up—some alone, others with their entire families, or with a few of their children old enough to help. Thomas Reesor joined the group as guide and advisor and the venture was under way.

That was the beginning. There were many difficult days, months, and years ahead, but it was this group that founded the settlement of Reesor in Northern Ontario in 1925.

16

Emily Carr and her English sheepdogs in her garden. "It was at Emily Carr's that we stayed the night. She had this little monkey that took an immediate dislike to me, and it kept trying to attack me. Emily Carr finally took it and locked it up in another room until we left." (Joe Garner)

17

Commercial Street in the early 1900s, the main street of Glace Bay, Cape Breton. "Life was not a fleeting thing then; and there was a permanence we don't have today. I believe that Cape Breton is still one of the few places in Canada that hasn't become 'North Americanized'." (Dan McDermid)

18

Like their fellow countrymen here, many of the Mennonites who came to settle in Canada knew little of the conditions they would find in this new country. "They had come from various parts of Russia and had come through a lot of harrowing experiences during the troubled years of the Russian Revolution." (Erna Tows Dyck)

19

Mennonite family making apple butter near Stouffville, Ontario, in 1912.

Mabel Lucas Rutherford was one of those who volunteered for overseas duty in the First World War. "Every morning I got the newspaper and kept looking for word of those chosen to go. Finally, there it was. I had all I could do to keep from standing up and cheering."

One of Ontario's best-loved lieutenant-governors and the first woman in the Commonwealth to hold the position was the Honourable Dr. Pauline McGibbon, who held the office from 1974 to 1980.

Indian settlement on the Fraser River, British Columbia. "It was during the Depression that the government hit upon the idea of reserving big tracts of land where they could put natives, and where we could live out our lives in the way they thought we wanted." (Chief Stephen Knockwood)

A view of Portage Avenue and the Winnipeg Street Railway in the 1880s as Leonard Knott knew it.

24

A typical scene on Kensington Avenue, Toronto, in 1925. "As they weren't permitted to own land, Jews in Europe did a lot of this collecting of junk, which was really recycling." (Dr. Harold Segall)

25

The Quebec Conference in August 1943. "King said, in fact, that his relationship with Churchill and Roosevelt would win an election for him any time. That was the kind of thing he was thinking of, rather than a share in the conduct of the war." (Colonel C. P. Stacey)

West and Peachey Alligator tug, Simcoe, Ontario. "The Alligator was so named because it was practically amphibious. It was built to pass over logs and booms, and could go close enough to shore to winch the trapped logs and get them back into the main stream." (Lorne Smith Eady)

Presbyterian Church at Eversley, Ontario, with its proud minister. "The minister's family always had to live up to great expectations in the community. They were supposed to be shining examples of everything, including the way they looked and the way they behaved." (Rev. Dr. E. A. Thomson)

28

The shameful expulsion of Japanese Canadians to camps in the interior of British Columbia and Alberta continued from 1942 to 1946. "On the second or third day after Pearl Harbor we were all ordered to leave our homes and go to Vancouver on the mainland. This applied to all Japanese families, so there was a great deal of confusion and crying as we all hurried to pack and get things down to the dock." (Helen Sakon)

29

Major David V. Currie of the South Alberta Regiment (at left, with pistol) was awarded the Victoria Cross for his action at St. Lambert-sur-Dives on August 19, 1944. Here he supervises the rounding up of German prisoners.

30

A one-room school on an Indian reserve in British Columbia around 1910. "The biggest mistake ever made with regard to native people was the Indian Act they created a long time ago. When you apply it to all Indians, even those on the highest rungs of the economic ladder, it serves to hold Indians back." (Elliott Moses)

Chautauqua at Manitou Lake, Saskatchewan, July 1922. "It's necessary to understand the isolation and deprivation of farm people at the time to understand what Chautauqua meant to them. This was world-class entertainment coming right to their doorsteps." (Marjorie Winspear McEnaney)

Erna Tows Dyck They Had Come from Various Parts of Russia

One of the hardy Mennonite settlers in Reesor, Ontario, was fourteen-year-old Erna Tows Dyck, who accompanied her father and brothers on the pioneering trip in 1925. Although young Erna was impressed with the settlement's progress, the community was eventually unable to support itself by pulpwood-cutting alone. The settlers also realized that their seventy-five-acre lots could never produce sufficient food to sustain them. Reluctantly they moved from the north to larger farms in western Canada and southern Ontario where they have prospered.

I was fourteen and my brother Cornelius was fifteen when my father took the two of us to the north, where we were to help establish a new settlement with a group of Mennonite men. About midnight on the second night the train stopped in the wilderness and our group got off. As a temporary arrangement, I was put in the care of the Warkentin family, which went on to the next station, the village of Mattice. Here we were met by a Mr. Christianson, who, lantern in hand, guided us over a long railway bridge to the other side of the wide river. It was a very dark and high bridge, floored by widely spaced ties, and unprotected by side rails. Crossing was frightening, and seemed interminable. When we finally got to the other side, we found shelter in a small cabin owned by Mr. Christianson, where I remained for a week with Mrs. Warkentin and her children.

In the meantime our group, left at the edge of an endless forest, stood forlorn and crestfallen in the dark for a while. They had brought only one small tent for shelter. This was soon put up, but it could only admit a few of them. The others had to make do with what scant protection was offered by the trees. They became the helpless prey of mosquitoes and black-flies, for it was the month of June when these pests are at their worst. Only with the dawning of the new day did they discover a vacant log cabin quite nearby.

This cabin had solid log walls and a roof and there were openings for windows and an entrance, but these contained no sash and glass, and no door. The newcomers did not know who owned the cabin, but, seeing that it was abandoned, they appropriated it for a temporary home. In a week's time, my father brought me to his makeshift abode, and I became the first female of this settlement. All of us slept on the ground, for the cabin had no wooden floor. Moss was to serve for mattresses, and logs were laid on the moss layer to mark off individual sleeping areas, so that each one could know the extent to which he could stretch and roll. I was assigned a "stall" in the farthest corner of the cabin, where I could hide behind my father and brother. How glad I was to have the security and assurance of their protective presence!

One by one the men selected homesteads for themselves and got them registered in their names. When this was done, they began building on their own lands, usually working in pairs, since one man could not handle the heavy logs alone.

In the evenings, however, they all came back to the shelter of the cabin and we would sit beside the fire in the middle of the cabin. The room was always filled with smoke, as we had no chimney and, besides, we needed the smoke to keep the mosquitoes from eating us alive. In this way we ate our suppers, and listened to the stories these men had to tell. They had come from various parts of Russia, and had come through a lot of harrowing experiences during the troubled years of the Russian Revolution. Some tales were sad enough to move me to tears, while others were exceedingly funny. When we sat beside our makeshift tables and partook of the meals we had cooked over the open fire, rabbits and squirrels would come into our midst to snatch food remnants we'd throw them. They had no fear, for they had not yet come to know man. Partridges would sit close to the door and would not move until they were dropped by a thrown stone or stick, to be added to the food supply. Nature was as free and unspoiled as God had made it.

During the day, the men were usually away working on their homesteads, and I was alone in the cabin. One day one of the men came back early, pale-faced and reeling. He had cut a deep gash in his leg with the axe. I stood there helpless, not knowing what to do. We had nothing for dressing wounds. Nothing! I saw him take a bottle of liniment and pour some of it into the open cut. Seeing the poor man bend over double with pain, I thought his end had come, but he remained in the cabin for only a few days, and went back to work again.

My father had chosen his homestead quite close to the cabin, and soon discovered that someone—probably a trapper in days gone by—had left a little log shanty. It had a flat, slanting roof, only one window and a door, but it was something that now belonged to my father and us. My brother and I lost no time moving into it, and were elated to live in privacy in our own cabin. Here I could run my own little household. I cooked, baked, and did our laundry, and in spare hours walked over to the building site some two hundred yards away, to help with construction of the house.

I don't know where Dad got the two-wheeled chassis we used to transport the newly cut spruce logs. We would put the heavy end of the log on the axle bar. Dad would hold up the smaller end, and, with Cornelius and me pulling at the tongue, or shaft, we would take each log to where we wanted it at the site. It took a lot of logs to build the two-storey house for our family of ten. The logs were carefully fitted, one upon another; the chinks between them were filled with moss and then sealed and smoothed with a slurry of clay. Later when strips of strong building paper were tacked over the inner side of the wall, this in turn was covered with printed wallpaper, and the rooms became quite presentable.

One day after the main house walls stood ten feet high, and we were busy on the gable and roof section, Dad slipped on a beam and fell, hitting the upper rim of the wall with his chest. He became very sick almost at once, and a bad night followed. I couldn't sleep. It was impossible to call a doctor, as the closest one was thirty miles away and there were no roads. Suddenly he spoke and said, "Should I die here, take my fondest greetings to Mother, will you?" I felt helpless and hopeless. But a miracle happened! Dad spent a few days on his sickbed in the shanty, then got up and continued to work on the house. It was later discovered that he had only fractured two ribs.

Everyone worked diligently to have their houses ready for the first cold weather in the fall. Our provisions had to be packed in from Mattice, seven miles away. We walked in on the railway bed, trying to adjust our steps to the various distances between ties. Coming back we carried packsacks with our purchases. I remember how tired we would get on those fourteen-mile shopping trips.

When the houses were finally finished after three months of hard labour, preparations were made to have the families come up from southern Ontario. The wives of the men were notified when and how to leave. A time of anxious waiting set in as there was no station. Dad estimated the day on which the group should arrive. When train time approached that day, we lit a lantern and made off to the railway, determined to flag the train to a stop. The headlight of the train appeared in the distance, the lantern was kept swinging back and forth over the track, and two short whistle blasts indicated that the engineer intended to stop. Our excitement reached a climax when the train ground to a halt—but then, none of those we had expected arrived. We could do nothing but hope for better luck the next day.

I tidied up the house for a second time, for I wanted everything in tiptop shape when Mother arrived. I baked a batch of raspberry squares from berries that grew wild around the place, and at train time we were all back at the track again, signalling with the lantern, as on the night before. But this time, whistling loud and long, it passed us at full speed. We looked at one another with dismay, wondering what had gone wrong. The next evening we were all there again. No disappointment that time. The train stopped, and all of our loved ones stepped off, one after another! What a joyous reunion it was!

From then on, things began to get better. Winter soon came and the men began to cut pulpwood for the mill in Kapuskasing, which provided us with much-needed income. More young people arrived, and a good deal of visiting and socializing set in, all of which adds up to many pleasant memories.

Mabel Lucas Rutherford "Canadian Nursing Sisters Are Always First Class"

Not only Canadian *men* went off in search of adventure
and excitement in the First World War. Young women
also answered the call, and they generally found more
than they bargained for. Mabel Lucas Rutherford of Oak-
ville, Ontario, remembers her years as a nurse in casualty
centres immediately behind the front lines in Europe.

I received my cap and my RN in 1911 after three years of
training, during the time student nurses got no pay even
though they worked twelve hours a day, with plenty of
overtime thrown in. However, I wanted to be a nurse, so that
didn't bother me at all. When war broke out in 1914, I had
three years' experience behind me, and there was nothing I
wanted more than to serve overseas.

When the war began, I was in the country on a holiday. My
sister wrote me and said they'd been phoning and wanted to
know if I'd join up; but she said, "You forget about that. You
can't go." "Oh, can't I?" I said to myself. I heard about the
Toronto University group that was forming a hospital unit. I
gave my name in without saying a word to anybody at home,
and I waited. Every morning I got the newspaper, and kept
looking for word of those who had been chosen to go, and
there'd be nothing, until finally there it was. My name was
right there with all the others who had been chosen to go with
the Number Four Canadian General Hospital Unit.

I had all I could do to keep from standing up and cheering,
and waving the paper around. What a moment that was! I
spent a few days calming down my family, and assuring them
that I was going to be all right. They accepted the inevitable,
and I went off to get measured for my blue uniform with the
brass buttons, and finish the other business of signing up.

Our entire unit—doctors, nurses, orderlies, and all—was
soon sailing across the Atlantic on a leaky old tub called the
Kildonan Castle that they'd pulled out of mothballs. It was a
dreadful old boat, but it got all seventy-five of us there, and
we landed in Plymouth. From there we went by train to
London, and about a week later, we were in France.

Ten of us nurses went to a hospital in Rouyn, which was just behind the front lines, and it was there I got my first taste of war. The wounded men were pouring in daily, and I was very anxious to get to work helping to relieve their suffering. The ten Canadian nurses were taken out to Number Six British Hospital and I found myself in a ward run by a little Irish nurse. She said, "You can wash the lockers by the beds." I was shocked. I thought—is this what I came over here to do? But I didn't say a word. I just washed the lockers. For two or three days, the English nurses in the ward kept giving me the cool treatment and the slob jobs.

I didn't know what this was all about, because I wanted to nurse patients, not do housekeeping. Anyway, it finally came out. It seems there had been a group of Canadian nurses who were there before, and I guess they were a bit wild, breaking all the rules, and telling the English nurses how to do things. Naturally, this didn't go down too well, so when they left and we came in after them, they thought we'd be just the same, and they were going to let us know where we stood right from the start.

However, they didn't know that were were known as "The Holy Fours" from the Number Four Hospital Unit. It was a nickname we were given because of our "no-nonsense" dedication to duty. The head nurse came to me after a few days of this locker-washing, and said, "Will you take this patient's temperature?" I replied very sarcastically, "Do you think I'm qualified to do that?" Anyway, I did it, and very gradually they accepted us all into their midst and we got to be very good friends.

Oh, I'll never forget how hard we had to work. We got those injured boys straight from the front, and we'd keep them for a few days before they were shipped on to England. I'd work from seven in the morning till eight or nine at night, and when I'd stagger into bed, I'd always think that I'd never be able to get up again. But when morning came, you'd just start all over. It was the thought of those poor suffering boys that kept you going.

I remember one patient they brought in who had been found lying in a field, where he'd been for two days. One of his legs had to be amputated as it was gangrenous. There were terrible wounds on his other leg, and his whole body was peppered with shrapnel. It took hours to tend his injuries, and do you know, I became so close to him during the three days he was with us that when he left, I cried, and he cried. I never did find out if he survived after he was evacuated to England. That was the hardest part of the nursing service. You'd get very wrapped up in trying to save an injured soldier's life, and you never knew what happened to them after they left your care. That happened so many times during my four years behind the lines, and no matter how many times you experienced this, it never got any easier.

Another bad time was when our unit was put aboard a hospital ship which ended up in the middle of a fierce battle at Salonica. The battleship *Agamemnon* was beside us, and word came from the Turkish enemy to move our hospital ship away as they were going to shell the *Agamemnon*. We moved quite a distance, but not far enough, because the shells were falling in the water all around us. That kept on for four days, and we, of course, couldn't get near enough to get any of the injured from the battle to our ship.

When they finally got them to us in small boats, I don't believe I've ever seen sicker men in my life. They were terribly injured, and they had malaria, dysentery, and almost everything else you can imagine. When they started to bring them aboard, I was on the upper deck, and one of the injured said to me, "Don't let your uniform touch any of us or our baggage, as I can't guarantee that you won't get lice." We didn't pay much attention to his advice, but another nurse who shared a stateroom with me had gone down in the hold with some of the boys, and found herself alive with lice. Every night from then on, after working with the patients we'd have to strip everything off and head for the laundry. It was awful.

After Salonica, our ship moved on to Malta, where were were able to get ashore for the first time in a long while. We thought it would be great to get into the barracks, but we nearly starved to death there. There was just about nothing for us to eat, so it wasn't long before our ship was on the move again—back to Salonica. We had an awful storm, and everybody on board was seasick. When we reached land, it's hard to describe the relief we all felt. I remember that night we had fried potatoes just like Mother used to make at home. After the hunger of Malta and the seasickness, we all agreed it was the best meal we ever had in our lives.

After the euphoria of being on land and getting a good meal, we discovered that Salonica had something else that wasn't so good—Canadian-style winters. We arrived in November, and there'd been a blizzard, and an awful lot of the men had been sent from Egypt. They had been given winter clothes, but they thought they were going from Egypt to another warm place, and so they had sold their clothes or given them away. A great many got badly frostbitten, and were sent down to our hospital tents. They had to lie on straw piled on the frozen ground with army blankets over them, as we didn't have beds set up yet. They were in a bad way, and some had to have their feet or toes amputated. We only had a small coal-oil stove in that big tent, so it was awfully cold. We wore sweaters and coats over our uniforms, and performed all of our duties with gloves on. There were lizards running all over the place, and one night when it began raining, the water just poured in, as the tents hadn't been pitched properly.

It was bad, there's no doubt about that, but the thing is, you get used to it, especially when you're all doing it together. Even the blood and the gore, and the amputations—we got used to all that too. You don't get hardened; you simply learn to live wtih it. The one thing we wanted at the end of the day was a good bath, but that wasn't available. All we were allowed was a quart of water each. When I'd wash up with that, I'd pour what was left in my hot-water bottle to take to bed to keep my feet warm.

I can't deny the horror if it all, but, you know, we actually learned to enjoy ourselves too. We had one tent which was sort of a community affair. We'd gather there when the day was over, and play cards and other games. That's where I learned to play bridge, as a matter of fact. The biggest reward of all for us was to see the joy on our Canadian boys' faces when they knew that there were Canadian nurses looking after them. They were lonely, sick, mutilated, and tired, and we were like a touch of home to them, I suppose.

One night, when the other patients had been moved out of these cold tents into barracks buildings, I found myself left alone with only one patient, who was dying. He was too sick to be moved. Suddenly overhead I heard a noise we had come to dread—a German Zeppelin. When we heard this, we were supposed to go to the dugouts. Now, the only fear I ever had was that of being buried alive. I could bear the thought of anything else, but the thought of being buried alive was something I had nightmares about. I couldn't go to the dugout and leave my patient, so I stayed alongside him and prayed while the bombs fell all around. I was never so scared in my life, but finally it was over, and we were both alive. Just then, I found out that we weren't alone. An orderly crawled out from under one of the beds and said, "Sister, you know you should have gone to the dugout." I couldn't help laughing. I didn't laugh very long though, as we suddenly heard the Zeppelin again, but before we had time to get frightened, we heard a great noise, and when we looked out, we saw it go down in flames and crash into the river.

My memories are not all unpleasant. I remember a young orderly who was so nice and helpful all the time. He was always smiling and wanting to do things for us, and he was with us for quite some time. I remember him especially, as that young man eventually became the prime minister of Canada. His name was Lester Pearson. His ambition then was to join the Royal Flying Corps. He was just a nice boy then. Most of those "fighting men" were really just boys, you know. Pearson was a private, but before he left us he had received his corporal's stripes. He was so proud of them.

I was proud myself simply to be a member of the Canadian Nursing Sisters, who had been part of every conflict that Canada had been involved in since the 1885 Riel Rebellion. We worked hard, and I felt we did a good job. I was sent back to convalesce in England after four years, and while there, I met my young brother, who was now a soldier himself. We were both so overjoyed at seeing one another again.

One time I travelled down to London to spend the day with him. I wore my uniform so that I could travel first class at a reduced rate on the train. Brother Bill took me to a dance, and afterwards when he took me back to the train, he began to put me in this first-class section. In there was one of these English generals, all gold braid and brass buttons. He looked at me in my nurse's uniform, and then turned to my brother in his private's uniform, and very haughtily said: "Has this person a first-class ticket?" My brother looked him straight in the eye and said, "Canadian nursing sisters are always first class." I took my seat, and never spoke a word to the general all the way on the trip back, and he said not a word to me.

I never did get back to the fighting areas after that. The war came to an end while I was still at the hospital, and I soon joined my unit to sail for home. It was an eventful four years.

Chief Stephen Knockwood We Were Promised So Many Things

The people who fared worst in the conquest and settlement of the New World were the aborigines. Our record in that regard is no better than that of any other conquering nation; and many of the wrongs inflicted by our ancestors remain in effect to this day.

Today the Micmacs of Nova Scotia and New Brunswick number around twelve thousand, the majority of whom live in Nova Scotia. Because they lived on reservations miles from centres of population, most Indians had little contact with white people. Sometimes they would come into town selling baskets or berries, but because they had little facility in the English or French languages, there was no bond of understanding established between the cultures. As the prosperity of more recent Canadians increased, native Canadians found themselves denied the opportunity to share it. On their reservations in the woods they became the forgotten peoples, victims of poverty, isolation, and alcoholism. Chief Stephen Knockwood, now in his late seventies, lives on the reservation at Shubenacadie between Halifax and Truro.

We were here before anybody else. The native people, I mean. We had a good society with laws for living and everything else, and, according to all the stories that are passed down from father to son, we had a good life until the white man came, and just pushed us to one side. We weren't conquered in the way that nations are conquered. We were pushed aside, because I don't think we understood what was happening. When our lands were occupied by strangers, we didn't offer much protest, because it didn't occur to our people that these lands were actually being taken away.

Indians always had a tradition of sharing, so they must have felt they were simply sharing their land with the newcomers. Of course, that's not what happened. As more settlers came, the natives were pushed farther and farther away until they found they couldn't even fish in their own streams.

Well, all of that took place over hundreds of years little by little, until we natives gradually became the outsiders on our own lands. I don't think anyone was deliberately trying to hurt the natives; it was just that they didn't know how to deal with us in a fair and reasonable way. Because of this, we became a "problem" and somebody was always coming up with a "solution".

It was during the Depression that the government in power at the time hit upon the idea of reserving big tracts of land where they could put natives, and where we could live out our lives in the way *they* thought we wanted. These lands were usually very marginal lands, not good for much of anything, and usually far away from population centres, where nobody could see or hear us. Maybe they had good intentions, I don't know. But it certainly hasn't worked out, in my opinion.

Back in the 1930s, I was living here in Nova Scotia as part of the general population, with the Scots and the Irish, and all the other races. Things were really tough for everybody. Many people were hungry. There was no work, and just about no help at all from the government. Many were starving—not only Indians. There was a lot of desperation, and people would grab at any straw just to stay alive. Then, one day, I read in the newspaper that the government was creating "reservations" for Indians and that we were all going to live there in houses of our own, and that we would be well looked after. That was the first time I heard anything about this. Nobody asked if we wanted it. They just said that this was what was going to happen. Of course, when people are hungry and have nothing, something like that sounded pretty good.

We thought that finally something good was being done for us, so we accepted the offer gratefully and started moving to the reservation, which was located in the woods halfway between Halifax and Truro. We were too far away from either of those two cities to be able to use them, but we were told that this didn't matter as everything we would need would be right there on the reservation, which was in Schubenacadie.

They said they'd build good houses for us, and a factory, a hospital, a bank, and all kinds of things, so that we'd have a happy, good life. We were promised so many things. Well, when we got here, we found that the houses were really just shacks made of rough lumber, the land was full of rocks, and there was no factory, no hospital, no bank, and we were buried deep in the woods miles from anywhere.

It was just a shack town, but the people came, expecting that all of these things that were promised would eventually come. Their mood was optimistic and hopeful. Everyone threw themselves into the business of making a good community. We didn't have much, but we were happy, thinking about a brighter future.

In 1935 when I got here, there were about fifteen families ahead of us. There was a lot of timber around, and there was a sawmill. One of the first things the men did was get together to build a church. We cut the trees and hauled them to the mill, and had them cut into boards and began on the church, which was a big one. It was forty feet wide and seventy-five feet long. The day we poured the concrete was a great day. Everyone was up at the crack of dawn. Every man mixed and poured concrete all day long, and by nine o'clock that night, the job was finished. The women kept us fed and even the children helped. We had the basement of our church finished. It didn't take us long after that before the whole church was completed, and the community started to take shape.

Those early days were happy days. There was a great spirit of co-operation. We didn't have much but everybody shared. People worked on their houses, planted gardens, and were very interested. I thought it really was going to work, but gradually people came to realize that what the government had done was simply get rid of "the Indian problem" by shoving it off in the woods.

The industries they had promised never came. The hospital never came. Nothing came. There was nothing for the people to do but sit around trying to pass the time, and it never got any better. The people were totally disillusioned, and that's the way they've remained over the years.

Reservations are not good places for natives. Young people miss out on education and job opportunities, because they are too far away. I keep telling the young ones to get out. It's not the place to start a family. But they're scared to leave, because once they get off the reservation, the government cuts off all help. Then, on the outside, nobody wants to give them jobs, because, they say, Indians can't cope. So they stay on the reservation, as it's the lesser of two evils.

Marjorie Winspear McEnaney The West Was Full of Optimism Always

Some of the new settlers who came to western Canada left a financially comfortable middle-class life behind them. They endured the same hardships on the prairies as any other newcomers did, and they suffered the same deprivations when the Depression hit in 1930. Marjorie Winspear McEnaney remembers her childhood growing up in the young West as well as her years with the popular Chautauqua movement that peaked in the 1920s.

My parents chose Canada as the place to go to escape the rigid class system of England. They were, as I like to call it, "middle-middle class". Father was a businessman, a draper, who sold high-quality clothing. He didn't make a lot of money, but he made enough that he was expected to send his children to private schools and that sort of thing, which restricted him to a class. Anyway, Father was an independent sort who wanted more freedom than that. He had been reading the CPR publicity about what a wonderful country Canada was going to be, so he and Mother made the decision to put the Old World behind, and give Canada a try.

They sold their business, packed up the children, and sailed away in 1911. I was three years old at the time, but I remember it all—perhaps because it was all so very exciting. That was one of the peak years for immigration to Western Canada, and people were coming in from all over the world.

The CPR had a great deal to do with that as there was a tremendous amount of publicity in Britain. They had to get settlers over here to help pay for that railroad, and the goodies offered made it quite tempting. Free education was one, and I think that may have been the one that tipped the scales as far as Father was concerned. He had four children to educate, and if you were in the middle class, it had to be in private schools, a considerable outlay for a man who ran a small draper's business. It wasn't the free land that attracted him.

With the money from the sale of the business, he set up a ladies'-wear store in Claresholm, Alberta. However, with the type of merchandise he was offering and the prices he was asking, he lasted about six months. There wasn't much call for high fashion among the homesteaders, and he folded. Then he was talked into buying some lots on the outskirts of Calgary, with the idea that streetcars would be out there soon, and the roads would therefore be paved too. Well, that did not happen and that became his second failed investment.

Then he bought a general store in Namaka, Alberta, which is forty miles east of Calgary on the CPR main line. This was to be his first success and our home for the next nine years. The store did very well, and Father became more or less the "chief cook and bottle washer" of the town. He was justice of the peace, postmaster, chairman of the school board, and a lay reader with the Anglican Church. He was a very religious man, who looked upon the local Indians as souls to be saved, which they didn't appreciate, as they were already getting enough religion from the Anglican schools on the reserve. But when he showed them how to measure their hay crop so that they would get a fair price for it, he became very much liked indeed. Before that they were being short-changed by some unscrupulous people. They appreciated Father so much that they gave him an Indian name—"Po-Po-Kaken"—which was an indication of their gratitude.

Namaka was only a little hamlet, really. It had no police force, except for an occasional visit from an RCMP officer who would ride by. It had a tiny one-room school, and the population was not more than thirty. However, it was the supply centre for all the homesteaders in the area, so at times it would be quite busy with pedestrians and horses and wagons coming and going. It was surrounded by this beautiful prairie land where you could look in all directions and see nothing but prairie and sky. I loved the flora and the fauna, and as a small child I had all the time in the world to explore and become friends with the birds and the animals. It was simply lovely.

The one exception to that was the gophers. Someone told us that we could get a bounty of one cent for every gopher tail we brought in, and we spent a great deal of time pouring water into their holes and flushing them out and killing them for their tails. To this day, I can't understand how I did that, as I can't kill anything bigger than a fly now. What's more, I can't recall collecting even one cent for those tails. I think we got that cold-blooded attitude from our elders, as there was this feeling that there was no end to the riches of the West, and nature was the enemy. Coyotes and poor little badgers were the enemy too, even though I don't think they ever did much harm. The ducks were friends because they could be shot and eaten.

The real enemy was the weather. It could be unbelievable. We had a tiny frame house without a basement. It just sat on the prairie and one of the big fall activities would be getting the manure from the stable and piling it all around the house for protection from the icy wind. Even with that, the wind would find plenty of cracks to squeeze through. We always wore the heaviest of woollens, inside and outside. I can remember temperatures of sixty degrees below zero Fahrenheit. In the summer, of course, it could get unbearably hot, as the sun beat down, and there were no trees or anything to interfere with it, but I loved it all.

One thing I loved to do was hitch my little sleigh onto the back of the big sleighs that took the wheat to market. You could ride that way for miles; then you unhitched yourself and tied onto another wagon that was going back. You might get a little anxious about the return ride if it was getting dark, but as far as I can recall, I always did get one.

The homesteaders in the area were a mixture of nationalities. Some were from England, and a tremendous number came from Montana and other states. When World War One came along, they didn't want any part of it. They said it was Britain's war, and anyone around there who was English, including us, was very unpopular. They didn't like the war and the shortages and the rationing it caused. But when the United States came into the war in 1917, the depressed price of wheat went up to two dollars a bushel. Thanks to the two-dollar wheat, we English suddenly became popular again.

Our friends in the district, however, were mostly English. Mother seemed to befriend the young English remittance men who were sent out by their families because they had been more or less black sheep at home. Some of them had come from very good families and she'd be delighted to have them in on Sunday evenings for a session around the piano. My brother played the cornet; another brother played the violin; my sister and mother played the piano; and my father had a marvellous voice. I was content to listen as I didn't have any talents in that direction. But they were wonderful, warm, cosy evenings that helped to chase away the feelings of isolation.

We were teased about our British accents by the other settlers, and my mother was often the butt of jokes in the store. There was one time she told a group of the home-steaders that she was afraid that some little chickens she had were dying. They were sympathetic and advised her to try giving them a little coal oil. A week or so later, when she was in the store, she was asked how the chickens were doing. "They died," she said. "Didn't you try the coal oil?" they asked. "Oh yes," replied Mother. "I had an awful time getting it into them, and I gave them about a cup each." Well, they almost died laughing, and the more they laughed, the more embarrassed Mother became. She was a greenhorn from the city of Birmingham, and a city person had a very hard time in learning the ways of the prairies, but in time they did learn to cope.

Everything was constantly changing in the West. New communities were springing up all along the CPR line about every twelve or fifteen miles, and it fell to the railroad to name all these new places, so what they did was simply do it in alphabetical order. North of Calgary, for example, these communities all begin with As and down south with Cs, and so on.

We stayed in Namaka until 1919, when Father sold the business, and we moved to Calgary, where my brothers and sister had already gone to attend high school. Now it was time for me to go, so my father felt it was time for the family to establish itself in Calgary too.

My principal at the Calgary school was a man who later became very powerful as a religious broadcaster on radio, and a Social Credit premier of the province. His name was William Aberhart, better known as "Bible Bill". He was a very strange person. I believe he had a good deal of concern, but there was also a tremendous ego there, and the radio for him was a projection of that ego. He seemed to want and need the adulation that he certainly got through his broadcasts. He wielded tremendous power through those programs, and I've always felt that because of Aberhart's broadcasts, the federal government stepped up its plans for the formation of a national system, with proper controls over those who would misuse the airwaves.

It was around this time that I moved east to attend the University of Toronto, and after I graduated I became involved in one of the most interesting and exciting phases of my life: Chautauqua.

J. M. Erikson, who founded the Canadian Chautauqua movement, was bringing the Chautauqua shows down into eastern Canada for the first time. The American companies had been coming to the east up until then. They began as a religious movement at Lake Chautauqua in New York State, but they expanded and became travelling mass-entertainment shows of music, lectures, and drama to those who seldom had an opportunity to see anything except local entertainment. They reached their apex before radio, but they continued successfully until they were killed off by the Depression of the thirties.

However, when Mr. Erikson recruited me in 1930 from the University of Toronto, they were still going strong, and he hired me and my sister right off, as we were the first ones he interviewed who knew what Chautauqua was all about. Coming from Western Canada, where the movement was very strong for years, we had often attended and enjoyed the shows which moved in a circuit from one town to the next.

A ticket for the season was two dollars and it would last a week in each place, with eleven programs. For a town to get the show, they had to sponsor it and take responsibility for sale of the tickets and guarantee the expenses. The Chautauqua organization would send them help to do this in the person of a young lady who'd organize ticket sales and give out the advertising.

Then, a few days before the show, another girl would come in and organize a final drive for sales. That's the job I had. I was also in charge of the artists while they were in town, and I had to get the stage props, and make sure the tent man got the help he needed so that the tent would be erected in time. It was great fun, but not at all easy, especially as I joined just as the Depression was taking hold.

People wanted the Chautauqua, but the simple truth was that they couldn't afford it. When they signed a contract to have it come back the following year, they would be full of optimism that their financial problems would be over by then—the West was full of optimism always—but when the next year rolled around, they'd be even worse off, with dust storms and grasshopper plagues having destroyed everything. Despite that, though, they would come up with the money somehow to enable the show to go on, and sign up for another for the following year.

It's necessary to understand the isolation and deprivation of farm people at the time to understand what Chautauqua meant to them. This was world-class entertainment coming right to their doorsteps. They would look forward to it from one year to the next. The acts were extremely polished and very good, which is understandable when you realize that some of the performers had been doing the one act in the United States and Canada for as long as thirty years. They could do it well even in their sleep.

The various Chautauqua circuit managers would meet in Chicago in the winter and decide on the acts they would engage for the following year, so that performers moved from circuit to circuit, and their acts were always fresh. In those pre-radio years all of the United States presidents brought their message to the people speaking from the Chautauqua platform on the third night of the show, which was billed as the "Inspirational Lecture".

Chautauqua had been operating in the States from late in the nineteenth century, but it wasn't until 1917 when J. M. Erikson decided to establish the Canadian movement, which used American acts for the most part, as we just didn't have sufficient talent in Canada at that time.

In the period I was with it, from 1930 to 1934, the Depression became so very bad that hardly any towns were signing contracts, and even in those towns where they had signed, they couldn't come up with money to fulfil them. The management couldn't continue without money as expenses were so heavy, with artists to be paid and so on, and the whole thing simply died in 1934. It was a wonderful period in our history though, and I'm so glad I was a part of it.

Leonard Knott Two Different Worlds

When Leonard Knott was born in Winnipeg in 1905, the
city was an unofficial marshalling yard for the immigrants pouring into the almost empty plains in search of
free land. Winnipeg was a big city even then, predom-
inantly Anglo-Saxon and resentful of the foreigners who
were passing through on their way west. When Leonard
Knott became a news reporter for the *Toronto Star* in
1927, he discovered another world beyond Winnipeg.
Winnipeg wasn't the West, or the East—and the people
who lived there didn't even feel very Canadian.

By the time I was old enough to venture into the north end
of the city where all of the immigrants came through, that
stream had pretty well died down. Around 1912, Winnipeg
was pretty well a segregated city. The south end was all
Anglo-Saxon, and the north was all Eastern European, and
Jewish, and Icelandic, people from all over the world. There
was no mixing at all, and in a sense there was a lot of snobbery
and bigotry. There was great suspicion of all these foreigners
who were pouring in. Many wanted these "peasants in sheep-
skin coats" to get what they needed and get out of the city
onto the prairies where they said they belonged. In the south
end of the city, we didn't see them at all. The bulk of them kept
on going through to the West.

Winnipeg was really the distribution point for the people
and supplies heading west. The largest rail yards on the
continent were there; and most of the wealthy in the city were
connected with the grain exchange there. The streets were
mostly paved in the downtown area, although in the residen-
tial communities, there were still mud or gravel roads and
board sidewalks. Most of the downtown "skyscrapers" were
but three or four storeys high, but a couple rose to twelve
storeys. It was a very flat place laid out in a regular pattern
with no winding crescents or boulevards. The north end had a
frontier appearance, whereas the south end looked as if it had
been there forever. It was really two different worlds.

There were close two hundred thousand living there at the
time, and I thought it was probably the biggest city in the

world. We had a concert hall, a symphony orchestra, wonderful Icelandic male-voice choirs, and big-name artists came there from all over the world. I thought it was the centre of the world, another Vienna, sophisticated and cosmopolitan. In fact, it was only at these artistic events that the various races mixed. There were no ethnics that I knew of in business, except in the small shops and stalls in the north end. At the university the student population was almost one hundred per cent Anglo-Saxon. This was partly due to economic reasons, but mainly because of prejudice. People didn't want anything to do with these foreigners. We young ones didn't know we were being prejudiced when we called them all sorts of bad names. We simply thought that's what one was supposed to call them, and, of course, I never met any of them.

Most people in Winnipeg at the time didn't know anything about the land to the west of them. It was wild country in their minds, a place fit only for these foreigners that they didn't want. I was a bit luckier, as my father was a representative for a fur company, and he would travel all through that territory on business right through to Vancouver, part of the way by train, and part by horse and wagon, or sleigh in the winter. When he'd come back, he'd have all kinds of stories, so I knew more about the West than I did about the East.

When we wanted a holiday, Minneapolis would be our big city to visit. While I was at college, a gang of us would go down to cheer the Minnesota team. It was very much a north-south thing, rather than east and west. Minneapolis was so much closer—overnight by train—whereas it was two nights and three days on a train to Toronto.

The land west of us was practically empty. In my student days I would go harvesting near Yorkton, which was little more than a village. The West was just a lot of flat land where one had to go out and stook all day, harvest till midnight, and then get up again at four, and begin all over. About four times a year there might be football or hockey games with the universities of Saskatchewan and Alberta, but never with British Columbia, as that was too far.

Aside from these few contacts, Winnipeggers seldom rubbed shoulders with Westerners. The West was the hinterland. As far as we were concerned, Manitoba was Canada, and when one went away, one went to Minnesota. Our Canada stopped at the Ontario and Saskatchewan borders. To those west of us, we were always considered Easterners, and by those to our east, we were thought of as Westerners, an attitude that remains to this day.

Because of our position in the middle of Canada, we had to develop on our own. We had plenty of good writers there, good theatre, both amateur and professional, and all the travelling road shows, which, as far as we were concerned, made Winnipeg an important cultural centre. We had a group called the Winnipeg Kiddies Choir which travelled all over the country, and we looked on them as great cultural ambassadors.

I became an Easterner in 1927, when I finished university and took a job as a reporter with the *Toronto Star*. I had been there earlier during summer vacations when Ernest Hemingway was a reporter, but the fact is I don't remember that much about him. He was just another reporter then, and hadn't really done anything special. I don't recall what he looked like either. I must say, though, that two of the other staff men, Morley Callaghan and Greg Clark, apparently recognized seeds of greatness, as they both became close to him and encouraged him—Greg Clark especially. Greg was always at him to spend less time on journalism and more on writing.

The *Star* was a wild place to work in those days, a real old-time newspaper office where one felt lucky to have a typewriter and a place to sit, and reporters were reporters then. They weren't investigative reporters, or social scientists or Ph.Ds. Their jobs were to get the news—simply that. And the vision of a 1920s reporter sitting at a desk in his shirt sleeves, pounding a typewriter with two fingers, a fedora hat on his head, and a cigarette dangling from his mouth, is literally true. They didn't want to be journalists, or specialists, or columnists, or anything else. They wanted to be newspapermen, because they enjoyed it. The only columnists we had were a couple of preachers, and a gossip columnist was unheard of at the *Star*.

There were no women on the staff, because Mrs. Atkinson, wife of the owner, "Holy Joe" Atkinson, didn't approve of women working on newspapers. Gordon Sinclair was the women's-page editor. Several years later they hired their first woman editorial worker in the person of Alexandrine Gibb, a sports writer. Prior to that, the only women workers were switchboard operators and office workers. It was very much a male preserve.

We'd literally run two storeys down the stairs, into a cab and back again, as fast as we possibly could, to make the next edition. Newspapering then was hard work, but very romantic, competitive, and often dangerous. It was all rush and hurry, but very enjoyable, and I think it made for great newspapers.

They would send out gangs of reporters on stories. On a shipwreck, we'd be out hiring every tugboat and tying up every telephone line to keep the other papers from getting a story as good as ours. In 1929 I went to report on the search for the MacAlpine fliers who were lost in the Arctic. When I got to Le Pas, I immediately hired every pilot in the area to work for the *Star*, so that when the Toronto *Telegram* arrived, there wouldn't be a plane that they could hire. To keep the pilots happy, I would fly around with a different pilot each day.

There was no such thing as working for a set number of hours either. You worked continuously until you got your story—and there was no overtime pay. Reporters thought nothing of working around the clock with never a complaint. It would have been repulsive to a reporter to have to hand over his story to another man because his shift was up. That was *his* story, and he wanted to stick with it. That was part of the excitement of the job, and most of them who got in at that time never did everything different for the rest of their lives.

We were part of a fraternity that worked together and played together. I remember that every Friday night at the *Star*, about twenty of us would go over to this little hotel room and play poker or shoot craps all night long. If you went broke, someone would give you enough money to get home, and the others would continue playing till seven in the morning, when the game would be shut off so we could go to work.

Drinking was part of it too, and there would be a few "fabulous" drinkers who might be compelled to go to rest homes once in a while to be "dried out", but most of the guys were just average drinkers, who'd have a belt once in a while from a bottle that they kept in their desk drawer. In those days, the papers didn't fire men for getting drunk. They'd

135

send a man to a sanitarium for a few days to dry out and clean out, but when that was over, he was expected to be back at his desk and on the job. There was not much of this going around to bars, because they were too expensive. However, I don't think there was as much drinking then as there is today.

I went to the Arctic the year the Depression hit to search for MacAlpine, the lost mining man and his exploration party, the biggest story I covered for the *Star*. There were dirigibles and everything else involved in that search. I was there for eight weeks before we gave up, and the funny thing is that three months later, they walked out themselves, accompanied by some Eskimo people. The year 1929 was also the year of what we call the "Christmas Massacre" at the *Toronto Star*, when the managing editor, Harry Hindmarsh, discovered a group of us playing craps in the darkroom. Under "Holy Joe" Atkinson's policies, the *Star* was strongly opposed to drinking and gambling. About a dozen of us were fired for playing craps that time, just a week before Christmas. I was one, and Gordon Sinclair was another. Everyone was hired back after a couple of weeks except me, as I had decided to move to the Montreal *Gazette* in the meantime. There I felt the results of the Depression. I began working for a pretty good salary of sixty dollars a week. After six months, our salaries were cut ten per cent, and after another six months, cut ten per cent again. The editorial department had no union, but the print shop did, and there was no way they would accept a cut; so management just cut *our* salaries that much more to make up. I started to worry that I would soon be working for nothing.

Compared to a newspaperman in the thirties, you could move around a lot in the twenties. If you wanted to make a move, you'd simply send a message ahead to the editor of the paper where you wanted to go, stating that you'd be available on such and such a date. Nine times out of ten a message would come back saying yes, and telling you when you could start. That all changed when the Depression came, as jobs were so scarce, and people who had jobs simply did not move from them. With all of this salary-cutting at the *Gazette*, and the same thing going on at newspapers all over the country, I decided that maybe it was time to try my hand at something else, and say good-bye to the job I loved to do.

Dr. Harold Segall Free for the First Time

Jewish immigration to Canada has almost always been the result of Jewish persecution in the Old World. In Russia the Jews survived massacres and regular pogroms as they did in Germany and most of Europe. And the Jews' desire to settle in Canada has often been hindered by lies and false promises. For example, one group of three hundred Russian Jews arrived in Winnipeg in the spring of 1882 because the government had promised them free land on which they could begin new colonies. The group was part of a Russian back-to-the-land movement called "Am Olam". Adherents believed that no people could be eternal without ties to the land. After a two-year wait here for land, they were finally assigned a tract at Moosomin, but by that time most of the group had drifted off to the cities or elsewhere to find other occupations. Eventually only twenty-seven families were left to begin the Moosomin colony, and it soon failed because of their insufficient number. The remaining settlers had no choice but to turn to peddling or an occupation contrary to their "Am Olam" ideals. The anti-Semitism of Europe had apparently survived the ocean crossing.

However, the Jews did come and they survived, and their descendants today are prominent in all fields of endeavour. Dr. Harold Segall is one immigrant who has become a world-renowned cardiac surgeon. He graduated from McGill in 1920 and then studied heart disease for six years at Harvard, and in London and Vienna. At a time when few knew much about the diseases of the heart, Dr. Segall brought the latest knowledge back to Canada and opened pioneering clinics in Montreal.

I was born in Jassy, Romania in 1897, but Canada has been my home since the thirtieth of July, 1900, when our family landed at Quebec City. The reason we left Romania was that my father, who had a very good job as book-keeper-controller for the big estate of a prince, suddenly found himself out of work when the prince decided that he wanted to go back to Germany, where he had come from originally. Father couldn't get a civil-service job as he was a Jew, so he did what many were doing at that time; he joined the big exodus from Russia and Romania to America.

He came by way of steerage, and during the passage he learned from fellow passengers that when you arrived at Ellis Island in America, you had to have either a relative to claim you, or ten dollars in your possession, or you would be returned to where you came from. Well, he didn't have a relative, and he didn't have ten dollars, but he knew that the boat would be stopping in Halifax before going on to New York. And that's why he came to Canada.

He got off the boat in Halifax, and boarded one of the CPR immigrant trains heading west. In Montreal he got off to see if he could link up with some fellow Romanian immigrants who might be living there. He was successful in this, and they helped him find a place to live and a job as an apprentice presser in a garment factory. He couldn't work as a book-keeper, of course, as he didn't have either French or English.

He had to be in the factory at four o'clock in the morning to prepare the charcoal-heated irons, and he worked a six-teen-hour day. Those were the days of the garment-industry sweatshops in Montreal and New York and all over the eastern seaboard. They fed on immigrant labour, and I have to say here, too, that many of them were run by Jews who had been here from an earlier time. So it wasn't just anti-Semitism that the new immigrants had to contend with. The sweatshop my father was working in was run by a Jewish family. The shops exploited immigrants regardless of race or religion.

In any event, my father was able to save enough money to bring my mother, my brother, and me over by steerage after nine months. He continued at his job, and he told me later that the only thing that sustained him was the knowledge that he'd find a way out.

After two years he met a butcher in Montreal, also from Romania. This man knew something of the junk business, the buying of old rags, metal, and bottles. As they weren't permitted to own land, Jews in Europe did a lot of this collecting of junk, which was really recycling.

He and this butcher formed a partnership, and it was a good one. My father did all of the business end, as he had an education, and the other man, who was illiterate, looked after the rest. When my father had so many dozen bottles, he would move them to a bottle company, and the same with the other stuff, the rags and the metal, and so on. This partnership lasted for many years, until around 1919 when Father left to start a retail shoe business, which he stayed with for the rest of his life.

His story is typical of many of the immigrants who came to the city, and were forced to start at the bottom rung of the ladder. There was nothing lower for them, so their lives were devoted to upward movement. When he arrived here, Montreal was an open city, with lots of immigrants in the labour pool, and the Jews were as welcome as any of the others. There were very few controls, and one hardly needed a passport. The CPR was well in place by that time, but the competing railroads, which were trying to get a start, needed plenty of immigrant labour also.

Barriers to immigrants didn't come until after World War One when the Americans decided they had a large enough population, all the labour source they needed so that the population could grow on its own. To keep people out, they started using all types of barriers, including the testing of immigrants for I.Q. They'd have immigration officers who spoke English only testing Yiddish-speaking people for their Intelligence Quotient. Not many would pass, of course. The only ones who could get by these false barriers were the English-speaking immigrants, and those from Germany and Scandinavia who had learned English at school. So a lot of people came to Canada instead, and our country gained from that.

A great number of Jewish immigrants brought a somewhat higher degree of education than the average, and it's interesting why that should be so. It happened simply because there were so many restrictions placed on them and their activities in their countries of origin. They weren't allowed to have certain jobs, or go to certain places, or to do things that other ordinary citizens could. They had to live in ghettos and on specified streets where the gates were locked overnight with nobody permitted to go in or out. They weren't considered a part of the city, and they had to pay rent for that street—so much a head for the privilege of living there—in overcrowded conditions that saw as many as ten living in a room. Whatever happened to, or for, them had to take place inside the ghetto.

Now, as bad and unfair as all of this seems, it had some good results. The very survival of the Jew as a Jew is because he had four walls around him. There was a texture of life inside that ghetto where everybody depended on each other. They lived for one another closely packed together, without contact with any other culture. They suffered a good deal of deprivation, as they really had no country, and were dependent on the good will of others simply to be permitted to live in the ghetto, but they had a very strong degree of identity.

This kind of lifestyle had an important side effect. They had no secular education and did all their correspondence in Hebrew. Whatever one had, especially in the way of education, was passed on to the other. You take the Jewish tradition of bar mitzvahs, where a boy of thirteen has to be able to read and understand a portion of the Bible. To ensure that a boy could do this, the parents and others in the ghetto saw to it that the child learned reading and writing, and a certain amount of arithmetic. Despite the fact that they were barred from outside schools, they usually had more education in general than other children in the city.

Other children could attend schools, but they very often didn't attend schools as they didn't need it to get the kinds of jobs that were available. The blacksmith, the carter, or the farmer didn't need it. Only a few, privileged ones knew how to read and write; but every Jewish male was by circumstance an educated person. Although the Jew is intrinsically no different from any other person, he was always forced to be smarter in order to survive, simply to keep food on the table.

Now that explains a great deal about the early Jews, such as my father, who came to this country and were willing to take jobs in sweatshops working sixteen hours a day. Here, for the first time, they experienced freedom, and they knew that by exercising their knowledge and using their wits, nothing could keep them from moving up the economic scale. Mind you, they didn't have total freedom by any means. Political freedom they did have, and I can tell you my father was very proud to get his citizenship papers as soon as he was eligible—five years after his arrival.

The economic marketplace, with these sweatshops, wasn't what you'd call free—especially the way they'd be laid off between seasons and develop debts. Workers could never catch up, and they were eventually slaves to the economic system. That's a different kind of absence of freedom.

Only after a major fire in a sweatshop in the United States were the unions able to cure some of these ills, and get a stronger voice in the running of the Montreal sweatshops. So it was out of a background of all of this that my father was able to break away, and become a full-fledged Canadian with a business of his own. Free for the first time, you might say.

I grew up on St. Timothy Street in Montreal in the middle of a French community. A neighbour boy called Antoine was four years old, the same as I was. The name I went by in French was Anatole. I had no toys, but we would play together in the yard. My pastime would be picking up old nails and pieces of wood, and nailing boxes together. Antoine was an only child with four doting grandparents, and he had lots of toys, and I could play with them when I was at his house.

One day he came out and said that his mother told him not to play with me any more. I asked why and he replied, "Because you're not a Catholic." I didn't know what this was all about, but I said, "Oh yes I am. I'm a Jewish Catholic." He thought about this for a while, and then he went back to his mother. He came back with a big smile, and said, "My mother says it's okay. A Jewish Catholic is all right." That was okay with me too, and we continued to play together as friends, although I didn't have the slightest idea what a Catholic was.

Aside from that little incident due to ignorance more than anything else, I never felt any kind of anti-Semitism as a child in Montreal, but I did suffer a bit because I wasn't French. A group of us, Jewish and Christian boys, would have to walk past three different French schools on the way to our own English-language one, and we often had to battle our way through. However, that wasn't because I was Jewish. It was because I wasn't French.

In those days, even at university, there were constant battles between students at Laval and the University of Montreal. Now, although I say that Jews found freedom in Canada, that is not entirely true in the field of education, or the workplace. The French schools didn't want the Jews, and the Protestant schools didn't want us either, mainly because we were poor and schools are maintained by taxes on property, which of course we didn't have. So that was discrimination based on money, or the lack of it. In the end I was able to attend English schools, including McGill University. It was easier for me to get in there than it was to get into the French system. That's the only reason I became an Anglophone rather than a Francophone.

I could have gone either way. I think a lot of people who could have made a great contribution to the Francophone community were lost that way. The French in Quebec wouldn't really give non-French-speaking immigrants a chance to grow, and it's easy for a Jew to understand how they feel. They are surrounded by alien cultures much as the Jews were in the ghetto, and they have always felt that they must protect what they have.

I have always believed that all Francophones should be bilingual for their own sakes, surrounded as they are by a sea of English. There was some solid advice given one time by a Roman Catholic bishop of Quebec City. He said to his people, "Learn to speak English, but learn to speak it badly, so that you'll never lose your identity."

Colonel C. P. Stacey King Was a Very Complex Individual

Mackenzie King, as he was known to everybody, was born in Berlin (Kitchener), Ontario, in 1874, and became prime minister in 1921. Except for the period from 1930 to 1935, he remained prime minister until he retired in 1948. He died in 1950.

To the public, King presented a picture of the dullest of the dull, the greyest of the grey. But he was a shrewd politician who knew how to keep the Liberals in power. Not until many years after his death did King attract great public interest, when the diaries he had kept for fifty-seven years were opened to public scrutiny. These records revealed that King believed in a spiritual world, that he took advice from his long-dead mother, and that, as a bachelor, he had led, in his own words, "a very double life".

Colonel C. P. Stacey, now seventy-eight years old, is an eminent Toronto historian and one of the first people to have seen and studied the King diaries. Today Colonel Stacey ranks as one of Canada's most respected historians, author of *The Official History of the Canadian Army in the Second World War* and many other books, including *A Very Double Life*, his biographical study of William Lyon Mackenzie King. Like many of his fellow Canadians, Colonel Stacey is fascinated by King's complex character. A conversation with the historian gave me a clearer picture of the "grey" man who played such a major part in shaping the Canada we live in today.

Mackenzie King was a very strange man. He was not a man of gigantic intellect. People often ask me how a man of second-class intellect could remain prime minister for over twenty years. Well, I don't think it's a gigantic intellect that makes a man a suitable prime minister. Bertrand Russell, a man of enormous intellect, wouldn't make a particularly good PM. King was a man of good sound intelligence and tremendous political shrewdness. You could call him an intellectual in some ways, though, because he was a highly educated man.

He had more formal education than any prime minister we ever had, I suppose. The closest competitor would be Trudeau.

The connections that King had! He spent a great deal of time in both Great Britain and the United States and he had very good friends there. He worked as an industrial consultant in the United States during the First World War and it was during this time in his life that he made the most money—about fifty thousand dollars a year. King certainly didn't do as well as that as prime minister; fifty thousand dollars was a lot of money in those days. When he retired as PM in 1948, the pay and allowances for PM were only nineteen thousand dollars. And that was at the end of his career as PM. It was much, much less when he first went into the job.

King claimed to be a person who had a deep feeling for the poor, although you could also say that his social legislation always came along when it could be politically valuable. He was fond of quoting the fact that his book *Industry and Humanity*, which came out in 1918, outlined the whole future welfare state that he helped to introduce. Well, it took him a long, long time to translate those ideas of 1918 into practical legislation. But along with his theoretical regard for the poor—and I think there was considerable sincerity in it—went a practical association with the rich.

In 1899, when King was still a graduate student at Harvard, he was invited to Newport, Rhode Island, by a couple of students who were members of the enormously wealthy Geary family. So King found himself pitchforked into this tremendously wealthy society at Newport, associating with the Vanderbilts, the Rockefellers, and all kinds of other rich people. This was pretty heady stuff! He had already started keeping the diary, and you find some rather funny remarks in there, rude remarks about the rich—their manners and customs, how little regard they show for the less fortunate, and so on. Yet, at the same time, it's pretty clear he was enjoying every minute of it.

Reggie Vanderbilt lost his father while King was at Newport, and King wrote him a letter of condolence. It's rather funny when you consider that King was an absolutely penniless Canadian graduate student. And, do you know, he never lost those connections, particularly with the Rockefellers, and these two things go alongside each other in King's life—the regard for the poor and this considerable obsession with the American plutocracy.

Now King also enjoyed greatly dealing with eminent British politicians and the Royal Family. And as he became an older, more senior politician, he had a fair amount to do with the Royal Family. When he got a little mad he was capable of making rude remarks in his diary about the institution of the monarchy; but nevertheless it's clear that King enjoyed these contacts and that he had a genuine deep regard for the family. In 1947 he describes in his diary how he went to Princess Elizabeth's wedding: "The guests were far better conducted than many other guests at other weddings that I have attended."

King loved to have his picture taken with royalty, and with Churchill and Roosevelt during the war. He considered this a great political advantage because these two people were enormously popular in Canada. In fact, I think it's fair to say that both Roosevelt and Churchill were far more popular in Canada than Mackenzie King ever was! He knew this, and it embarrassed him. People during the war had a habit, which he greatly resented, of referring to Churchill and Roosevelt as "our leaders". He thought that this was not the way Canadians should talk because, after all, he was their leader. But he also realized that, faced with this situation, the thing for him to do was to sort of cosy up to them and make it quite clear that he was on very close and intimate terms with both leaders. This was very noticeable at the time of the first Quebec Conference in 1943. Some people felt that King should insist on being on a basis of equality with Churchill and Roosevelt when they came to meet with the combined chiefs of staff in Canada. Well, King didn't particularly want a share in the direction of the war. If he had done that, he would have had trouble with Roosevelt and Churchill, and the friendship to which he attached so much importance would have been disturbed. He said that, as far as he was concerned, his objectives were served by the fact that the Canadian people would see him as host to these great men, and they would be convinced that he was in close cahoots with them.

King said, in fact, that his relationship with Churchill and Roosevelt would win an election for him any time. That was the kind of thing he was thinking of, rather than a share in the conduct of the war. I think, in a way, what he was saying was true. I think that this association was a great political advantage. I don't think that that friendship was a terribly intimate one, and I don't think King ever felt very close to either Roosevelt or Churchill.

One of the funny little evidences of this is the fact that they both called him "Mackenzie". They were the only ones who ever did. King's friends all called him "Rex". He liked to be called Rex.

Mary Pickford came to Ottawa once after the war, and King liked her, and he told her that his friends called him Rex. After that she called him Rex and he called her Mary, but he never got onto that basis with Churchill or Roosevelt. He very occasionally called Roosevelt "Franklin" over the phone, and when he did, he mentioned it in the diary. I can't find it mentioned anywhere that he ever called Churchill "Winston" or "Winnie".

King was a very complex individual and to generalize about him is very difficult. You could prove almost anything about Mackenzie King by extracts from his diary. You could make him out to be a very warm-hearted man, or a very cold individual. I don't find King an attractive person, but I'm not a King hater either. We've had a good many King haters, and some of them are still around. I always felt that he was a rather unattractive individual, and after reading his diaries, I still feel that; but I also feel that he is absolutely fascinating.

Dolly Court Dooey A Hard Life for Mother

The men who chose the North as a starting point for new lives were often young and adventurous, ready to do anything to break away from more southerly occupations that offered no future for them or their young families during the Depression. These men faced a constant battle in the North with nature as the enemy. For the women who followed their husbands' dreams, life was just as hard in different ways. Theirs were lives of "making do", of raising children and boosting morale. Dolly Court Dooey of Shillington, Ontario, went north as a young child and she gives credit to the women who kept those isolated families and communities together.

When I was six years old, my parents decided to come to Canada. The year was 1911. They signed an agreement to work for a farmer in Blenheim, Ontario, so when that year was up, my father decided to take a homestead grant in Northern Ontario. He went first to clear part of the land and to build a shack so that mother and we children would have a place to stay when we got there. He was there all winter and it wasn't till June 1913 that we were able to join him.

We got off the train at Matheson, which was really just a collection of shacky-looking houses and muddy streets. There was a blacksmith shop and a few stores and a big wooden hotel where we stayed for one night. In the morning we boarded the train again for a place called Homer's Siding. Father had arranged for a man to meet us there with a team of horses and a wagon, so we bumped along over trails and stumps to his home and spent the night there. The next morning, we piled all our things in a boat for the next part of our journey up the Crooked River to Father's homestead.

By this time, we thought we were coming near to the end of the world, as we never in our lives experienced anything like this. You must remember, we came from a crowded English city, and aside from that year on the farm, we were used to seeing people—lots of them. Now, we could see nothing but trees and clouds of mosquitoes. By the time we got to Father's place we were bitten and bleeding, and everybody, including

Mother, was in tears. All we could think of was getting inside the house and away from those mosquitoes.

But we found that Dad had only the frame of the log building up. There was no roof, no windows or doors, and more mosquitoes than we had seen before. Dad had warned Mother to bring plenty of cheesecloth with her to make tents over the beds, but as she didn't know anything about mosquitoes, she didn't think it was important, so she didn't bother. I'll never forget the agony of that night! We rubbed some tar oil on our skin, and we used baking soda, and water and salt, to take the sting out, but nothing seemed to help. Dad had also warned Mother to bring lots of warm clothes, but she said, "It can't be that cold in June," and we went just as we were. Well, it *was* that cold in June, and in the nights we thought we would freeze to death.

Anyway, Dad got permission from the bosses at the lumber camp where he worked for us to live there with him for the summer and things looked a bit better. My two brothers came up from the south in the meantime, and they finished off the shack so that we were able to move in there before the cold weather came. It was nice and cosy, even with the five children and Mom and Dad. Our stove had a door on the front, which we left open at night so we wouldn't have to use the coal-oil lamps. That was important, because the only place you could get oil was in Matheson, fifteen miles away through the woods. Anything that had to be purchased came from there, so we were careful how we used everything. Nothing was wasted!

It was a hard life for Mother because Dad and the boys were always out in the bush cutting pulpwood or something, and all the rest of the chores were left to her. How she managed I just don't know. I often think how wonderful those women were at that time, so important to the success or failure of their men. The men were realizing their ambitions and dreams, but the women were along *only* because of the ambitions of their men.

The spiritual side of our lives was supplied by a missionary minister who came through the woods from the other side of Moose Lake, visiting families all along the way. I remember one time the Bishop came through with him, and my mother had dinner ready for them when they arrived. It was a Sunday and she put out the best she had, which was tin plates and little milk cans that were cleaned out to serve as cups. The Bishop sat at one end of the table, and while we were eating, a great spruce bug fell from the poles of the ceiling right in front of his plate. My mother nearly died of embarrassment, but the Bishop just laughed and brushed it off onto the floor. Poor Mother never forgot that to the day she died. You know, those women just had to make up their minds to make the best of everything, but it was very hard, especially for women like my mother, who came from the city and knew no other life.

These women knew how to make shift with nothing. There was no running off to stores to buy things when you didn't have them. You had to look around and see how you could make those things that were needed out of something else. Many of the women, those who didn't have sons to help, went out in the woods and worked side by side with their husbands. They'd pick up an axe or a saw and work just as hard as their men. My mother had sons, of course, so she didn't have to do that. Her big talent, after she got used to the life, was making new clothes out of old, and she did a wonderful job. I'm sure if it hadn't been for women such as my mother, who stayed on with their husbands no matter how hard their lives were, none of these communities would have survived.

Lorne Smith Eady The World Had Changed

The twentieth century has been a century of greater
change for Canada, perhaps, than it has been for most
countries. Since 1900 we have progressed from covered
wagons and teams of oxen breaking virgin soil to a
high-technology world of outer space. The amazing thing
is that there are many people alive today who have lived
through it all. Lorne Eady, born in the Ottawa Valley in
1895, remembers some of the changes from the turn of
the century to the Depression.

When the century turned, I was five years old, being
prepared for school, learning to tell the time and read the
calendar. As Father spent most of the year away working, my
Irish grandparents helped raise me along with my mother. My
Eady grandparents were from England, very religious, and
the very opposite in many ways from my Irish grandparents
with whom I lived. However, I loved them both, and learned
from both sides of the family.

My grandfather Smith, a witty Irishman from Dublin, was
an entertaining man who could turn a dull gathering into a riot
by simply walking into a room. One day I asked him why he
drank so much instead of taking just enough. His answer was,
"Too much is just enough." He had a fine watch, and he told
me there were only two such watches. "The King has one," he
said, "and I have the other, and he has to call me for the
correct time."

They were among the late settlers who took up Crown land
and populated the Township of Horton and the Ottawa Valley.
This was in 1860 when the territory was nothing but a wilderness called Upper Canada.

I can vaguely remember a number of things before 1900,
but that year was especially memorable. I started school in
the early spring because in those times there was so much
snow during the winters that roads could be blocked until
some kind farmer would break a trail. It was almost three
miles to school, and the same distance, of course, home again.
I could have used snowshoes but that would have been hard

work for a five-year-old with a schoolbag full of books and a lunch. It meant a nine-hour day away from home as well.

The school was close to the Ottawa River and when we were let out at noon hour, I noticed a raft being towed by a small boat called an "alligator". On the raft was a cabin and in it, a stout cook in a white apron who was ringing a bell. Beside the cabin was a cow tied in a stall and at the front of the raft three men were fixing chains. I was very interested, and when I mentioned it the response was, "Oh, those rafts have been going down there for years," and so they had; but that was the last timber raft to make the trip.

In the early stages of the lumber industry, logs were cut and hauled onto the lakes during the winter months. The ice would support them until the spring thaw, when the drive crews would direct the logs into the different rivers. During the high waters of the spring, the rivers were packed with logs and as the water receded many of these were lodged behind rocks and fallen trees. The alligator was so named because it was practically amphibious. It was built to pass over logs and booms, and could go close enough to shore to winch the trapped logs and get them back into the main stream, where they could be guided into a boom. When this was done, the alligator would give a number of blasts on its steam whistle to alert a larger towboat which would pick up the boom and haul it further down river to the sawmill.

Grandfather Smith was a good teacher and he wanted to show me everything. He got me up early so we could sow the grain by hand at daylight. On the white snow he could see to spread the grain evenly. The grain would attract the sunlight and sink far enough into the snow to be protected when the crust froze over at night. He learned this as a farmer's son in Ireland, and was well trained in pioneering as a settler.

The land was rich, and when the crop grew and ripened, there seemed to be a right time for everything—even cutting. I saw my first thrashing in the fall of 1901. Before that time, thrashing had been done by flail and the grain was ground into flour after it had been cut by cradle—all by hand. That year things were greatly changed. Horses were a new source of power to drive the machine that separated the grain from the straw. A teamster stood on a platform and kept the horses

151

going round him in a circle, only stopping them occasionally, to rest and water them.

Straw was very important then, and was used for many purposes. In the fall, bed ticks were filled and the new straw was used as bedding for the animals as well. The art of building a strawstack was also important, as the stack had to be balanced. Cattle eat around a stack at body level and, in so doing, make it into the shape of a mushroom. If not properly built, it will topple over on them.

Grandfather Smith had me stay away from school on thrashing day. It was dusty work, as the grain had to be hauled to the barn to keep it dry. The men needed drinking water, and this was the job I was given.

Mother, Grandmother, and my Aunt Bell wore pure-white aprons, and waited on the dirtiest group of men you could wish to see. The dinner they served took a week to prepare, but because the men's work was hard and the hours long, it was all eaten in one hour.

After everything was finished, my grandfather asked me how many men had been there. I said, "Twenty-three." "How do you know?" he asked, and I told him that I had counted their hats. He said, "You are getting to be useful."

The next year, there were further changes. Our remaining oxen were replaced by horses, which were stronger and faster. Equipment suitable for oxen was inadequate for horses, so there was now more demand for wagons and sleighs. That year's thrashing was very different; a steam engine was used. It still had to be drawn by horses, and the same method was employed for the separator. The same number of men were there as in 1901, and the same white tablecloths and white aprons, but the output of grain was much higher, and now eight men were needed on the strawstack. For all the years the Smiths farmed the land, there would be new and different ways of doing things every year, but, sadly, it wasn't destined to go on forever. The farm wasn't capable of supporting the number of people needed to make a living from it. That fall saw the closing of the Alex Smith farm, to which every member of the Smith family had contributed part of his or her life. My father and mother had tried to run it as a cattle ranch, but time had run out. It was finally turned over to the Township of Horton as a park. For the Smith farm and many other farms in the Ottawa Valley, the fields were too small and too rough for modern equipment, and it was no longer practical to work them for grain or stock.

Renfrew had always been a prosperous place, surrounded by the finest farm and grazing land. The two main railroads, the CPR and the Grand Trunk, that passed through it facilitated shipping, and the town became a centre for factories. There were woollen and textile mills, machine shops, foundries, a planing mill, flour mills, blacksmith shops, and hydro-electric power. It was known as a millionaire town, and from 1909 to 1911 it had the first professional hockey team in Canada. It was also noted for fine horses and cattle, and for its farm products, especially the butter, which was known worldwide and took many awards.

What was happening in and around Renfrew in 1910 was happening in other towns and cities in Ontario where the impact of technological change was being felt after many prosperous years. Surrounding farms were the first hit. Farmers who had employed five farm helpers could now, with the aid of machines, manage with two. Those who were let go came into the towns looking for work and food. There was no unemployment insurance, and the result was that many of these men resorted to theft. The years 1911, 1912, and 1913 saw a steady increase of able-bodied men coming in on freight trains, and leaving the same way as the local authorities hurried them out of town.

In 1914 automobiles were coming into use for pleasure driving, which was limited to towns as there were no highways, just country roads. Automobiles were not welcome; they frightened the horses, and most people could not afford such luxury. In spite of such reactions, cars sold through catalogues, and they were all black. By 1916, there were twenty-six different makes in Ontario alone, even with the war going on.

Everyone expected the war to be over soon, but the war did not end. People didn't realize what was involved until the names of the very men we had paraded to the station a few months before appeared in the casualty lists. I was never convinced that a lot of those men joined the army because they were patriotic, but to get food, clothes, and a place to sleep—in this, a so-called country of plenty, something was radically wrong. It was not long before the town band was meeting the wounded, some of whom had lost their legs and were returning in wheelchairs.

It became obvious that this was a different kind of war, and that we were ill-prepared for it. It was not a man-to-man war; it was mechanized. The German army was better trained, and better equipped, and we were losing the war in 1915 because we did not understand that the methods had changed.

It had been no small feat to start from scratch in 1916 to outproduce the enemy by the fall of 1918, but we did; and when the war ended, a pattern for rapid production had been set. The "war to end all wars" saw most of the major powers, victor and vanquished alike, equipped with far greater industrial capacity and potential than when they had entered it. The world had changed in those twenty-three years since my birth.

The years 1919, 1920, and 1921 were exciting. From the armed forces and the factories, the United States and Canada released the greatest number of educated and skilled people the world had ever seen. Initially, there was severe unemployment while there was an adjustment from wartime to peacetime production, but times soon picked up, because of the shortage of almost everything that had not been made during the war years.

The Technical Alliance became a consulting firm to big business, advising companies to expand, in order to fill the need for cars, trucks, and housing. People spent money like water, thinking that bad times were over forever. Everything looked rosy.

At the same time, and in contrast to what had taken place from 1910 to 1912, when unskilled men were walking the streets looking for work, now, ten years later, skilled unemployed men were walking the streets. Modern methods had eliminated many jobs. Here is an example—a man operating a machine by hand in 1914 was able, by 1917, to look after six automatically operated turret lathes. That same operator had become a toolsetter, and even a toolmaker. Near disaster had shown that man had the ability to become more efficient. Resistance to change had been overcome in the face of common danger, but what should have meant benefits to all mankind had proven a mixed blessing.

Helen Sakon A Four-Year Nightmare

On December 7, 1941, the Japanese bombed Pearl Harbor,
an act that outraged the United States and brought that
nation into the Second World War. Pearl Harbor was to
have a devastating effect on those of Japanese origin living in the United States and Canada.

In our country a form of national hysteria took over.
The Japanese on the west coast especially were looked on
as enemies. Their property was confiscated, and they
were ordered from their homes and herded into hastily
built camps in the interior of British Columbia to live out
the war years under guard. Helen Sakon of Kapuskasing,
Ontario, is a survivor of those traumatic years.

At the time of Pearl Harbor, I had been married for some
time, and my husband worked in the bush for a lumber
company and we lived in one of the company houses. We had a
small baby and another was on the way when the four-year
nightmare began for us.

I think it was on the second or third day after Pearl Harbor
that we were all ordered to leave our homes, and go to
Vancouver on the mainland. I had no idea what this was all
about. I really didn't. Anyway, they told us to take everything
we owned, and take the boat to Vancouver. This applied to all
Japanese families, so there was a great deal of confusion and
crying as we all hurried to pack and get things down to the
dock.

Now, I considered myself as Canadian as anybody, as,
after all, I was born in Vancouver. My husband was born in
Japan, but he also considered himself Canadian, as he'd lived
on Vancouver Island a good number of years. In the years
leading up to the war, it was very hard for Japanese in B.C. to
become naturalized, as there was a lot of prejudice.

Anyway, exactly one week after Pearl Harbor, we were in
Vancouver where nobody, including the government, knew
what to do with us. We were frightened, but so were ordinary
Canadians who lived on the coast. They were worried about
invasion, I suppose, and Japanese submarines, which were
said to be operating off the coast, and anybody of Japanese
descent became suspect.

Anti-Japanese propaganda filled the newspapers and the average west-coast Canadian was being educated to fear "the enemy in their midst". As far as they were concerned, I suppose, every Japanese they saw was out to murder them. It was so bad that an Oriental of any kind was afraid to venture out on the streets. Some Vancouver politicians used this for their own purposes, and made speeches about "the yellow peril", as they called us. Mr. Green, who later became external affairs minister in the federal government, was vehement against us. He was a high-school teacher at the time.

To show it was doing something, I guess, the government passed all kinds of orders-in-council. One of these said that anyone born in Japan would be sent to road camps away from the coast. My husband was sent to one in the Rockies, a place called Lampier, while I was left behind with my three-month-old baby. We were herded with thousands of other Japanese into the Pacific National Exhibition grounds, where each family was given space in horse barns and places like that. Families that came from the island were put into the building where they show cattle during the fair. I remember it was all concrete, and it wasn't pleasant, especially with the baby and expecting my second. Those who had parents living in Vancouver could stay in their family homes, but even though my parents had a house, I chose to stay in the barns at Hastings Park. I wanted to be there when my husband came back from the road gang.

By this time they had a system for families living in the park to be shipped out first to these ghost towns and camps in the British Columbia interior. Our baby was due in October, so I wanted all of that to be over and us to be settled somewhere before the baby came.

In the meantime, they began evicting Japanese families from their homes in Vancouver. My mother and brothers and sisters received their orders to get out by a certain date. It was such a mixed-up time. Then I heard that my husband was shifted from the road gang to a place in the interior called New Denver, where he was put to work building these places for Japanese families.

It was the churches in Canada who interceded and they raised quite a fuss about families being broken up and separated. The churches had a lot to do with having the men brought back from the work parties and reunited with their wives and children in these settlements. It's a good thing I was so busy with the baby during that period as it kept my mind off these other troubles. They took our cameras and radios, and they kept searching for guns, which nobody had. Even before we were allowed into Hastings Park, we had to go through a process where we registered all our belongings with something called the Custodian of Alien Property. We were told it would all be there for us when the war was over.

It wasn't, of course. We received a letter from the Custodian which said that my mother's house had been sold. It had been sold all right, but for only a fraction of its worth. They never asked if they could sell it—they just did. There are so many things that were done that even today I can't understand why. I keep telling myself it was wartime, and war brings on irrational behaviour, especially as there was so much propaganda plastered around Vancouver. That town was full of posters warning against spies, and there were caricatures of sinister-looking Japanese faces. Emperor Hirohito of Japan was depicted as a monster trying to scoop up Canada in his hands.

I must say, though, that the RCMP, who were in charge of looking after us, treated us kindly. First off we had to register and get a number. Mine was 02371, and that number had to be on everything we owned. We were at a place called Lemon Creek and we had to report to the RCMP once a month in these ghost towns and camps. There were two thousand of us there in these little pre-fab houses, and if there were less than four in a family, your house had to be shared with another family. We had an older couple and their daughter with us. It was only one big room and a wall down the middle, with us on one side, and them on the other. There was an outhouse in the yard, and there was a pump where we all went for our water. Often there would be a quarter-inch of ice on the floor in the morning, as the wood stove we had would go out while we slept. We lived there from 1942 until 1946.

We were the last to leave. You were given the choice of going to Japan or staying in Canada—east of the Rockies. They wouldn't permit us to go back to the coast when the war was over because the people there didn't want us, they said. Then stories began that the people in eastern Canada didn't want us either, and that if we went there we would get awful treatment. We decided to go to Northern Ontario, where we found people couldn't have been nicer to us. Even at the camp in British Columbia, it wasn't all that bad. I was busy with the children, and my husband worked in the bush as he had always done. He wasn't paid much but it was enough for us to get by on. The Slocan Valley was beautiful, and many of us grew very fond of it. However, we couldn't stay there after the war, so many of the Japanese went back to Japan, disillusioned and bitter. They didn't stay there, though. Most came back to Canada because they found that they weren't Japanese any more. They couldn't stand life in Japan, so they came back as fast as they could. They were Canadians—especially those youngsters who were born here.

In my case, having been born and brought up here, but being treated like the enemy, I suppose I could feel very bitter. But what good would that do? When the madness of war was over, we were able to rebuild our lives in a lovely community. To dwell on things would only bring more unhappiness.

I'd like to go back sometime and see the west coast again. The last time I saw it was in 1942 when we left for the camp, but I'd love to see it again, as a tourist. I'd like to visit, but not live there, as Northern Ontario is my home now. I love it very much, and that other part of my life is forty years in the past.

Vern Dooey Railroad Tracks Curled Like Hairpins

Everyone who has ever lived through a forest fire seems to have the memory of every moment indelibly etched in his or her mind. Every smell, every crackle of flame, every sight and sound, remain with that person forever. For the survivors, memories of the fire are reminders of their proximity to death.

For the early settlers and today's northern residents in many areas, daily life was difficult enough without the devastation of a forest fire. Vern Dooey was a young man of nineteen when fire swept through the town of Matheson in 1916, and up to that time, he had already had his share of hard knocks.

When I was born in 1897, my parents were living in the southern part of the province, and I suppose you could describe us as poor people. We didn't have much of anything, and as Dad said, "It doesn't look as though we're ever going to have much." So that's the way it was until he heard about this homesteading land that was available up in the northern part of the province.

I remember well there was a lot of talk about it at home, as I was about fifteen years old at the time. It was 1912 when the decision was made. Mom told Dad to go ahead and to take me along with him, because by this time I could do the work of a man. We took the train and located our homestead site and then started in with the axes, clearing off the place where we'd put our first shack. I'll never forget the mosquitoes and the blackflies—clouds of them—and the more you'd sweat, the more they'd come. But we kept at it, as we had to get some kind of a shelter built before the winter came. Along with this, we had to gather what food we could, small game and fish and berries, as we weren't able to take that much with us and we couldn't buy much because we had only twelve dollars in cash.

But we did it, and by gosh before the first snow began to fly, we had a shack built and we sent word down to my mother that she should come up and join us when she could manage it. Dad and I just settled in to wait and to make things as good as we could for the rest of them when they arrived. We plugged up all the cracks so the wind couldn't come through, and we laid in lots of wood and kept hunting and fishing for a reserve supply of food, but, oh my, I'll never forget how lonesome I got that first Christmas, and I stayed that way till my mother and the others arrived in January of 1913. That was a great day, I can tell you. It was like having the Christmas we didn't have— the sheer happiness of all of us being together again. It was just a shack, and we were crowded, but being together made up for that.

That first winter was really something. I can tell you, we were happy to see spring arrive, but right away, in April, we had a fire and we lost just about everything we owned. We gaffled what we could out of that, and fixed up the shack so the womenfolk would have a place to stay, and we went on from there. It was a bad start, but things improved a little bit at a time.

It's a funny thing, y'know, but except for that first Christmas up here, I always felt at home. I loved the timber. I loved clearing the land, and I loved horses. We bought our first horse in February of 1913. A little French-Canadian black stallion. Our neighbour brought a horse in from Grand Bend that was the first that crossed the river here. Then Walter Statton brought a team up, along with a sawmill. Getting a new horse was more of a thrill then than getting a new car today. He was a wonderful horse.

By 1914, the community started to take shape. They built a store, and they built a school and a community hall, all with volunteer labour. Most of the other settlers here were Anglo-Saxon, and we all got along well. There was a great influx of people in 1914, even a bunch of Norwegians who came in from New York—Peterson and Knudson, and all the others; and they built shacks and houses. They were cracker-jack carpenters. They built most of the school and the hall. They could put on more lumber in a day than the rest of us could in a week.

It slowed down after the war began. A lot of our boys enlisted. I tried, but I was turned down as they said I had an "athlete's heart", so I had to stay behind. We carried on as usual, pulling stumps and piling them up in big piles to dry out so we could burn them. We were burning something all the time, trying to get that land cleared. You could always smell smoke no matter where you went. When the timber was cut, we burned the slash, and when we cut these right-of-ways out for the government, there'd be big piles of logs burning, so nobody worried that much about it; but in 1916, on July 23, all of that changed. That morning, it was suffocatingly hot at six o'clock. The sun came up just a big ball of fire, and you could hardly breathe. There had been no rain for weeks, and everything was as dry as tinder. By noontime, you couldn't get your breath at all and you had to get down low to the ground if you wanted to get a breath of air. I never seen anything like it before.

It kept gettin' hotter and windier as the day went by, and that's the way it was when the fire struck. It hit the town of Matheson first, and it jumped across the tracks and wiped out that part of town too. It was so hot that the railroad tracks just curled up like hairpins. Those wooden houses simply exploded with the heat and there was no place to run to. The fire was everywhere. The wind was from the southwest that day, so after it burned Matheson, it kept on going down, burning everything in its path. At Val Gagné fifty-six people had crowded into a rock cut for the railway in an effort to escape the flames, and they died right where they were! The fire just sucked all the oxygen out of the air and those people suffocated. It swept down through Montuse, Kelso, and Porquis Junction. At Iroquois Falls, the only building left was the mill. It was made of concrete, and all the women and children and the cattle and the milk cows went in there and were all saved from that fire. One woman had her baby born in there that day.

When the fire would hit a tree it would explode—no matter whether it was evergreen or a leaf tree. It was so hot! Most of those who lost their lives were hiding from the flames in basements or root cellars or wells. The oxygen just cut right off. The best thing one could do was get down near the ground with wet blankets to cover you. There's always a space at the ground where the oxygen is good, you see.

After it was over, the wagons had to go round pickin' up the bodies. I'll never forget the sight of all those coffins with the bodies of people who were just like us. They had come up here looking for better lives, working so hard to better themselves. They *were* bettering themselves, too, until the Matheson fire.

It seems to me, though, that you always got to pay in some way for betterment, but those poor people paid far too much. Our home escaped, but hundreds of settlers' homes were burned to the ground. When I went into Matheson the next day it was an awful thing to see—dead horses lying all over the place and one end of the town was blackened ruins. The railway station was gone, stores, everything, and the wagons were already goin' around pickin' up the corpses. Three hundred twenty-five of our people had lost their lives. We had other big fires before and after the Matheson fire, but in my mind, that was the worst.

The day after the fire while everything was still smokin', help started to come in from the outside. Blankets and clothing and food. Lumber for new homes and things like that. Some people, not many, gave up trying to live in the North after that. But most just dug in and began all over again.

We were all shocked and, to be honest, frightened for our lives when these fires came along; but most of us figured that that was part of the price we had to pay for the privilege of living here. If I was born again, this is where I'd want to be—in Shillington, Northern Ontario. I love it here!

Eleanor Daigle Tin Lizzie Carried Us Through

On the prairies in the 1920s, horsepower was supplied for the most part by live animals. There were some cars and trucks, but for the average homesteaders, a motorized vehicle was a dream of their wildest imaginations. Cars cost money—a commodity that the homesteader saw little of. Most of their buying was done by barter, eggs and butter being the coin of the realm. But horses were slow and limited in the distances they could travel, and a homesteading family dreamed of the day they could speed down the trails of the West in their own Ford "Tin Lizzie". Eleanor Daigle and her family, now of Waterloo, Quebec, were some of the fortunate people to own a car at the time.

We had a farm near Weyburn, Saskatchewan, back in the twenties. We were young, our children were young, and there wasn't much money. We had a fair number of stock though, and a young man who helped us on the farm had an old Ford car that he had taken the back seat out of, so it was his transportation and truck combined. But what he really wanted was a horse of his own, so he could go galloping off over the prairies. We had lots of horses, but what *we* wanted was a car, and I suppose it was only natural that we should strike a deal. We traded him a nice horse we called Topsy for his truck, and we gave him five dollars to boot. He was happy, and so were we.

Now Lizzie wasn't in great shape, but with winter setting in, you couldn't use cars much on the roads anyway. My husband decided that he'd do all the repairs himself, while the snow was on the ground. He did them all right, but as we had no outdoor sheds at the time, he did them in the house, and I spent the whole winter with parts of the engine and the car scattered all over my kitchen floor.

When spring came, old Lizzie was raring to go, and she was willing to tackle anything. My husband used her to do the ploughing and I would pile the ploughshares into the back seat and take them to town for sharpening. I took her everywhere, even if I didn't have a licence. It never occurred to us that we might need one. Lizzie took us to church and the children to school. She hauled our eggs and butter to town, and our flour and sugar back. She was our pride and joy, as well as our best workhorse.

Nobody ever said Lizzie was easy to get along with. Once in a while she'd have a blowout that I couldn't fix, so I'd just remove the tire and run her on the rim on the gravelled roads.

Saturday night was the big night for us. We'd pile our two boys, both still under the age of ten, in the back seat with pillows and blankets. After them would go a crate of eggs, and a box of our butter for our shopping spree at Shibley's store in Radville. If we were feeling especially rich, the four of us would take in the current movie in town. Those were the days when all members of a family could see the same movie without feeling uncomfortable. Tom Mix might kiss his horse, but never a girl.

When we were finally ready to go home, we'd have to jack up Lizzie's hind wheel, and crank her in front to get her started, and run around fast to let her hind wheel down again before we jumped in to drive away. I remember one time we didn't do it all quite fast enough, and my little boy and I ran her smack into my husband's new binder. I think that's when we decided to sell Lizzie for something else.

It was a sad parting, somewhat lessened by the thrill of her successor—a touring car, with button-on curtains. She stayed with us a while, doing all of the jobs Lizzie had done, but eventually she too was replaced by one of the first Fords with a hard top. This Ford was tall and skinny, and our neighbours laughed, saying she was going to tip over in a high wind—but she never did. Those were the good old days. The ones that followed weren't. The grasshoppers came and ate our crops, and the dust storms blew our soil away.

We traded our car for an old Ford truck, another Lizzie, which needed a new engine before it would take us anywhere, so my handy husband, Tony, got busy again, and bought an engine from a wrecked truck, which was called a Star. He installed the Star in the Ford, and we all laughed again, and said that Tony made a Star out of Lizzie.

Times were terrible, and many proud farmers were forced to go on relief. We didn't want to do that, so we sold what we could, and gave the rest away, except for the few things we could load in the truck. We said good-bye to our house and our barns, and anything else that was left, and headed east in our truck towards Quebec, where my in-laws lived. We ate in the truck, and we slept there too, just like a band of gypsies. We had four boys by now; the oldest was twelve, and the youngest eighteen months. It wasn't awful; it was fun! People all along the way were so good and kind to us wherever we stopped. And do you know, we still didn't have a licence to drive.

During the part where we went through the States, we were told that we would have to buy a fifty-cent licence for every state we passed through, but if that were so, it never happened. Nobody bothered us until we got to the bridge at Montreal, where a policeman stopped us and asked for our licence. We told him our story, and where we had come from, and he just took my father-in-law's address in Granby, and said he'd be in touch with us, and let us go. We never heard anything more about it, though.

When we arrived at our in-laws' we had $2.75 left in our pockets, and we had been on the road thirteen days. Our old Tin Lizzie truck carried us through.

The Rev. Dr. E. A. Thomson Child of the Church

For the new settlers, no community was complete until it
contained a school and a church. The clergyman was
often the most important person in town, looked up to
and respected by all. He was the symbol of all that was
right—a god-like figure who could do no wrong, father
confessor, and arbitrator of disputes. The standards that a
community set for its clergyman were even stiffer than
the ones that he set for them. The Reverend Dr. E. A.
Thomson, former Clerk of the General Assembly of the
Presbyterian Church in Canada, grew up as a minister's
son in Ontario during the Depression.

In our family, becoming a minister was almost as natural
as breathing or eating. The Thomsons were ministers right
back to the formation of the Presbyterian Church in Scotland
two hundred years ago, and they were always on the front
lines of social change.

When the Scots came to Canada, most of them under
dreadful conditions, pushed off their lands in the old country,
there were Thomson ministers with them, trying in whatever
way they could to ease the hardship and never living any
better than the people they served. My own father was a
minister for more than fifty years in Hastings, Ontario. His
salary was never more than six or seven hundred dollars a
year, so, as you can imagine, nothing was ever wasted. We
were never hungry, but we never had more than we needed
and there were no luxuries whatever. None! We ate a lot of
oatmeal porridge, milk and eggs and potatoes, but meat was a
real treat.

There were five children to feed and clothe, so it was
always a case of "making do". There were never any new
clothes as far as I can remember. Everything I wore had been
worn by somebody else before me. Things kept passing from
one child to the other and most had originally been made by
Mother from something that Father had worn. As for her
clothes, they were always the same. I don't know how they

managed, but I used to say that Mother always kept her clothes until they came around the second or third time in fashion. But somehow or other she always managed to see to it that Father looked his best. People expected that he should look a certain way, and she saw to it that he did.

The truth of the matter was that the minister's family always had to live up to great expectations in the community. They were supposed to be shining examples of everything, including the way they looked, and the way they behaved. They shouldn't look untidy, and sometimes dirty, like the other children. They were expected to be neat and clean at all times, and to always behave well, because they were "the minister's children". It was like living in a glass house all the time, always on show. It was a difficult role to live up to in a small community. We sometimes felt that we were expected to be *too* good; but, of course, we were like everybody else. Some of us were good, and some of us weren't. Father and Mother knew this, and were always very understanding of the difficulties we had to face. Father, after all, was a minister's son himself.

They managed to educate all their children despite the lack of money, even though we all had to leave home for our secondary education, which meant paying our room and board away from home. They made tremendous sacrifices to see us pursue careers in law, medicine, and theology. They took nothing for themselves, except the absolute bare necessities of life. Back in those early days of this century, many, many people were like that. There were farmers who could barely write their own names, who would sell their last possessions to keep a son or daughter in school.

I was ordained in 1917, and my first parish was a small place called Monkton, Ontario, near Stratford. It was in the snow belt of the province and the storms were intense. As a minister, I always had to make sure my visitation to farmers' homes was done before the river froze up and navigation was closed, which usually happened by the end of November. After that it was difficult, if not impossible, because they didn't even try to clear the roads, and everyone was locked in for the whole winter.

The church was very, very important to everyone in the community in those winters. It was the only outlet for activity for just about everybody. Aside from horses and sleighs, the only kind of vehicular traffic that moved was the CPR train. There'd be many weeks when that wouldn't move either as the snow was piled up higher than two-storey houses. We often had to tunnel our way out of our homes and to the church. There'd be sewing bees and quilting bees, church suppers, and many other events going on for all age groups. The church really brought people together, and the minister felt himself to be an important part of people's families.

It was during the Depression that the churches really came to the fore in the lives of people. All of the churches of all denominations! When the Depression came, I was in Elora, Ontario, and we began to hear the terrible stories of hunger and hardship among the farmers of western Canada, who were also hit by drought and dust storms. I formed a committee which sent carloads of food out there to these people, who were literally starving. The first thing we did was raise twenty-five dollars to buy one hundred bags of potatoes at twenty-five cents a bag. It was enough to fill one railway car. We kept up the effort, canvassing people again and again, and everyone was so generous. All of the denominations banded together and between the townspeople and the farmers of the Elora district, many, many carloads of food made their way out West. All of this food was being collected and sent by people who didn't have very much themselves.

But that's the way it was during those years. Everybody helped each other to the best of their ability. The ministers asked to have their salaries cut, so they wouldn't have more than anyone else. They were hard, hard times, and yet we came through. I'm proud of the way the churches helped to alleviate the hardships of the Depression.

Elliott Moses A Bad Act

Elliott Moses of the Six Nations Indian Reserve near
Brantford, Ontario, was a leader respected in both white
and Indian societies. He refused to accept the second-class
status conferred on his people by white men's statutes,
and instead showed his people how to earn respect. In his
more than eighty years, Elliott Moses helped to forge
bonds of understanding between two widely separated
cultures through wise and peaceful persuasion.

The biggest mistake ever made with regard to native
people was the Indian Act they created a long time ago. With
all good intentions it was assumed that all Indians were the
same no matter where they lived in Canada, but, of course,
that wasn't so. There's a great difference between the
nomadic tribes of the far North and the tribes of the south
such as the Six Nations of Brantford. There may be two
hundred years of progress separating them, but the Indian
Act, which covers all Indians, was designed to protect the
interests of those who are lowest on the scale of development.
When you apply it to all Indians, even those on the highest
rungs of the economic ladder, it serves to hold Indians back.

For example, when my wife and I were married, the home
we were to live in and the rest of the property needed a lot of
improvement. We discovered when we went to the bank that
we couldn't get a loan, because the Indian Act, as a protection
to Indians, said that our note or anything else that we might
give in the way of security could not be regarded as a legal
document. In other words, if we decided not to pay the money
back, the bank couldn't foreclose to collect it.

So, naturally, we couldn't get the loan, and neither could
other Indians who wanted to improve their homes. In our
case, we sold a couple of insurance policies we had and were
able to do the work that way. But that's a case of how the
Indian Act works against the people it's supposed to benefit.

That's one of the reasons why so many homes on reserves,
even today, look to be in such poor condition. Indians can't
borrow money in the same way as anyone else. In the beginning, there might have been good reasons for making Indians

not responsible for their financial dealings, but as we have advanced, those reasons are no longer valid.

One time when I was young, I needed a bushel of alfalfa and a bushel of red clover. I went to a dealer and he said that, as I was an Indian, he couldn't take a chance on me. This was a terrible blow to me, because I was just getting started in farming, and I had no idea that I wasn't going to be able to operate on credit as all the other young white people were, many of whom were friends of mine. The dealer took down an old account book from a shelf and dusted it off and began going through it, page by page—until he came to the name of Moses. He pointed to the name and I said, "Yes, that was my uncle." He told me that my uncle owed the firm ten dollars and that he had no way of collecting it. I said that my uncle had been dead for ten years, and anyway, that had nothing to do with me. He said, "I'm sorry, I can't help you." It was a very demeaning experience. However, there was a firm next door that was willing to trust me and I got what I needed.

The thing was, though, that if I had decided not to pay, there was nothing that firm could do to collect, because as far as the Indian Act was concerned, I could not be held responsible. I did pay that firm, however, and over the years I gave them many thousands of dollars of business because of their trust in me. At the same time, I couldn't blame them at all if they didn't.

Now just to show the other side: I remember a time when a number of Indians had teams of horses out hauling gravel for the Number Six highway. It was all teamwork as there was no big machinery in those days. The Sherra Milling Company, which was nearby, supplied these Indian teams with hay and grain for their horses while the work was going on, and the men paid the mill every week. But when it came to a last bill after the work was finished, some of them didn't go back to pay. The result was that the company found they couldn't force these men to pay because of the Indian Act. At the next company meeting, a resolution was passed that they would not trust Indians any more. That, of course, affected all of us, most of whom wouldn't cheat anyone; but you couldn't blame the company for the stand they took either.

Charlie Shires This Great Wall of Flame

Canada's Northland always held a certain appeal for those who yearned for adventure; but not until this century were there any large-scale attempts to establish a population there. The distant North was forbidding until the coming of the railroad and the airplane. When these two means of transportation enabled industry to move north, employment and government encouragement brought the settlers. Charlie Shires was one of those who came to Cochrane, Northern Ontario. He was ready for anything—except fire.

I guess the north country looked like the land of opportunity when I came to Northern Ontario. Everybody was talking about it—about the free land and the cheap land, and how it was the land of the future. I was about twenty-one or twenty-two, and full of adventure, I suppose, and I thought I should give it a try. I lived in southern Ontario at the time, so I thought, "Why not?" I was young and I just wanted to go somewhere, anywhere at all. So away I went, and got myself one hundred and sixty acres of homestead in a little place called Hunta, about twelve miles by rail from Cochrane. That was in 1911, the year that Northern Ontario was almost wiped off the map by fire.

We knew there was fire around. The weather was hot as hell, and there was plenty of smoke, but that didn't seem to frighten anyone. There was always smoke at that time, because farmers were burning stumps, and the railroad was burning slash and things of that nature, but boy, nobody expected what we got that day.

I was working at something in the field when I turned around and saw this great wall of flame coming in my direction. I dropped what I was doing and ran to the barn to let the cattle loose. They were making a hell of a ruckus, and when I opened that door they just came crowding out of there, heading for this little lake in front of the house where I lived. They just seemed to know they were in danger and what to do. We decided to follow their lead and we all took off too, with the fire licking right along behind us. We grabbed blankets from

171

the house, as someone who'd been in a forest fire told us to do that. We jumped in the water and soaked those blankets and pulled them over our heads. I guess we'd have burned to death if we hadn't done that.

The flames followed us right down to the water, and they just jumped across that lake like it wasn't there. My God, I'll never forget it! We thought the flames would stop at the water's edge, but, my God, they just reached across the water and ignited the trees on the other side. They were crackling and exploding with loud bangs like shots from a cannon. There were balls of fire flying through the air and fire on all sides of the lake. There was so much heat, we thought we might boil to death if we didn't burn first. I don't know how long it took for the fire to burn past us—maybe an hour or so—but finally it did, and we were safe.

In that short time, everything that had been green and growing was just a mass of blackened ruin. The trees were just tall, black sticks poking out of the ground. It looked like a battlefield. At that point it occurred to me that without that little lake, I'd have been burned to death. It just seemed like the whole world was on fire and that everything God and man together had created and built was wiped from the face of the earth. I was lucky to be alive.

When things cooled down a bit, I went around looking over my one hundred and sixty acres that had cost me fifty cents an acre, and I got to thinking about all the work I had put into it. I had been trying to clear the land, and get rid of the trees, and all I had up to then was stumps. Stumps everywhere. Piles and piles of stumps. Working by yourself, trying to get stumps out of the earth, is killing work. It was all mine though, and so was that little shack I put up to live in. That was part of the agreement with the government—build a place to live in, and do so much work every year. I worked even harder than I was expected to. There were stump piles there as big as a house.

After the fire, I looked around and said, "I better get to hell off this land before I starve to death." It just made me realize that what I had been working on was just not enough to support a family. A few days later I walked up the road a little closer in to Cochrane, and bought a bigger place from a fellow who wanted to get away. That worked out fine, although it was tough going for a while. I fixed up the old buildings, cut lumber on contract and planted potatoes, carrots, and turnips, which we sold in Cochrane.

Even after that fire or any of the others we had, I never thought about leaving the North. The North was good to me. I had a nice wife and after a while, nine children—every one of them good. The fires were bad, but there's always something bad no matter where you are.

Sheldon Luck Born to Fly

More than any single group, the bush pilots opened up the
Canadian Northland. With their tiny planes, they flew
into uncharted wilderness taking with them prospectors,
developers, miners, and supplies. Many of them were
fliers who had earned their wings in the First World War
and were unwilling, or unable, to take up more pedestrian
occupations when the war ended. They could see that the
airplane was the perfect vehicle for exploring the vast
and mysterious North.

Back in 1922, when I was about ten years old in Edmonton, many of these fliers from the war were using the airport there as their base; and the unquestioned hero of them all was hometown boy "Wop" May. He was one of the top aces of the war, and a living legend. I'd go over to that primitive airport day after day just to get a glimpse of him taking off and landing, and I knew even then that flying was going to be my future. I just knew that some day I would fly those planes.

"Punch" Dickins, another war ace, also used that airport, and these fellows didn't know it, but my heart went along in the passenger seat when they took those little planes up into the sky. Later on, in my teens, I saw Wop May at a social function, and I kept watching for an opportunity to talk with him. When it came, I told him of my ambitions, and he didn't disappoint me at all. He was everything that I wanted him to be, kind and encouraging, and he said, "It's a tough game, but if you want it badly enough, you'll get there."

My biggest hurdle was my father, who was a poor Methodist minister whose ambition was to see me follow in his footsteps. Not only that: he hated the idea of airplanes. As far as he was concerned, the Apostle Paul hadn't mentioned airplanes in his early letters to Christians; therefore, there was no place for them in our lives. If I had wanted to be a fisherman, he would have said, "That's okay, Peter was a fisherman;" or "Be a carpenter. Jesus was a carpenter." I kept after him, though, until he finally agreed to a compromise. He told me that if I could reach my goal without financial help from him, he'd give me his blessing. That's all I needed.

I was nineteen by this time and the Depression had just begun. I took any job, no matter how little it paid—digging ditches, shovelling manure, anything—and nothing paid more than thirty-five or fifty cents an hour. I'd work all day, and sometimes all night just to get money for another hour of instruction, which cost twenty dollars an hour on a dual machine. I'd shovel manure in the day and at night I'd help around the local theatre. At one point one of the travelling stock companies hired me as an actor to replace one who got sick. I was paid four dollars a night, so five nights of that gave me another hour of instruction. This kind of thing kept up even after I soloed and received my licence, because in getting a job, the more hours of solo flying you have, the better.

My first job as a professional flier was doing what was called barnstorming. We'd take people up for their first ride in an airplane, fly them over the city and around a little bit, and take them down again after a few minutes, and they'd pay two dollars. This was big business in the early thirties, when only about two per cent of Canadians had ever been up in a plane. They'd flock to the airports on Sundays, and you were hard-pressed to find time to take all who wanted to go.

Outside of that, my first commercial flying was done the year that William Aberhart and his Social Credit party went into power. I was hired to fly candidates around to meetings all over southern Alberta. Planes were just beginning to be used for election campaigns in the early thirties.

We'd land in a farmer's field close to the hall where the candidate was to speak, and take off again across this bumpy field when he was finished. I was flying little Puss-Moths at that time, three-seaters, built by DeHavilland—monoplanes, as they were called, with inverted gypsy engines. Great little planes that could go just about anywhere, and do anything.

We had to be careful about haystacks on those early airfields. You see, they weren't paved strips at all. Even the airports in places such as Calgary were simply fields, and they had to be kept mowed. The result was that more than once a pilot would slam into a new haystack that hadn't been there when he took off.

One of the myths of that time is that Wop May and Punch Dickins did their first flying into the Northland in patched-up World War One planes. This was not so at all. These men were too sensible for that sort of thing. They were real pioneer pilots concerned with safety and good flying practices, and they set the standards for men such as myself who came afterwards. They knew those old war planes weren't fit for the Arctic.

I met Wop one night in Edmonton and he said, "Let's go down to the hotel and have a drink." In the course of the evening, he talked about the search for Albert Johnson, the Mad Trapper, which captured the imagination of the whole world back in the early thirties. May was the pilot that the RCMP hired to lead them on that search. He told me that he felt terrible about the way Jonhson was tracked down. He said he felt like an eagle circling around, waiting to pounce on a defenceless rabbit: "It all seemed so unfair." He felt that it wasn't sporting. That gives you an idea of the kind of man he was. Wop wasn't excusing Johnson for his crimes, but he didn't relish the idea of getting him that way. Johnson killed two Mounties in cold blood, but as Wop said, "The man was crazed, and not really responsible for his actions."

A lot of extremely fine and unusual men were engaged in flying then. I think that their prime motivation was a love of Canada and opening it up. There was very little money in it, and most of us couldn't have done it without the full backing of our wives, who were often called upon to keep food on the table for our families. It's as simple as that.

I remember one time when my wife, two children, and I were living in a small cabin on the shore of a lake in northern British Columbia. The president of our company had flown a new plane up to me, as mine was getting pretty shaky and needed repairs. Well, he landed this new plane on the water, taxied in to the dock, and came to our cabin. He told us the company was in real trouble and finding it impossible to meet the payroll. Now, my pay was only a hundred dollars a month, and two cents a mile, hardly enough to feed us. He asked if I was willing to take just enough for the bare necessities for a few months, with no salary at all to help save the company. Well, this was a shocker, because even as it was, we were always scraping the bottom.

Isabel never hesitated a moment. She said, "By cutting corners and cutting them again, we could get by until the

Do not stand on Exhaust Pipe

Wilfred R. ("Wop") May, above, one of Canada's greatest early bush pilots and the pilot who tracked the Mad Trapper of Rat River in 1932. "Back in 1922, when I was about ten years old in Edmonton, many of these fliers from the war were using the airport there as their base; and the unquestioned hero of them all was hometown boy 'Wop' May."

*The early homesteaders on the prairies were forced to build
their new homes out of whatever materials were handy.*

*Ford being towed on the prairies, 1923. "Nobody ever said
Lizzie was easy to get along with. Once in a while she'd have a
blowout that I couldn't fix, so I'd just remove the tire and run her
on the rim on the gravelled roads." (Eleanor Daigle)*

This informal gathering suggests the range of the prairie population in 1905, the year that Alberta and Saskatchewan became provinces.

"Colonel Sam" McLaughlin in the driver's seat of a 1908 McLaughlin-Buick on his one-hundredth birthday in September 1971, just four months before his death. In the back seat are, left to right, daughters Isobel and Hilda.

The prairie settler's first home was often built of sod cut from the land. "First he ploughed a furrow, and then cut sods about a foot and a half long. He then laid these in exactly the same way that bricks are laid." (Hilda Urquhart)

Settler Maurice Ingweld in his first log home in 1908. "My dad was a greenhorn who came to Canada looking for something different than the life he was born to in the shadow of England's Wells Cathedral, where his father was organist for fifty-three years." (H. "Dude" Lavington)

Settlers scraping buffalo horns at Unity, Saskatchewan, in 1910 (while the earnest young man on the right squeezes a bulb to take the photograph). " One of the first things we noticed was the tremendous number of buffalo heads that were scattered around our land, thousands of them with the horns attached, bleached by the sun." (Hilda Urquhart)

40

As a child, Bill Lewis used to play on the grass-covered mounds that outlined the ruined Fortress of Louisbourg before its restoration began in 1961.

41

Louisbourg today.

42

A log city carved from the New Brunswick wilderness, circa 1870. "They settled along the shore, with the sea in front and their farmland in back, with a small bit of land and a big lot of sea." (Gleneatha Green Hettrick)

43

The bunkhouse of a logging camp similar to those remembered by Magne Stortroen and Hartley Trussler.

One of the greatest timber barons, J. R. Booth stands beside one of the last shipments of great white pine. "They cut everything down and then selected only the finest for the square timber they wanted." (Hartley Trussler)

weather turns cold on eighty dollars a month, and if that will help, we'll do it, because it's important that Sheldon continue to fly." So that's what we did. The company was able to turn itself around, and before the snow fell that winter, they paid us back the money we had sacrificed.

We didn't have radio in our planes at the time, and there was an awful lot of seat-of-the-pants flying in that very mountainous part of British Columbia. I get shivers still when I think of some of the situations I was in fifty years ago. I might be pulling my plane up to dock in some out-of-the-way airport when the Hudson's Bay Company factor would come tearing down to tell me of an accident somewhere. The Hudson's Bay people all over the North had wireless, even as far back as the twenties, and consequently were the only ones equipped to know what was going on. The factor would say a man had been badly hurt and they had to get him out to hospital.

So I'd take off, often in terrible weather, and wonder if I'd ever make it. But you always did—or at least, I did. I was very lucky. You would have to find your way there at night, land with no radio in the dark, and take off again in the dark. You had to know what the ground conditions were—a big rock here, a lake there, or a waterfall somewhere which would tell you where you were—and you seemed to develop an equilibrium that enabled you to keep your plane going straight, even in the dark, or a blinding snowstorm. That was something that came after a lot of flying, and all of those early pilots had it. Mind you, there were a few times I felt I was lost, and it was on these occasions that I reverted to the fervent prayers my father had taught me, and everything would turn out all right.

I did crash twice but walked away without a scratch from planes that were totally wrecked. One time I took off in a Boeing 40H4 from a little bay that we were using as a runway. I was just out over the trees when my engine quit, and smoke came billowing out from the back of the plane. I came down smashing through the tops of trees, and my plane landed, burning and upside down, in the bay. When I came to, my face was in the snow on the lake surface. You see, I was in an open cockpit near the tail, and I looked and saw that my engine was pushed all the way down into this cargo of fish that I was carrying. If it hadn't been there, that engine would have crashed right into me. I crawled out and walked away with nothing but a sore stomach from the pressure of my seat belt.

A few days later, Grant McConachie came out to make up a report on the accident, and after walking around the wreckage a few times, he looked at me and said, "Sheldon, anyone who can walk away from something like this was born to fly." And you know, I guess he was right. I flew for fifty years, everything from Puss-Moths to jets, and I wouldn't trade one minute of it for anything else.

John Charyk Good Little Schools

Memories of small, roughly constructed buildings called one-room schools are fondly recalled by many pioneers. In these tiny educational institutions there were often as many as eleven grades taught by one teacher to forty or fifty children. These schools with their overworked teachers formed the backbone of the early educational system. John Charyk, now of Calgary, Alberta, began his teaching career in a one-room school in the small prairie community of Bindloss, Saskatchewan, in the 1930s. He has also written two books about one-room schools.

I went back fifty years later to look at my little school, and it was still there, but it was no longer a school. It was just a deserted building, but for me it was full of memories of eager youngsters and happy times, and I couldn't help feeling sad. As I sat on the step outside, I got to thinking about how that school came to be built, a story that's repeated thousands of times across the country.

The name selected for the school district was "Social Plains". At the time it was built, in 1913, there was no railway in the area. The community of Bindloss didn't even come into being until 1915. The closest railway town was Medicine Hat sixty-five miles to the southeast. You could get to Medicine Hat by wagon road, but most of the settlers found it more convenient to use the South Saskatchewan River to raft their supplies in, their flour, sugar, groceries, clothing, and anything else they needed. They were very isolated on these homesteads, so simply staying alive required a lot of planning and a great deal of effort. However, one thing they wanted more than anything else was a school so that their children would have a chance to better themselves.

They banded together in the spring of 1913, and formed a school board to purchase lumber and other supplies from a company in Medicine Hat. Two of the homesteaders constructed a raft from this material and floated it down the river to a place called Tucker's Landing. The raft was then taken apart, and the material was hauled the remaining six miles to the school site by horse and wagon.

The actual task of building the school involved the whole

community. Everyone did something. John Antiumpi, a home-steader who was also a skilled carpenter, was put in charge of construction, with all the other volunteers acting as his helpers. Wesley Vaughan, who had been a mason prior to taking up a homestead, was put in charge of lathe-and-plaster work and building the chimney. The outside was covered with cedar siding, and when it was finished, it was as good a little schoolhouse as you'd find anywhere, and the settlers were very pleased with the results.

That's the way all of these schools began. There was very little expenditure, but a great deal of effort, sacrifice, and love. Naturally, with so much amateur work, many mistakes were made. Doors were hung wrong, windows were put on the wrong side of the building, the pitch of the roof might be too steep, the chimney might be on the wrong end, the black-boards were sometimes hung too high for the smaller students, or ceilings might be too high or too low. However, they were schools, and that was the important thing. Out of those imperfect little buildings came some very fine scholars who moved on to build the Canada we know today.

The provincial ordinance relating to the formation of public-school districts left the responsibility of naming each district to the local residents. When a school was first contemplated for a rural district near Carlyle, Alberta, in 1904, the problem of a coulee complicated matters. The homesteaders to the west wanted the school built on their side of Squaw Coulee, while those on the east were adamant that it should be on the east side. The school authorities from Regina, Northwest Territories, who came out to help organize the district, were unable to make much headway because of the location deadlock. Soon after, the commissioner of the Council of Public Instruction for the Northwest Territories forwarded an ultimatum to the organizing school committee: the council's official would come once more, but this was the committee's "last chance". In the meantime the two factions settled their differences and decided to build the school on the bench land near the base of the west hill. What did they name their school? It just *had* to be the "Last Chance School District".

It was at an organizational gathering held in February 1911 at the Albert Lindquist homestead that a name was chosen for the newly formed school district near Bow Island, Alberta. A blizzard had come up during the course of the meeting, so they all stayed and enjoyed the hospitality of the Lindquist family and the comfort of a giant heater. This particular model of heater went by the captivating trade name of "Good Cheer", so it didn't take them very long to make up their minds to call the school "Good Cheer" as well. It became "Good Cheer S.D. 2531".

A play on words was responsible for the unique name of a school district near Lloydminster, Saskatchewan. At an organizational meeting held on May 10, 1910, an official from the Department of Education told the gathering of home-steaders the value of an education for their children, and throughout the meeting kept emphasizing, "You need a school!" Apparently one potential rate-payer must have agreed with him, for he put forward a motion that the commu-nity organize a school district. The motion was passed and another enthusiastic supporter immediately shouted, "Good! Real good! Now that we have a school, let's use the name that our honourable visitor from Edmonton has been dinning into our ears all through this meeting: 'You need a school!'" Every-body had a good laugh, but when the inventive name was brought to a vote, it was adopted almost unanimously. Thus, the "Uneeda S.D. 2177" came into being.

There were so many ethnic groups in a community north-east of Lloydminster, Saskatchewan, that they could not agree on an appropriate name for their school district. The problem was that all wanted their particular origin to be reflected in the designation. Meeting after meeting ended in one stalemate after another and the situation seemed hope-less. It wasn't until Charles Despard came up with the unique title of "Tangled Flag" that people began to voice their approval. They thought the name aptly described the ethnic make-up of not only the local district but also most early communities in the West. Agreement became unanimous when "Tangled Flag" was modified slightly to read "Tan-gleflags". This name eventually became known as one of the most colourful and relevant in the province.

There was considerable opposition to the forming of a school district near Endiang, Alberta. The residents figured it would be too hard for them to pay the necessary school taxes. At an organizational meeting held on April 25, 1912, the word "rustle" was bandied about. One indignant prospective tax-payer stated that if a school was built, the people of the district would have to rustle cattle to pay their taxes. A parent who had four children of school age and wanted a school in the worst way replied, "I agree! Sure, we will have to rustle hard, but not cattle, only on our own homesteads. I read somewhere that hard work conquers all. Our children will thank us some day." The protest of the first speaker was turned down, but his shady suggestion will be remembered for a long time. The school was named "Rustle S.D. 2720".

When the first school district at South Hill, near Ogden, east of Calgary, was being organized in 1914, nearly all residents of the area were employed at the Canadian Pacific Railway repair shops in Ogden. Feeling a close allegiance to their employer, they applied for the name "CPR". Upon learning it was illegal to use Canadian Pacific's name, they came up with a designation spelled "Cepeear".

A school district founded near Central Butte, Saskatchewan, in 1912 was named "Robin Hood". Since the livelihood of the majority of people in the district was derived from wheat farming, they thought it only fitting to name the school after the Robin Hood Flour Mills located in nearby Moose Jaw. When the trustees sought permission from the milling company to use the Robin Hood trademark, they were given a courteous yes. In fact, Laurence Irving, who attended the school from 1916 to 1924, remembers rather proudly that the obliging company took it upon itself to donate a new Union Jack for the school's flagpole on a patriotic occasion. The Robin Hood Flour Mills didn't want to forget their rural-school namesake.

Some district names ran absolutely counter to the natural geographical features that characterized the area. The Violet Dale School District 3499, near Czar, Alberta, is a good example. James Graves, a father of seven children, was one of the early homesteaders in the area from the woods of Minnesota. He could neither read nor write, but he was determined that his children would have "book larning". Hence it was not surprising that he became the mainspring behind the district's efforts to establish a school during the last years of World War One. The instant the new school came into being, Mr. Graves was given the honour of naming it for his new daughter, Violet. In spite of the fact that the school site was situated on the highest knoll in the surrounding flat country, he chose the name "Violet Dale".

Isobel McLaughlin Very Friendly with Mr. Olds and Louis Chevrolet

Isobel McLaughlin, a daughter of "Colonel Sam" McLaughlin, founder of General Motors of Canada, is a ranking artist who studied and painted with the Group of Seven. Born in 1904, she grew up with the motor car, and remembers a time when motor cars were little more than horse carriages powered by small engines.

My grandfather, Robert McLaughlin, was the man responsible for getting our family into the business long before the turn of the century. He was a carriage-maker who became famous for the quality of the horse buggies and sleighs that he made and sold right across Canada. My earliest memories are of these beautiful little sleighs—all black and shiny, with gorgeous hand-painted decorations.

He had a slogan for his company that said "One grade only—and that the best". He really meant that, too, because he was a real artisan who looked on every piece he made as a work of art and he just couldn't abide shoddy work. If it wasn't perfect, he wouldn't allow it to leave his small factory. He felt that even one bad product would be a smirch on the family name. Well, some of those qualities obviously rubbed off on his children because when the family started putting engines in those buggies, it wasn't long before McLaughlin Buicks were rated among the best early motor cars in the world. My father and uncle George really believed in the company slogan.

Of course the first cars were just sleighs and wagons with wheels and a motor instead of horses. It was my father, the youngest son, who persuaded grandfather to switch over to cars with a Buick engine. At first they just called them "McLaughlin"; then it was McLaughlin-Buick, and finally just Buick. Later, of course, it became General Motors. In those days of the early automobile, quality was much more important than speed of production, as the percentage of people buying cars wasn't great.

I suppose Father's other great interest was his family, but this was to be his greatest disappointment, too. He always wanted a boy, but all he got was five girls, and five very lively ones at that. Naturally because we were in the business of making cars, we all felt we should have one of our own as soon as possible. In those days, however, boys were allowed to drive at sixteen while girls had to wait until they were eighteen. That was a great bone of contention with women everywhere, but in our house, with six women and one man, it was a constant subject for argument. It wasn't Father's fault that that's the way things were, but if you could hear the discussions, you'd think it was. Whenever that started, Father would find some excuse for disappearing down to the factory, where he spent most of his time anyway.

He was totally involved in the production of every car in those days. That was possible, of course, because they produced so few. Dad was a strong-willed man, and those early cars were very much the product of many of his own ideas. His background was Scotch and Irish, and I think he inherited his fighting determination from that mixture. He was always marvellously healthy, and that helped to give him tremendous drive.

I can't say that I was terribly interested myself in the car industry although it was always a thrill to see the new models. We'd give our opinions on them to Father, but I can't say he paid much attention to what we said. When I was old enough, Father would give me his latest new car after he had it for a while, but the thing was, I didn't always want it. I'd become attached to one of the earlier models and wouldn't want to let it go. Sometimes I'd get away with this for as long as three years before he'd insist I start driving one of the new ones. Then I'd give the old one up, but not without a fight. The cars were changing radically every year in those days, and I didn't always like the changes.

Although the different companies were in great competition at that time, Dad knew, and was great friends with, many of the other makers. He was very friendly with Mr. Olds and Louis Chevrolet and he would never downgrade their product. Of course, family loyalty made us think the McLaughlin cars were the best, and when I'd see that name on a car, it made me very proud of him. I never thought of it as my name—it was his; and for a long time it was the most popular car on the road.

We had one that was a big open touring model and Father would take all of us for drives on Sunday afternoons. In many places the railway line would run parallel to the highway, and we thought it was the most thrilling thing when Father would race the train. The engineer would be waving at us and we'd wave at him. It was great fun for all, except Mother, who kept asking Dad to slow down. It seemed awfully fast to us, but I suppose it wasn't by today's standards. The highway wasn't even paved in those days.

My biggest interest while everybody else was talking about cars was art. I first got interested while studying botany in school, and discovered I loved drawing plant life and other things in nature. After I finished high school, I studied in Europe for a while and returned home and began taking classes with the Group of Seven. This was before they even thought of themselves as a "group". They were just a number of artists who did work together and exhibited together. They happened to be seven but they never did form themselves formally. The first one I knew was Arthur Lismer, because when I came home from Europe and was studying at the Ontario College of Art, he was there along with his very able assistant, Yvonne McKague. When a group of us students later broke from the College of Art, due to disagreements with much of the teaching, Yvonne became our permanent teacher when we formed the Art Students League.

This was a very radical thing for us to do, and we received a lot of criticism from the established art community. However, we had our own reasons for doing it. In the Art Students League we got to know most of the artists of the day but the Group of Seven gave us our inspiration. They were interested in design and form, and in painting the Canadian landscape in a Canadian way—not in the way Europeans were doing it. After all, Canada was a different country. Of course, they were criticized because of their style, but anybody who has travelled this country knows that the Group captured perfectly the spirit and the colour of Canada in their work.

Arthur Lismer or Lawren Harris or Alex Jackson would come with us on sketching trips on a weekend. We got a sort of free criticism and encouragement from them, and I must say they were wonderful with young people. They were well-recognized artists at that time, in the twenties, but they were still not in a position where they didn't have to earn a living, with the exception of Lawren Harris. Jackson worked with a printing or advertising firm in Montreal, and the rest were in commercial-art work or teaching.

The funny thing about our relationship with the Group members is that we were all quite young and we considered them old and mature. When they'd come to visit the Art Students League, we were just a bit intimidated. The truth of the matter is that most of them were in their thirties at the time, but I suppose to a young student that's old.

Before the Group, most of the art being sold in Canada was European. Sir William Van Horne, for example, was a great collector of Van Goghs, Cézannes, and the most magnificent Egyptian sculptured cats I've ever seen. Those people bought the very best of European art, and there was a great market for Dutch art, some of which was magnificent, and it became a fashion to have these things. That's what the Group fought against—to break that spell and get Canadians thinking about Canadian art. The fact that Canadians today are thinking this way is due in large part to the Group of Seven.

The Right Honourable Daniel Roland Michener Reserve Your Curtsies for the Queen

As official head of state and representative of the Crown in Canada, the governor general is "above politics" and the office's function largely ceremonial. After Confederation, Lord Monck was Canada's first governor general and all of those who followed him in that office until 1952 were from the English aristocracy.

The pattern was broken with the appointment of Canadian-born Vincent Massey, who served from 1952 to 1959. He was followed by Major-General Georges Vanier, who served from 1959 to 1967. It fell to Roland Michener, a Methodist minister's son born in Lacombe, Alberta, to bring the office to the level of the people. Mr. Michener, born in 1900, served from 1967 to 1974.

I've always been proud of my Canadian roots, which stretch back on my mother's side to the United Empire Loyalists who settled near Niagara. There were also Pennsylvania Dutch, as they were called, on her side, but they were really German, and a family named Roland, who came from France by way of Pennsylvania. Scottish settlers on my father's side also settled in Pennsylvania before coming to Canada after the War of 1812. So it was in the Niagara area that my mother and father met. She was a teacher, and he was training for the ministry.

They married, and headed for the West as so many were doing just before the turn of the century. My father's first church was at Banff, with another small mission at Chilliwack, so his first year in the ministry was spent travelling back and forth between those two places. Their home during that year was a small log house at Banff. The year I was born, 1900, he was sent to a church at Lacombe, which was then located in the Northwest Territories, as Alberta didn't join Confederation until 1905. My father didn't enjoy good health, and it was at Lacombe that he finally had to give up the ministry and take up life on a farm just outside Red Deer, Alberta.

He soon realized, however, that he was no farmer, so he moved into the town of Red Deer, where he made enough money by bookkeeping to keep the farm going. That developed into a very good business in real estate and insurance at a time when the prairies were filling up with people, so I really grew up in the infant town.

The first settlers came in 1884. Most of the early ones in the town came from Eastern Canada. Dr. Leonard Gates from Nova Scotia was the founder. He came with ten children, and filed on the land which is now the centre of Red Deer. It became a prosperous, well-run, healthy little place of about three thousand while I was growing up, the centre of a farming community located halfway between Calgary and Edmonton. Our family did well there. Father became very involved in politics and he eventually became a senator. I graduated in Arts from the University of Alberta in 1920 and received a Rhodes Scholarship to attend Oxford. From that, I went into the practice of law, and then politics, which I loved very much.

I became Speaker of the House of Commons for a period, and then I was made High Commissioner to India. It was while I was in India in 1967 that Governor General Vanier died, and I learned that I was to succeed him. Now, I was greatly honoured by this appointment of course, but I had always felt that the office had great potential which was never fully realized. I thought it could be a great unifying force in our huge, sparsely populated land—particularly with Canadians occupying the post.

I felt that a Canadian who had lived here all of his life would be able to view the office from a different perspective, and, as the senior government person above politics, be able to accomplish things that an elected representative could not. I could be welcomed by all Canadians, no matter what their political affiliations, and it occurred to me that this would be the most useful role I could play as a Canadian-born governor general. My constitutional role was one that always went smoothly, as it's one's duty as head of state to do what you're advised by your government, as long as it has the confidence of the House of Commons. The governor general is not called upon to dismiss a prime minister, or refuse his advice.

We don't have too many symbols of national unity. That role—symbolic of the entirety of Canada, of our collectivity—presented the opportunity to do something meaningful. When I took office, we had our new flag, of course, but there weren't many other things.

I began with a big plus: 1967 was Canada's centennial year and this gave me a great chance to get out and meet people all over the country in a time of overall happiness. My wife and I travelled constantly and took part in literally hundreds of affairs in the tiniest hamlets and largest cities.

When I made my inaugural address, I said that that would be my objective, and I said I hoped my office would be a meeting place that Canadians would consider theirs. I invited everyone to come and visit me at any time, where they would find a neutral meeting place for discussion of diverse ideas and differences. Well, people responded to my invitation, and during my time, thousands and thousands came to Government House as visitors and as guests.

I don't think I ever became overwhelmed by the importance of my office, or my own importance, because I never considered myself anything other than an ordinary Canadian who had the good fortune to find himself in a somewhat exalted position. I started out by asking people to forgo the curtsy, which I wasn't used to, and neither were they. I told them to reserve their curtsies for the Queen and to greet me the way they greeted each other. One of the first to respond to this was the wonderful Charlotte Whitton, the mayor of Ottawa. She promptly came up and curtsied, saying that this was the way that *she* always greeted everyone. We had a laugh over that, but it helped break the ice, and ease the way for a lot of others who wanted to simply shake hands.

During all the time I spent in office, I never felt any sense of insecurity or of being threatened in any way. I never felt as though my life was in danger—in a time of political unrest and terrorism all over the world. I remember at one time my wife and I were on a tour of the little outports of Newfoundland—right up to St. Anthony through the Straits of Belle Isle, and down the North Shore as far as Sept Iles on the St. Lawrence.

We were there for a couple of days, and found it a fine community of young people with secure employment in mining and shipping. The police warned me that they had heard that a couple of men were going to throw eggs at me to show their disrespect for the monarchy. Apparently they brought eggs and went to a spot on the route where my car would be passing. While they were waiting, they visited a pub for fuel to better their aim, I suppose. They did too good a job, because by the time my car came into view, the best they could manage was to crawl to the edge of the road. Neither had the ability to throw an egg, but one of them did take one from the carton, and rolled it across the road in front of my car. The police called it an assault but not a very serious one. As a matter of fact, I didn't even see it, as I was looking the other way when it happened.

It was a wonderful seven years for me, and if I succeeded in bringing the office of governor general closer to the populace, I am satisfied that I did just what I set out to do.

Dan McDermid The Highland Heart in Cape Breton

The Scots brought a way of life and a new language with them to Nova Scotia, as well as a determination to rebuild the society they had lost. They brought their bagpipes, their tartans, and their Gaelic to "New Scotland", and they fought to keep all their traditions alive. Dan McDermid of Cape Breton tells about some of the changes that have come to his island.

Gaelic was the first language of my parents when I was growing up here in a little rural community called Wreck Cove. Although that was in the early part of this century, it could just as easily have been the last century. The style of living had hardly changed at all from the times when those early Scottish settlers landed at Wreck Cove more than a hundred years before. When people began learning English by reason of necessity, a mixture of English and Gaelic was spoken. They had to learn English because after a century of isolation in these small Cape Breton villages, the new roads and better transportation of the twentieth century were bringing the outside world to their doorsteps.

They spoke English reluctantly. It was Gaelic they were comfortable with, and the result was a gentleness and a rhythm to rural Cape Breton English that you'll find only in the Gaelic mother tongue. My father said that the Gaelic language was "the language of the poets", and as an illustration he used the Twenty-third Psalm: "The Lord is my shepherd; I shall not want." In Gaelic it translates, "It is God Himself who is my shepherd. He will take care of me." There's an added dimension there that doesn't carry over into the English. It's a very expressive language.

From the day I began to talk until I was about ten, I lived in North Sydney, where only a few spoke Gaelic, so I didn't have the language at all—until we moved back to Wreck Cove, which was a Gaelic community. The children at school spoke Gaelic, and it wasn't long before I was speaking it most of the time, although I usually spoke English with my father, who wanted me to retain that language. But Mother and I always conversed in Gaelic, and my grandmother, who lived at Wreck Cove all of her life, never did learn English. Many of the older people in rural places did not ever learn English, as they never met many English-speaking people. They lived in undisturbed isolation.

When change did come, it came in what I feel was a cruel and thoughtless manner. First the teachers were suddenly obliged to teach in English in the schools. Children were told to stop speaking Gaelic, which was described as "a second-class language". Children were hurt by this, of course, but when they'd come home, the old grandmother, who couldn't speak any English whatever, would be outraged when children spoke what they considered a foreign language. "Speak your mother tongue," they would say. The children would be in a dilemma. I have great admiration for the French-speaking Canadians, who have retained their language in spite of many difficulties they faced in doing so. Shame was the weapon that the teachers used in killing the Gaelic language; even though school was the only place they could ever hear English.

I only went to school five or six terms myself, so that whatever bit of education I have was acquired by reading. Many Cape Bretoners of my generation have the same kind of experience, and that's strange, as the Scots here in the early nineteenth century were a people who placed a great emphasis on education. My own great-grandfather who came in 1835 belonged to debating societies and things like that. The thirst for better education died because the emphasis had to change to just staying alive. They were poor, and, as soon as a child started to mature, he was put to work. I was doing a man's job in my father's sawmill when I was fourteen, and after that I was in the lobster factory, and education became something sort of secondary.

Then, too, the teachers were of pretty low quality. They were for the most part local girls with half a high-school education, trained at normal school for a few months to learn the art of teaching. They couldn't impart much knowledge as they didn't have much themselves. These young teachers had been led to believe that Gaelic was a peasant language, so when they began to teach they were even more adamant than *their* teachers had been about not speaking Gaelic.

Isolated communities were little worlds unto themselves, and the most powerful person there was most often the clergyman, who usually was the best-educated. Very often he became something of a dictator, legislating not only religion and morals, but everything else. There was, for example, the Reverend John Fraser, who served from around the turn of the century up to the First World War. He was the minister who baptized me. He was the kind who would bawl people out from the pulpit before the whole congregation. One time, Big Rory MacLeod and my grandfather, Alistair Morrison, met outside the church after one service, and Big Rory said, "It was me he was after today." My grandfather said, "Oh no, you're quite wrong. It was me he was after." Whatever the sin was, I don't know, but each of them was sure that the Reverend was on to them.

Another time there was a member of the congregation who, to put it delicately, got a certain girl in "the family way". He had accepted responsibility, but there was still a meeting of the parishioners called to deal with the matter, and the Reverend Mr. Drummond, who was there at that time, wanted to have the man excommunicated from the church. The fellow's name was Big John MacFarlane. At this meeting, which was something like those old hanging tribunals in England, Mr. Drummond, who was an overbearing, powerful man, was out for blood. He roared out in Gaelic, "Big John MacFarlane, stand up!" Big John just sat there, with his arms folded across his chest. Drummond repeated the order three times, and the third time he roared it out even louder, pounding the pulpit at the same time. By now, Big John was in a temper too, and he roared back in Gaelic, "I won't get up today, or tomorrow either!" The whole congregation was involved by this time, and one old lady seated directly behind MacFarlane jumped up from her seat, and slapped him across the shoulders and shouted, "Bully for you, Big John!" So, as you can see, there was at least a spirit of rebellion, even if the ministers were dictators.

The church was not only the centre and the meeting place; it could really be called the whole community. The church then derived from John Calvin and John Knox, where any type of pleasure was *sin*. There's the story of the minister who had three churches to serve, all along the same river. One winter he decided that he would skate from one church to the next. This of course brought up the question of, "Is it a sin or isn't it?" A meeting of the session had to be called to consider this important question, and it was finally decided that he would be permitted to skate if he didn't enjoy it.

Well, we can have fun talking of that kind of thing now, but there was a rather sad side effect to all of these restrictions that is evident to this day. Because the early Presbyterians were not permitted to make a joyful sound, there were no fiddles or other musical instruments, and dancing was definitely frowned on. The result of those earlier restrictions is that Cape Breton's lively musical scene today all comes from the Catholic Scots, who were always permitted to make joyful sounds. One exception we were allowed was the milling frolic, where the people would gather to pound and shrink wool to the sound and rhythm of songs. It could at least be said that this was entertainment with a practical purpose.

Even at a wedding, any dancing that went on would have to be held in the barn, away from the sight of the older ones. Someone might have a mouth organ, and, if there was no barn, the young ones might move down to one of the local bridges. Of course, we'd always have to pay for our indiscretions when the minister took his place in the pulpit the following Sunday.

In spite of all of this, there was a real enjoyment of life by those early Cape Bretoners, be they Protestant or Catholic. In the evenings we would gather in each other's homes and tell stories, with the kind of wit that only a Gaelic-speaking Scot can fully appreciate. We may have lacked music, but we had a great appreciation for laughter, especially laughing at ourselves—even the older ones.

As a child, I can remember evenings when two of my great-uncles would come to the house and it always was better entertainment than anything I've ever seen on television. Those people knew how to entertain themselves, rather than waiting to be entertained. Everyone had a ghost story then, and most of us believed them to be true, which made them seem that much more exciting. My great-uncle Donald McDermid was around seventy when I first heard him tell this story, and no one would ever doubt a word he said. He was an elder in the church, and very religious, a man who was never known to tell so much as a little "white lie". His story went like this:

He had been on a fishing trip with ten of his friends in the Bay St. Lawrence area in the late fall of the year. It was an isolated spot where they had a small shack on the side of a cove where they could sleep and prepare their meals. At nine at night, one of the men came in and said that there was somebody coming in from the direction of the forest. Now, as they were miles from the nearest settlement, the idea that anyone was coming that late meant that there must be important news, news of a death or something like that.

They all rushed to the front of the cabin, and sure enough, this stranger was coming towards them. They all saw him clearly, but none of them recognized him. One thing that Uncle Donald said he noticed, however, was that this stranger never looked towards them. His eyes were staring straight ahead, as if looking at something in the distance. He wore a double-breasted navy type of coat with brass buttons, and as he got to where they were standing, he just continued on, without pausing, until he came to the edge of a cliff where it falls down to the water of the cove. As the group watched—and they all swore to this—the stranger continued walking in a straight line—through space over the water and across the cove, and disappeared into the woods at the far side. Uncle Donald never did offer a theory as to the meaning of it all, but he did say it happened, and no one ever questioned that it did.

People scoff at stories of that nature today, but these people were closer to life, closer to nature, and open to the supernatural that I believe surrounds us at all times. Therefore they did have these experiences, which I think do not occur to those who do not believe in them.

Those early Cape Bretoners were very close to what they had gradually evolved from. The animals have this intuition, finely honed and Creator-given, and they obey it without question. Early man had it, but now we feel we can go it on our own, and because of this, we are losing it. I hope I still have some, and I believe strongly in hunches. We are suppressing this natural intuition, and this has put modern man in a very vulnerable position. Our knowledge is still very limited. Our ability to reason is very limited: all one has to do is to look around to see the truth of that. We're building machines to destroy ourselves, turning our backs on intuition that tells us that mankind is heading for disaster.

Those early Cape Bretoners knew exactly who they were, where they were, and where they were going in life, and in death. They may have had some misconceptions, but that was all part of what I referred to as evolving. My grandmother was as certain of where Heaven is as I am of where Glace Bay is, and equally certain of where Hell is. Life had a great continuity for them that doesn't exist in today's society. Life was not a fleeting thing then; and there was a permanence that we don't have today. Our kids now are uprooted every two or three years—here today, and two years from now, they're living in Moncton or Toronto. Two years after that, they're living in Calgary or Vancouver. The phrase "our pact of timelessness" was true of my early Cape Breton. Everything that was part of my life on any one day was fairly certain always to be there tomorrow and the next day.

Due to economic circumstances, I was forced to be away from Cape Breton for thirty-eight years, but I never stopped longing for home. On the day that I retired, my wife and I packed the car and headed back home to stay. I believe that Cape Breton is still one of the few places in Canada that hasn't become "North Americanized", thanks to the values laid down by those Scottish pioneers. They were great people.

Mrs. Thomas Metcalfe We Only Knew We Were Heading West

"If only we could get out to western Canada, things would be better." For the poor in the East, the West seemed like a pot of gold at the end of the rainbow, a haven where their troubles would be over. In an age long before radio and television, the government propagandists had done their job well. Newspaper advertisements told of the glories and riches easily attained in the new West. The temptation was one that many could not refuse in the years immediately preceding the Riel Rebellion. As a young girl, Mrs. Thomas Metcalfe, now of Bowsman, Manitoba, moved from Ontario to Manitoba with her family. She has never forgotten that trip.

When I was born in 1871, my parents were living on a small farm near a village called Thompsonville in Ontario. Life was very hard for them and it was just a struggle from one year to the other. The soil was rocky and they just didn't seem to be getting anywhere. There was all this talk about western Canada, and free land for anybody who was willing to work hard. Well, this appealed to my dad because, as he said, "I'm not afraid of hard work. That's all I ever done." So we just packed up everything in a big wagon—all our pots and pans, a few bits of furniture and the whole family, and headed west.

I was just a young girl at the time, and it was very exciting for all us kids when we started out. This would be about 1883, I think, because I was about twelve years old. It was the spring of the year, and none of us, not even Dad, had much idea of where we were going, or how far it was, or anything. We only knew we were heading west and that was about it. We might have changed our minds if we knew what was ahead of us.

When we started, we were all in good shape. The horses were nice and plump, and everybody was anxious to get on the road, but it wasn't long before we ran out of road. There was just trails to follow that someone else made before us. They were crooked and bumpy, winding around rocks, up and down cliffs and hills, and full of bumps and holes. The going was very, very slow. In parts of Northern Ontario, we were only making a couple of miles a day, and sometimes not even that. It was really tough. The wagon would break down and we might lose a day before Father got it fixed again.

Then there was the weather. Sometimes it would rain day after day, and then we would have days of terrible heat and we'd be all blistered by sunburn. We had to watch our food supply, too, as there was no place to get any more. We picked berries, and we caught fish, and sometimes Dad would shoot some rabbits.

We hardly ever saw any other people, except once in a while we would see some Indians go by with these two poles hanging from their horses and the other ends dragging on the ground. There'd be crosspieces between the poles and sometimes they'd have bundles on these crosspieces. Other times, there'd be an Indian woman sitting on them with a baby on her back. It seemed so funny to us to see these poles with the ends just dragging in the dirt, but as I look back on it now, that was a better system than we had with our wagon and wheels that was always breaking down.

One of the worst things of all was the clouds of mosquitoes and blackflies. They would come just like that—in clouds— and no matter what we did they would get at us. We had cheesecloth over our heads, but these mosquitoes still found a way to get through to our skin. We were bitten and bleeding most of the time from head to toe, and, of course, we were sunburned too. We were a miserable lot, I can tell you.

I don't know how long this went on, but it was months. The summer was almost over when we crossed the border into Manitoba: for that matter, we didn't even know we were in Manitoba. There was this fellow came riding along towards us one day, and Dad asked him where we were. "Dauphin," he said. "Where's Dauphin?" said Father. "Manitoba," the man answered. "That's good enough for me," my dad said, "we'll stay here." And so we did.

I don't think we could have made it much farther anyway. The wagon had been patched up so much, it was just hanging together. The nice fat horses we started out with were as skinny as rails, and you could count their ribs.

We were all sunburned and full of bites and bumps, and we needed nothing more than a good rest and some decent food. So we camped right there until Father arranged for our homestead grant. When we moved onto it and got things started there, as hard as all that was, it was nothing compared to that trip from Ontario. That was the hardest part of all.

Hilda Urquhart Father Was the Wrong Man in the Right Place

The Canadian government's barrage of propaganda to entice new settlers to the West was overwhelming. In Britain and Europe, posters showed carefree families enjoying life on the verandahs of huge homes with fields of golden grain, herds of cattle, and brightly painted farm buildings in the background. The fact that scenes like this could be theirs only after many years of back-breaking work and hardship was not mentioned.

The poor already in Canada, too, poured onto the prairies looking for places of their own. Even in Saskatchewan, where the government wanted settlers up north, families in southern parts of the province like the Qu'Appelle Valley sold what they owned and went in search of a dream. Hilda Urquhart, born in 1906, remembers her own childhood in Saskatchewan.

In 1910 my parents decided to take up homesteading. From all of the propaganda that Father had been reading, he felt that there was a lot of money to be made growing grain. The land was only a dollar an acre, and everybody thought that this was a chance to make a fortune. This new land was in the northwest part of Saskatchewan, so they sold everything they had accumulated over the years.

Father went out first by train to scout the land. Then he wired Mother, who followed him by train with us children. The rail line ended at Kindersley and our homestead site was another three days' travel by horse and wagon. We had two wagons to carry the family and the things we'd need to get started. Behind all of this, we had a cow and a few other farm animals tied on, so we were quite a procession. When we finally got to our destination, we had to search for most of a day to find our property. We knew it was somewhere in those thousands of flat, empty acres, but the only marker was a corner stake driven into the ground. Trying to locate that stake was like looking for a needle in a haystack.

Shortly after we found the land, a terrific thunderstorm

came up and there was nowhere to go to get out of this drenching rain. Father simply unloaded one of the wagons, turned it upside down, and we crawled under it. One of the first things we noticed was the tremendous amount of buffalo heads that were scattered around our land, thousands of them with the horns attached and bleached by the sun. They were plentiful there because Dad chose land where there was a stream and a watering hole. This was a wise move on his part, as many early settlers just couldn't make a go of it because they were unable to find water. He had picked his land with the help of a "locater"—a man who made a living by helping newcomers find the best homestead land.

Our land was slightly undulating, but it had no hills and no trees. There were no trees anywhere in that district, which meant one had to find something else besides wood with which to build a home. That something else was sod right off our land; but our first shelter was made with lumber from that second wagon. Dad had enough lumber from it to make a very small shack eight feet by eight feet, and he made it very well. He even put shingles on it which made it warm and airtight. Then he started right in to build our sod shack, which he attached to the end of this.

First he ploughed a furrow and cut sods about a foot and a half long. Then he laid these in exactly the same way bricks are laid. The sods would be upside down, with the grass on the underside. This was neater, and apparently safer, and, of course, stopped the grass from growing. The shack would have a regular frame of ordinary two-by-fours, reinforced by very thin shiplap or tar paper, and over all of this, a couple of layers of tar paper. Then, instead of boards or brick, came the sods. Inside, only the shiplap would be seen. My mother would eventually cover this with newspapers, stuck on with a paste of flour and water. That brightened up the place a lot, and helped to insulate it a bit too. There was one door and one window, purchased on our way from a man who was tearing down an old building in Kindersley. Everything was second-hand and Father thought himself very lucky, as lumber on the prairies was very expensive. When we got the stove in it, the shack was warm and cosy, and it wasn't long before it felt very much like home. We were in our "real" house and out of our shack when I saw that first fire, so we weren't in the sod house for more than a year, or a year and a half, but that was long enough for my baby sister to be born there.

The worst thing I remember is the fires that would sweep across the prairie faster than a horse could run. You felt so helpless, because there was almost nothing you could do about them. I remember one night we were standing on a small knoll near our home, and off in the distance we could see this fire, totally encircling us. Wherever we looked was this great rim of red lighting up the sky. All of the men, including my father, had to go and plough up the land in front of it so it wouldn't reach our homes, and they were gone for days. This would happen frequently, but the men always were able to save the homes.

When we moved to the three-storey big house, the sod shack was made into a chicken house, and when my sister was a little girl, she always told people that she was born in the chicken house. The money for the "big house", as we called it, came from our first grain crop, which was planted the second year we were there. We arrived after the planting season the first year, and, anyway, we were all too busy trying to do other things before the winter set in. Along with the sod shack, Father had to build a sod barn for the animals.

The first crop was hard to get in, too, as the land was virgin and hard and full of rocks. That was a complaint all over Saskatchewan—rocks of all shapes and sizes played havoc with the walking ploughs. I must say, though, it was interesting for us children, as we would find all kinds of Indian flints and arrowheads. But those stone-boats would have to haul stone away all day long. It was very hard going, and Mother was pitching in with Father on everything. She was very good at handling horses, and when she wasn't hauling the stone-boat, she was walking behind the plough. The children helped as much as they could. Even at five years old, I went out and stooked grain until all feeling left my fingers. My hands wouldn't open after a long day of that, but I loved doing it because it made me feel important.

My father was a Welshman who had a fairly good education at Christ Church in Wales, and even on the homestead, he kept on studying. He was a driving force in getting the school built, and he had the reputation of being able to help all of the teachers when they ran into problems, so that he was every teacher's guide there for years. We were there only about a year when Daddy went riding on horseback from one farm to another, building up interest in starting a school, and he didn't rest until it was built.

It was a one-room school called "Prairie Dale" and it was the centre of the community. All social events were held there, and even when there were dances, the children would be taken along. The seats would be shifted to the sides of the room to make room for a dance floor, and when we got sleepy, our parents would roll us up in blankets, and we'd sleep on the seats while they had their fun. Every once in a while, we'd wake up and hear the music, and see everyone whirling away on the floor, and we thought it was just wonderful. It *was* wonderful too, as the whole area where we lived had been nothing but empty prairie a year before, and already it was a thriving community of people, all of whom had the same goal—to build a better life.

Getting supplies was another difficult part of life. Kindersley was the closest place, which meant forty-five miles each way by horse and wagon. Everything had to be bought in large quantities. For example, you'd buy hundred-pound bags of sugar and flour, and so on, and you made sure that your list was complete, as if you forgot something, you had to do without it.

One trip that I recall was in the fall. We were returning from Kindersley with the wagon loaded, and a coyote who'd come very close let out a howl. The frightened horses took off, bouncing us and the wagon and supplies around. They kept on for the longest time before Father managed to stop them. Everything was coated with flour dust—us, the sugar, the coffee, everything! The result was that all winter long, and right on into spring, they were drinking coffee and tea that had a mixture of flour in it. Mother spent many, many winter nights trying to separate tea from coffee, because those bags had broken, and were mixed together with flour dust. Half the time they never could tell if they were drinking tea or coffee.

The weather was fierce in that part of Saskatchewan, so bad, in fact, that we didn't go to school. School was closed all winter, and didn't open until spring. Of course, we'd go to classes all through the summer then until Christmas, when it would close again. The weather was that bad. However, being children, we loved it. We'd be out of bed with the dawn, playing with our sleighs and digging out rooms in the snowbanks, and having a wonderful time.

There were five of us children—and all that that entails, plus helping on the farm, and sewing and knitting—but do you know, I don't believe Mother considered it a hard life. She was only about twenty-seven when we went there, so she was young and strong and took everything in her stride. I can't remember ever seeing her sit down and weep. I remember shortly after winter set in that first year, and Mother's churn was destroyed by the frost. Now, losing that churn was a tragedy, as we needed it to make butter and cheese. Instead of making a fuss, she simply improvised, and all of that winter we would all sit around, shaking these jars of milk to separate it. We made a game of it. If you didn't have something, you improvised and "made do" with what you did have.

One of our biggest joys as children was to sit with the new Eaton's catalogue, picking out things that Mother would make on her sewing machine. She wouldn't send for the articles. She'd just order enough material to make them herself. To us, that catalogue was everything. It was entertainment and education, too, for hours and hours, learning of all those products that we had never seen before.

Shoes were hardly ever purchased. We children just refused to wear them, because it was such a joy racing around the meadows in our bare feet. When school opened, and Mother decreed that we must wear shoes, I would be in agony with these awful things on my feet, and I'd put them on only when I was in the school itself. The rest of the children did the same. I can remember making a vow when I was six years old that when I got older, I would never allow anyone to make me wear shoes again!

The school was also where we had our church services. We didn't have a regular minister. Travelling ministers kept moving from place to place on horseback or buggies, putting on religious services wherever they went. I don't believe I ever got to know one of them well, as it was always a different one.

We certainly never felt those days were hard. Maybe it's because everybody we knew was in the same circumstances. For those who liked it, the whole thing was exciting and wonderful. For me the dawn couldn't come fast enough. We'd race out to the barn first thing to see if the new colt, or the new calf, had arrived, or some chickens had hatched overnight. If a little chicken would suddenly stick its head out from under the hen, we'd be screaming with joy. There was a small ravine that we loved, close to the house, and Mother knew that she could always find us there. The ravine had a spring, and nearby a great big patch of strawberries, which we watched like hawks until they were ripe.

All in all, I think one could say we were a very happy family at that time. At night, Mother would read stories to us until it was time for us to go to bed. One of her favourites, and ours, was *The Girl of the Limberlost*, and to this day I keep getting that book from the library. No one could read a story like Mother could. She had such a busy life, but she was never too busy to pay attention to our needs. She had such a lovely way with children. Instead of saying hello when we came in the house, she would have a little song to greet us with. I can still remember how I'd keep on singing "Blue Bells", or "Daisies Won't Tell", until I got on everyone's nerves. Poor Father would say, "Hilda, please change your tune." Because of all the singing in the house, however, the three of us Rolland girls were always part of the concerts at school.

Daddy also had a love, and a knowledge, of music, and he taught us to harmonize. This was a big part of our entertainment, as we didn't even have a gramophone. We had to make our own music. Singing came naturally to Daddy, being a Welshman, and although Mother wasn't Welsh, she loved singing as much as he. I remember the great joy in our house when one of the settlers, who had decided that he didn't like the life, offered to sell us his big full-size grand piano very cheap. Mother found the money somehow, and although she couldn't play, she knew that some day we would learn. It was a fantastic piano—black as ebony, and to us it was the eighth wonder of the world, sitting there with its lid up in our homestead living quarters.

Father was suited for everything except farming. He wrote beautiful poetry and he read all the great books he could get his hands on. He sang like an angel, and could charm the birds out of the trees with his beautiful voice. But alas, he couldn't farm and he couldn't make a success of it. After a few years, things got worse, and his temper tantrums were awful, and more frequent. Some of the children became terrified when they would see him coming, and he took out a lot of his frustrations on Mother, who'd become quite afraid of what he might do. She would stand right up to him, however, and fight back, until one day she said that she'd had enough.

She packed up us five children and moved on to the next little village along the railway, and said she'd never go back. She had no money, and no plan for survival, but she had an awful lot of spirit and determination. She was fabulous. She found a little unused building, and arranged with the owners to move in there. Somehow she turned it into a home and took in some boarders. She turned part of it into a kind of a rest station for farmers and their wives who needed a place to stop for a few hours while in town. They might pay twenty-five cents for this, but a quarter went a long way then, and she stretched every cent and got the most out of it. She kept us well-fed and well-clothed, although I often wonder how she managed.

Father discovered where we were, and he would come and beg Mother to come back, saying things would be different, and that he would change. One day he arrived with her piano on a horse and wagon as an enticement, but although she was nice to him, and friendly, she said no: her mind was made up, and she wanted to give the children a better chance than they could get on the homestead. It was then that she decided that we'd have to move, to get farther away from him and the homestead, which was, after all, only seven miles from our place in the village.

Although she had no funds, she had noticed that often there were quite a few train men who would hang around the station when the train came in for service. One day, she baked a big tray of her wonderful cream puffs, and offered them for sale to these men. They were snapped up right away, and they told her that if she came every day, they'd buy every one she baked. She baked every day, and added apple pies to her tray. When she had enough money to move, these same train men helped her, free of charge. They put the furniture and the big cooking stove and all of us on the train, and moved us to Loverna near the Alberta border, and she didn't have to pay one cent. Well, she figured that was far enough away from the homestead and Father. From that time on, she brought up the five of us all by herself, and she did it well too, making sure we had good educations, good moral standards, and so on. She really was a fabulous woman, simply fabulous!

In Loverna she found another building for us, and she put an ad in the paper offering overnight accommodation to the many travelling salesmen who were on the road in those days. Very soon the word got around that this was a good place to stay, and she got a good reputation for the cleanliness of her rooms and bed linens. The truth was that she didn't have second sets of linen, and she had to wash the bed linens every day, and hang them out to dry in the prairie air and sunshine. I remember hearing one traveller saying to her, "The reason I like to stay here is because those bed clothes are always so fresh you can smell the ozone in them. How do you do that?" She didn't tell him that they had come straight from the clothesline to the bed every day. She never cared how much work she had to do. Raising her family was her passion, and raising them well. She arranged to have the telephone switchboard office put in our house, and we all learned to operate it, too, so that in one way and another, we managed to get along.

Father eventually realized we weren't coming back, and he accepted it. I often wrote to him over the years, but never saw him again. He stayed on the homestead, but never did make a success of it, although I believe he became content with his lot. He wrote his poetry, read his books, and did what he always did best—he dreamed. It was too bad about Mother and Father, but they weren't suited for one another at all. I have good memories of both of them. Mother died at seventy-five, and I was very close to her. I just adored her, and never will forget how fine she was. I keep all of her letters. I read them still, and it's just like talking with her all over again.

Father lived to be over ninety, and I went back and was with him for three days before he died. He knew me, and when he first saw me, he smiled, put out his hand, and said, "How good of you to come." All he had left was the small piece of land his house stood on. Everything else was gone. I guess some people would call him a failure, but I don't. He was simply a man who couldn't live with the reality that never matched his dreams. He stayed until the end, and he is at rest now, in the ground that surrounds the little Prairie Dale school that he organized the settlers to build.

The Victoria Cross

The VC—the Victoria Cross—was first awarded by Queen Victoria on January 29, 1856, during the heyday of the British Empire. It is the highest of military decorations, given for the most selfless acts of individual bravery regardless of military rank. Since the VC's inception, Canada has been involved in many wars and conflicts, including the Boer War, two world wars, and the Korean conflict. Hundreds of thousands of Canadian soldiers have participated in these wars but only one hundred Victoria Crosses have been awarded. Eight of these men talked with me about winning the award.

Major-General George R. Pearkes (1917)

It's Fear That Keeps You Going

Passchendaele was part of the third battle of Ypres and it had been going on for a long, long time. British and Australian troops had been involved. We Canadians had come in to relieve them at the final stages of a long-drawn-out battle in which there had been very heavy casualties and very unpleasant conditions—mud and one thing or another with a lot of disappointments. The Canadian Corps was given the task of capturing this ridge which was by then considered the final objective for that year's offensive. The final effort was going to relieve pressure on the ports to the north. Others had not been able to get to the top of the ridge, or anywhere near it.

The Canadian Corps came in, and by skilful organization, determination, and good leadership were able to get to the top of this ridge, which overlooked quite a wide expanse of Belgium.

I was a company commander at the time, and we were detailed for an attack on the ridge at Passchendaele in Belgium, a little to the left of the actual village. It was a very marshy, swampy area, and we were the only unit left of the whole of the Canadian Corps, and there was a British unit to our left. Just before the attack started, the enemy barrage came down very heavily on our lines and particularly on the trenches, which were being held by the British. Consequently we suffered a good many casualties before the actual start.

I got hit myself just as we jumped off, but I was able to carry on for the rest of the day. To our left, the British battalion was practically wiped out. They couldn't advance at all, so we waded through the marsh as best we could and struggled up the hillside. The barrage was very, very heavy, but a group of us managed to get almost to the north of the village. That was it. That was the whole thing!

I felt cold, muddy, and dirty. I don't think I felt scared— just bewildered. You just staggered on in a sort of half-aware manner. I think it's fear that keeps you going, fear of being considered not competent, not being up to the job. You keep going because you feel it's your duty to keep on going. You don't think about it. Your men are going on because *you* are. You're responsible for the company, and the company has been given an objective, and you keep on struggling up to the top. You don't *think* of death. Never. You just feel you've got a job to do, and you've got to go on and see it through. King and country, and that sort of thing doesn't occur to you either. Not at the time.

When it was all over, I felt a little tired, I think. I was beginning to get stiff from the wound I got on the way up and I remember looking forward to getting back to a casualty clearing station. I don't regret having had to do any of that. I suppose if I were the same age now, I would do it all again. But I certainly felt no more heroic than anybody else after it was all over. The only feelings were those of relief and weariness, and glad we made it through.

Major-General George Randolph Pearkes died on May 30, 1984, in Vancouver, British Columbia, at the age of ninety-six.

Captain C. Norman Mitchell
(1918)

It Didn't Seem Heroic to Any of Us

The general sent for me and gave me my instructions. We were to make a night attack on Cambrai, part of a pincer movement. There was a canal on the west side of Cambrai, and the general said that the engineers were to go ahead of the infantry and unmine the bridge that hadn't been demolished so that the enemy couldn't blow it up.

We went up with infantry and when we got about five hundred yards from the canal, we left them. They went over and started a barrage to give us some cover and keep the Germans' heads down. There were four of us, Sergeant Teddy Jackson, Sapper Bloor, Sapper Murphy, and myself. Bloor and I ran along the right-hand side of the bridge feeling the railing and looking for signs of wires, and Jackson and Murphy ran along the other side. We'd phone them at every second post on the bridge. The bombs under the bridge were called "potato mashers", and all a German had to do was pull a cord to get the fuse going. We were certain the enemy had mined the bridge and our job was to find that wire. We got to the other side, and I sent Murphy back to guard the west end, and Bloor to guard the right. Jackson and I slid down the bank onto the footpath. The canal was about a hundred feet wide and when we got down there and turned our flashlights on up into the girders, sure enough, there was a big packing box obviously full of powder, and you could see all the fuses leading into it.

The Germans had obviously mined the bridge in a hurry, because the scaffold and a ladder had been left behind. We dashed up this ladder and, while I held the flashlight, Jackson spread all the fuses and found the electric wire and we cut it. Just as we were beginning to cut the fuses, we heard Bloor's voice. "Stand to," he said, so we slid down the ladder, and went up the bank. When we got to the top, Bloor was down in a shell hole at the end of the bridge, and there was no sign of anything around. He said that a couple of men had come along the side of the building and he had shot them. I went over, and sure enough, there were two Germans lying on the road. We knew then that we were "for it", but we waited and nothing else happened. Then I saw a man coming alongside this building on the right-hand side. I didn't want to shoot the poor fellow, but I had to.

Then there was another pause. I knew we couldn't stop the big attack, so I sent for Murphy who was at the other end of the bridge. As he came up and the three of us were standing there, a bunch of Germans came out from the back of the building. There must have been about twenty of them, and they were running towards us. The three of us were standing in a row, and we started yelling and firing and cursing too. That's what saved our lives! The Germans must have thought we were a whole battalion! Suddenly, it was all over. We could see a few bodies lying on the road, but the rest had disappeared! I got hold of Murphy, and told him to go back and tell two or three parties to come forward and give us cover.

When daylight came, we started to unload these mines. We took about five or six hundred pounds from those four girders! When we could see better, Bloor found twelve Germans with their backs up against the abutment of the bridge, so we took them prisoner, brought them over to the infantry, and that was that!

What we did didn't seem heroic to any of us. Before the thing, we were scared stiff; but while it was going on, it was just like a football match. If you get kicked in the shins you don't feel it, but when it is over, you start to realize what might have been!

Sergeant Raphael Louis Zengel
(1918)

I Don't Believe in War Any More

It was a very confusing time. A lot of action was going on, and we were attacking. My officer got killed before we even got started good, and I was going ahead with my company. I noticed there was a machine-gun firing at our boys down in the ditch, so I ran up behind, and saw a German officer and three men on this gun. I shot the officer and I jabbed the bayonet into the guy operating the gun, and the other two ran into a wheat field. I shot in their direction, but I don't think I hit them.

That was it! The whole thing! I waved to the rest of the boys and we kept right on going till the German resistance was broken. I was right in the front line after that up till the news of the Victoria Cross came through. They wouldn't let me near there after that. They wanted to be sure I'd be alive to accept it.

You don't think of being scared or anything like that. I'd been there three years and some months by that time. I was shelled, and I got blown up one time. I was wounded through the jaw when I was at the Somme, and I never once thought of death! I was afraid of getting a leg blown off, or crippled, but as far as death was concerned, it never bothered me. I believe in the old saying, "You're gonna get it when you get it." As far as doing it again, I dunno. That's a hard question, because I don't believe in war any more. War is no good. No good at all.

Company Sergeant-Major A. P. Brereton (1918)

I Was Just Ordinary

I don't know why I got the Victoria Cross. I was just one of the troops moving ahead, and there were lots of good men around me. I was just ordinary.

We were in advance at Amiens, and I didn't know anything about the VC—that I had won anything—until a month after. I didn't know what the Victoria Cross *was*, in fact. I thought at the time that the DCM was the finest medal in the world.

I really can't remember that much about the battle even. The day was ordinary, a little cloud, and sunshine. I do know it was a tough battle—plenty tough. We were trying to advance—gain ground and chase the Hun; which we did.

There isn't too much to say, because you were only one of many, and any individual effort wasn't that. It might have come out as that, but it wasn't an effort where you wanted to distinguish yourself. There was lots of action, and lots by others, too.

They gave two VCs that day. Freddie Coppens got one. There may have been another one too, but I'm not sure. I read the citation that came with it, but I couldn't tell you what it says. I'm not being modest. I just don't see why they gave it to me and not to everyone else who was there that day.

Brigadier Milton F. Gregg
(1918)

A Little War of Our Own

I got my Victoria Cross at the end of the war when the Allies were on the move forward very actively, and we were at the approach of the city of Cambrai. We of the Royal Canadian Regiment were on the left of the city. I was a lieutenant at the time, acting company commander. We got badly cracked up on the approach to our first objective, and while moving on to the second objective, we ran into serious problems getting through the German lines. It was hoped that the barbed wire would have been beaten down by the artillery attack, but it hadn't been. There were a few gaps in it, but that's all.

I thought I'd go through one of these gaps to see what would happen, and that's where things really did get going! A runner went in with me through a German trench—not really a trench, but a series of strong-points connected up by a series of little passageways, thirty or forty yards apart. We took them by surprise in the first hole that we jumped into, and we took them prisoner. We were able to gradually percolate, one by one, up through the other holes, leaving a sentry behind at each one, taking prisoners each time. By mid-afternoon we were able to declare that our objective was taken. However, we were completely isolated from the rest of our forces. We had several counter-attacks during the night, but we held on until the Princess Patricia's Light Infantry came up and went through the following morning. I was slightly wounded, that's all.

It was all very simple, really, and at the time, I didn't think it was anything very tremendous. There were, I think, twenty-four officers that went forward in the first attack. And two of us survived. So the two of us reorganized our men, and put on a little war of our own. The whole operation lasted five or six days. I never felt that I did any more than any of those other men.

Perhaps it's the training in war, but it seems that the

soldier is able to draw down an iron curtain over his sensitivity. Things that one was forced to see and casualties that you had to step over. In ordinary quiet times of peace, I'd probably faint, but then you became hardened to it, due partly to the fact that you were constantly suffering from fatigue. You were going on your nerves, and the fact that you didn't know if the next moment might be your last. You feel . . . hard, if you like, not as sensitive as you would otherwise be. But you're scared to death all of the time. You see all these dead soldiers around from both sides, and you think, "There, but for the grace of God, go I." Whatever it was, you had to do it, and you put it out of your mind completely afterwards.

When the war was over, I forgot about it completely and deliberately. The only time it comes up is maybe when you meet an old army buddy, or when anyone asks you about something to do with it. When I worked for the United Nations, I did not want people to know about the Victoria Cross, and I saw to it that they didn't. That had nothing to do with the present, or with those people who, for all I knew, might have been on the other side of the line.

You also put it behind you partly, because we were all youngsters then; we were just trying to serve our country in the only way we knew how. When all that is behind you, and you're back in civilian life, you worry when someone is offering you a job because of some quality he sees in you, or whether he is doing it just because you happened to win the Victoria Cross. That was something you didn't want.

That same thought has occurred to so many of the other lads who have won the Victoria Cross. It could also become too much of a prize in one's own mind, one that you could trade on if you were inclined that way.

There were many, many soldiers who deserved it just as much, if not more, than I.

Captain Paul Triquet
(1943)

The Bravest Man Is Always the Private

December 1943 was a very critical period for the Canadian Army and the Eighth Army in Italy as a whole. On the night of the thirteenth, we were all briefed about taking this crossroads held by the Germans. Others had tried before us but with no success.

At seven o'clock in the morning, after a terrific barrage, we started attacking, and immediately after we crossed the line, we found a very big platoon of Germans. There were at least thirty men with an officer, and they were so shaken by the artillery fire, they were all ready to give up. When I said to the commander, "Give me that gun before you hurt yourself," I even remember him throwing it to me right away.

We sent them all back as prisoners and moved ahead again, along with the Ontario Tank Regiment, which by this time was reduced to about eight tanks. My company was reduced, too, to about eighty-one men. Suddenly there were German tanks coming at us from a barn, firing their guns, and a lot of soldiers shooting at us with rifles. We lost about thirty more men at that point, and we had only just begun. Two officers were wounded, and I lost all my signallers and runners. The only means of communication left was the tank wireless. When my commanding officer asked over the wireless what we were going to do, I told him we would resume the advance. I knew we weren't strong, but I was under the impression I had a company following me. What I didn't know was that they had been stopped by the Germans.

So we were alone and advancing and firing and stopping and jumping around. The Germans were firing everything at us, and I kept losing more men all the time. Then I found out that the place we had just taken from the Germans was now re-taken by them and we were surrounded on all sides. There was no going back, so we started down to the only safe place around, this big farmhouse. As we tried to reach the farmhouse, my third officer was wounded, and we lost some sergeants and more men. When we reached the farmhouse, there were only sixteen of us left, plus six of the eight Canadian tanks. We got there at two o'clock in the afternoon, which meant that for seven hours we had been on our bellies most of the time, but at least I was able to tell my C.O., "We are here." By then, we had almost no ammunition left, and within a half-hour the Germans had launched a counter-attack. We were trapped there for five days, and by the time we were relieved, we had only nine men left.

When I was walking back after we had been relieved, I was amazed to see the piles of spent ammunition and guns that our army had used to keep us at those crossroads. They wanted to hold that point to launch a brigade attack, and they did. It was an absolutely vital thing for the whole Eighth Army.

I never expected the Victoria Cross for myself. All of my men were recommended for something. My only worry at the time was to organize a new company, because mine had been destroyed. You know, when you're caught in something like what we'd all just been through, you're always scared. But an officer can't afford to be scared. He does things the way he's been trained. The bravest man in war is always the private, because he can only follow and it takes a brave man to do that. You should always tell him something to keep him from being scared. While that battle was going on, I was jumping from one hole to another to talk with my men. The reaction you'd get was terrific! Anyway, anyone who's *not* scared at a time like that is a fool!

Major David Vivian Currie
(1944)

We Were All Scared

The action at that time was the sealing of the Falaise Gap. We were ordered into the Gap along with the Poles and other units to try and plug the escape route of the two German armies trapped in there. That was in France, and it was the final encirclement of the German armies there. We were ordered into this village, and told to cut the Germans off. For three days and four nights, this is what we did.

I was surprised to get the medal. I was just one of a lot of people there. We were all scared. Who wouldn't be? But you just do what you have to do in this world. Not just in war. I was with the South Alberta Regiment at the time, tanks. We were a reconnaissance regiment, and although a lot of Germans did get through, the whole operation was said to be successful.

Private Ernest "Smokey" Smith
(1944)

War Is Terrible

It was in Northern Italy where I got the Victoria Cross. It was raining when we crossed the river, and we were supposed to take up our positions about two miles beyond the river, which we did, and we got stuck there. That's where all the action took place and I was there for two days. They couldn't get any support over to help us, because the river had risen so high with all this rain. I had eight men going over, and I only had one man left, and he was badly wounded. So there was just myself and him stuck there until our relief came two days later.

It was a job to do, and you did it, and I was scared the whole time. Who wouldn't be? I'd been there right from the start—from Sicily right straight through the war—and had been in lots of battles. You're always scared, but you don't think about death. I guess you're geared up for it or something.

All battles are tough, for that matter, and I was no better than any of the others. I wouldn't do it again, because I wouldn't go to another war again! War is terrible, and it's useless! They used to happen about every twenty-five years, and whether or not that still applies, I don't know, but it solves nothing at all, and it hurts and wastes so many beautiful young people!

Mrs. Lenore Findlay Like the Inside of an Oven

Fire was the enemy new settlers feared most. There was
virtually no defence against it—especially in those areas
where the forests literally grew up to the back door.
Whole communities were wiped out in a matter of hours
as the raging flames consumed buildings, animals, and
people. One of the worst of these tragedies was the Matheson fire of July 29, 1916, in Northern Ontario. Hundreds
of lives were lost, and thousands lost their homes and all
their possessions, as did Mrs. Lenore Findlay's family.

We were very proud of Matheson. It had lots and lots of
lovely homes, including ours. My parents had a business and
were doing well, so we had a lot of nice things.

I was almost eighteen at the time, and we had never been
around a forest fire before. When everything got smoky, we
were really frightened. My mother, father, and brother were
at home, but I was visiting some friends. I came home with
some people who had a team of driving horses, and we found
ourselves driving through all this terrible smoke. Then the
wind got real bad, and fire could be seen in various places in
the bush, but it still hadn't reached the town yet.

After I got home and we had our dinner, the situation got
worse. At two o'clock in the afternoon the fire was coming
fast. My father said, "Get some heavy blankets, and we'll go
down to the river." He had been attempting to save the house
with buckets of water, but that was futile. When we got to the
river, we went right down by the water's edge, and we soaked
these blankets and pulled them over our heads. They would
dry so fast, we had to keep wetting them. Some people got
right into the water up to their necks, but I put only my feet in
and stayed covered with the wet blanket.

We watched the houses in Matheson which just seemed to
explode when they caught fire. The heat was terrible—like the
inside of an oven. The air, which was very hot even before the
fire came, was now unbearable. When those four walls of
flame surrounded the town, it was like being inside a blast
furnace. Despite that, I don't think that anyone burned to

death in Matheson. There were those who smothered in their root cellars, but most of the townspeople either got out on trains or down to the water. It was those outside the town who actually perished in the fire.

It was an awful fire, and it spread awfully fast when it reached here. After two hours, I would say, there was nothing left to burn. By four o'clock, everything was gone, except a few houses that survived on the other side of the tracks. It was just as you might imagine what the end of the world would be. It stayed, and didn't cool down till the rain came that night.

When it was all over, there was no house to go back to. We stayed the night in one of the homes that was still standing on the other side of the tracks. They took a lot of people in—at least another ten besides us.

The next day, when we went to see our home, there was nothing there but the basement. We found some things that survived the fire: a couple of teapots, some silverware, which was all bent out of shape, but still usable. Even most of the metal items—the pots and pans, and things of that nature— were melted, but we scratched around and got whatever was left. We needed them—to start over again. There was a clause in everybody's insurance policies that said, "not valid in case of forest fires". So everybody was in the same boat. We all had to begin from scratch.

H. "Dude" Lavington Home on the Range

Dude Lavington of Sorrento, British Columbia, figures
he's been a cowboy ever since he could crawl. Born in
Alberta in 1907, the son of pioneer parents, his childhood
memories are made up of horses and cattle, open range,
and the hardships of a new country.

My dad was a greenhorn who came to Canada looking for
something different than the life he was born to in the shadow
of England's Wells Cathedral, where his father was organist
for fifty-three years. I guess he was an adventurer, and the
New World seemed a good place to find that. He was around
eighteen or nineteen when he landed in the States, where he
worked for a while on the railroad, and later on ranches in
Iowa and Nebraska. This gave him a taste for ranch life, and
when he heard of the free land available up in Canada, he got
himself a covered wagon and a bunch of horses and set out for
Alberta in 1896, arriving in the southern part of the province
just as winter was settling in.

That winter was spent with a detachment of North West
Mounted Police. When spring arrived, he moved on again till
he came to the central part of the province and found himself
a homestead about sixty-five miles from Stettler. After he got
settled with a house to live in and some of the land broken, he
felt he had some roots and something to offer a woman; so he
proposed to a neighbour girl, Eva Cook, and they got married.
By this time, he also had some cattle and horses, so the
homestead was becoming something of a small ranch and,
although things were going pretty good for them, there were
tough times ahead.

My brother Art was the first child, born in 1906. I came
along in 1907, and a sister was born in 1908. That was a bad
year. It began with two-year-old Art getting kicked in the face
by a colt, and remaining unconscious for four days. Then
typhoid fever struck the area and my baby sister died.
Apparently I almost did too. Mother got sick and passed away
shortly after that, and Father was left alone with two baby
boys. Added to this, there was a bad prairie fire where he was
hard put to save our place. On top of all this, he sprained both
ankles on a runaway team of horses. It's a wonder he didn't

just pack up and leave. I think 1908 must have been the worst year of his life. He had no help at all, and trying to look after the two of us gave him a lot of problems. When he left the house to do his chores, he had to tie us to the bed, one to a leg, and far enough apart that we couldn't untie each other's strings. It's only now that I can appreciate how tough it was for him, and how lonely.

Neighbours were far away, and single women on the prairies were as scarce as diamonds. But he carried on, doing the best he could for the next couple of years, until his brother Charlie and his two sons came out from England and home-steaded near us in 1910. This gave him more freedom to get around, with the result that he had a new wife, and we kids had a new mum the following year. That meant that our life as wild colts was over, as the new mum was a lot stricter with us than Dad knew how to be.

About this time the railroad came along, and its path took it right through our property, and that made a big change in our lives. Up to this time, we had to travel sixty-five miles by horse and cart to Stettler for supplies, but with the coming of the railroad, the little town of Big Valley sprang up almost overnight. Settlers poured into the area, and gradually the wide-open range was a thing of the past. Churches and schools came with the new homesteaders, and before we knew what was happening, Art and I were going to this little one-room school four miles away.

Art was seven and I was six. We had an old pony called "Babe", and we'd climb up on him in the morning, and ride bareback to school. Babe may have been old, but he was smart. Whenever we forced him into a gallop, which he wasn't too fond of, he'd suddenly come to a full stop and we'd go flying over his head into a pile on the ground. Then he'd wait until we climbed back on him again, and he'd amble on to school at his own pace, waiting around grazing until it was time to take us home again.

Babe was a good horse, and it was on him that we learned to be cowboys. The reason we rode bareback in the beginning was that Dad figured that that was the best way to keep us from getting into accidents with our feet caught in the stirrups. As a result we could ride like Indians, and we even roped calves with nothing to hold onto but the horse's mane.

One of our tasks was dehorning young calves when they

were a week old. There'd be around a hundred of them to do every spring. We'd rope them and cut off the little button horns, and rub the stump with a caustic stick. We had to dehorn these cattle so that they wouldn't injure each other when they got older. One of us would stay mounted on Babe while the other was doing the operation because the mother cow didn't like to see us bothering her babies, and if she started to attack, the one on the horse would drive her off.

Dad was an animal lover and couldn't bear to see them suffer. Besides, it made economic sense not to have the cattle tear each other up. I remember one time, when I was eight years old, we decided to put on a show for the kids at school. Dad had never allowed us to wear spurs, so we put some nails into our boot-heels, and made poor old Babe buck all over the schoolyard. Some girls ran off and told the teacher. The teacher told my parents and the result was that we weren't allowed to ride Babe to school for a whole year. Walking four miles, twice a day, taught us never to abuse animals again.

When I was seven, an epidemic of mange hit the prairies. This was serious, and the government was forced to do something about it. As young as I was, I can remember every detail seventy years later because I was involved in the solution. Every piece of stock on the range had to be rounded up and dipped in a giant vat of sulphur and lime. The vat was on a ranch about forty miles away, and I was permitted to go along on the roundup.

The ranchers in the area pooled their stock, and made the drive together. Dad had four hundred cattle. Some had more, some had less; and as we moved in the direction of the dipping vat, the herd got bigger until there were thousands and thousands of animals as far as the eye could see. The whole countryside was one great moving mass, with great clouds of dust rising in the air as it shuffled along. I've never seen more animals together before or since, and the trick was to hold our cattle together so they wouldn't get mixed up with the others.

When we got to where the vat was, there were great long holding corrals where each rancher kept his animals until his turn came up. The vat itself was on the shore of a lake, and this stinking mixture of sulphur and lime mixed with water was boiled before it was mixed with lake water in the vat. The cattle were led from the corrals to a chute which led to the edge of the vat. The animals behind pushed and forced the ones ahead to dive off the platform into the vat. They'd go right under for a few seconds, and when they came up, they'd swim the forty or fifty feet to the far end where they could walk out.

About a week or so later, we put them through the whole thing again, as it took two dippings to cure the disease. After that we were allowed to head back home. Of course, other ranchers with their herds were arriving in the meantime, so de-mangeing the range took months.

On the way back home, when our cattle realized that they weren't being held any more, they began to feel their freedom. They had been held in those pens and forced to drink water that was dirty and muddy, and this lime and sulphur was still caked all over them. Well, when we came close to this big lake, they got a whiff of the fresh water, and they stampeded. They couldn't wait to get into it. Those poor, tired, dirty animals suddenly became a huge mass of running cattle, with horns flashing in the sun, hooves clattering, bellowing and crying, and making a terrible ruckus. You couldn't help but be thrilled by it all. When they hit the edge of the water, the ones behind pushed ahead until soon they were all in there, swimming for the opposite shore.

Now, we hadn't counted on this. Our plan was to take them around this lake, but what could you do? They were in there, swimming across that body of water, which was at least a mile wide. The cowboys on their horses, including me, had to dive right in after them and make sure the weaker ones made it too. That was the longest swim I ever made on a horse, and it was the most thrilling, too. I've never seen such a happy pack of animals.

Well, as we came out the other side and began getting nearer home, first one rancher, and then another, would cut his animals from the herd, and gradually the drive came to an end, and our four hundred cattle looked pretty small after seeing a herd that covered the whole countryside. That was my first and last experience with a mange epidemic.

It wasn't my last time with a herd, though. Almost every time there was stock to be handled, Dad would take the two of us out of school to help on the beef drive. As young as we were, we were considered a part of the working ranch. We had chores to do before breakfast, even on the coldest days of winter. We all had to help, even Mum.

I remember at one time we were helping our cousin Ralph to cut his beef on the range. Most of these animals were three or four years old, and most had some pretty mean-looking horns. One of these big, mean steers decided a little grey pony Mum was riding would be a good target for attack. He hit Mum just below her knee with his forehead, while one horn pierced the horse's shoulder and the other went into his ribs. Dad was near enough to see it happen, and he came galloping over and drove his horse straight into the steer and knocked him right over on his side. Mum was shaken up a bit, and her horse had some nasty gashes, but there was no great harm done.

Another time, Mum was out on the range with a hammer and staples patching up a broken gate. She was just about finished the job when she turned around and saw this big bull charging in her direction. We had all heard about this crazy bull that was loose on the range, and we had been told to keep a watch out for him, but we had never seen him before. Mum dropped everything and made a dash for her horse, and mounted him with the bull straight on her tail. That little horse, who was never known for speed, broke all the records that day, and both he and Mum came through without a scratch.

One of the clearest memories I have, and one of the funniest, is of one of the shortest bullfights on record. We were driving a herd of cattle along a fenced pasture, alongside this steep hill. Suddenly we heard a great racket, and when we looked up, we saw this great bull coming at top speed down the hill, with evil in his eye. One of our bulls cut himself away from the herd and just set himself up there, hunched and ready for this challenger. The other one kept thundering down the hill and met ours, head on. There was a sound like a clap of thunder, and I was sure the two of them would have broken skulls, but the running bull went up in the air and landed straight down on the other one's back, and then on the ground, with his feet in the air. Our bull was so stunned by the impact, he didn't follow up his advantage. The other one scrambled back to his feet, let out one mighty bellow, and lit out of there like the devil was after him. Most bullfights go on for hours, and at times even weeks, but that one was over in one second flat.

Bill Lewis Barrels of Rum from the Sea

The little town of Louisbourg in Cape Breton is perhaps
our most obvious reminder of the time when two of the
world's great powers were constantly at war. In the
eighteenth century Louisbourg was a centre of commerce
and a symbol of French dominance. The great fortress
built there seemed invulnerable, but it actually fell three
times before it was finally demolished by the British in
1758. Its French inhabitants were scattered. Only a few
stayed on and established themselves in small fishing
communities along the shores of Cape Breton.

Bill Lewis, now in his seventies, comes of a family that
has played a prominent role in the social, economic, and
political life of Louisbourg for most of this century. The
Lewises were merchants and fish buyers as well as may-
ors of the community. In fact, the present mayor is Bill
Lewis's nephew. Bill Lewis himself is an amateur historian; and although he has had nothing to do with the fortress's reconstruction, he is considered an authority on
the town's local history.

This little town of Louisbourg here on the rocky shores of
Cape Breton Island has more history per square inch than any
place in Canada. When France and England were battling with
each other in the eighteenth century for control of the New
World, the French built a great fortress here to be their
strong-point, the capital of their possessions in North America. It was also to be the mercantile centre for trade between
this new world and the old one in Europe, and for a while,
that's exactly what it was. In addition to its being a military
base, it was a thriving town with several thousand people and
a harbour that was always full of ships.

However, as the war heated up, ownership of Louisbourg
shifted back and forth several times between the two countries. The last time, though, the English were the winners, and
they demolished the fortress forevermore in 1758. Every last
stone was knocked down and there was nothing here for the
next two hundred years, except the outlines where the walls
and the buildings had once been. We would play there when I

227

was a child, and we vaguely knew about some of the history, but we certainly weren't that aware of it. The outlines of what had been there were only slightly raised lumps in the ground covered with moss.

I had to grow up before I got interested myself. For most of us who lived here, Louisbourg was simply a fishing town that had an ice-free harbour that was sometimes used in winter by the coal companies when the Sydney harbour was blocked by ice. That was enough to keep us prosperous. The Sydney and Louisbourg Railway that brought in the coal provided employment for plenty of our people; some worked on the coal docks, and others who weren't involved in the fishing industry found jobs on the boats that carried the coal away.

We were busy and happy with our lot, and very few thought of what Louisbourg had been two hundred years ago. We had enough to think of in the present day; however, as I got older, I began to read about it. The French should never have built their fortress here, as it was impossible to protect it from invading forces because of its geographic position. They had intended to build it at St. Ann's, on the Bras d'Or Lake, which would have been a perfect spot; but somehow, the decision was changed, and they built at Louisbourg. I often wonder how the history of North America would have been changed if it had been built at St. Ann's, which is quite a distance inland. I don't believe that the English could have ever taken it.

After 1758, some of the inhabitants went back to France, and others spread out to different parts of Cape Breton, where they began small communities. With a few fishermen and farmers who settled around the harbour close to where the fortress had been, Louisbourg barely stayed alive. Few if any of the original people stayed. The new settlers used the stone from the fort to build barns, or as ballast for ships, and after a while, it was almost as if the fortress had never existed.

The new village didn't amount to much in the years that followed. It always played second fiddle to the city of Sydney a few miles away. Our harbour was only used when Sydney's was frozen, and that was a shame, as Louisbourg is a better harbour in so many respects the whole year round. But no one could, or would, admit that. Despite all the faults of Sydney harbour, steel and coal continued to be shipped from there except when the weather made it impossible. As a young boy I remember seeing great cargoes coming here to be loaded on the boats, and then there'd be a shift in the wind, and the whole thing would be sent back to Sydney. That had the effect of lifting our spirits up, and then dashing them to the ground.

The same type of thing kept our population down, too. It's never been more than fifteen hundred and we've had a history of seeing our young people leave for greener fields. Our problem has been that we've never had a real focus industry of any kind. We've always been a little bit of everything, but not much of anything. We're a second-choice port, a tiny railway terminus, and a small fishing village combined into one; however, when it gets busy, it gets very, very busy.

I remember there were twenty-five big ships lined up in the harbour one Christmas Eve, and when another arrived, the pilot had to go out and tell the captain that there was no more room. The crews of these ships would come ashore, looking for somewhere to spend their money, and as it was Christmas on this occasion, they wanted just about everything we had to sell, including every turkey and goose. These were large ships, with big crews, and, boy oh boy, they certainly brought some life to Louisbourg that Christmas.

Louisbourg was a very busy place during the Second World War. We repaired corvettes, for instance, and we got many of the convoy ships ready for the Atlantic crossings. Sometimes there'd be more outside sailors on the streets than townspeople. The place would be hopping. When the war was over, though, that all disappeared.

We have a very rocky coast, and because of this we've had many shipwrecks—hundreds. Now, a shipwreck is a disaster for the people involved, but for those who live on the coast, it means gifts from the sea. The cargo comes floating in and those on land are there to receive it. One time that I remember, was the year of the flu epidemic in 1918, and a ship named the *Afghan Prince* went ashore. She was carrying a cargo of steel rails, and tobacco in big casks. The rest of the cargo was white rum and alcohol—in ninety-gallon drums. Before the customs chaps could salvage it, the locals had enough booze and tobacco to keep them going for months. What the customs officers did salvage, they put in our shed on the wharf under lock and key, and it was well guarded. Well, where there's a will, there's a way.

One night around nine o'clock, I was going past this shed when I heard something that made me stop and have a look. I could see these legs running, and when I went to see what was up, I came across these buckets under the shed that were filling up with liquid. Some fellows had drilled holes up through the floor right into the ninety-gallon drums of rum, and it was draining out into these buckets. By the time I came along, they had just about emptied two of the drums, and took it away to the woods.

Another time, very early in the morning, I was passing near the shed and I saw the watchman sitting with his feet in two galvanized buckets. When I asked what he was up to, he said, "Bill, this is the greatest cure for the rheumatism." The buckets were full of white rum, and he was sitting there with his feet in it, as happy as a lark.

All kinds of things went on. For some reason, people didn't feel that they were stealing when they took things that had come off a shipwreck. They felt that God or Providence sent it in just for them, as every Sunday morning they'd be the first ones in church—offering thanks, I guess.

One ship that went on the rocks was loaded with tea from India. Nobody here had to buy their tea that year. But if God gave gifts from the sea that year, He also gave plenty of hardship and misery. The influenza epidemic of 1918 hit just about every home in Louisbourg, and there were ships in the harbour where every member of the crew was down with it. I remember one saying, "Just give them some good rum, and try to make them comfortable." People were dying like flies. I had it myself, but I was one of the lucky ones who survived, and Louisbourg survived that disaster just as she had all the others in her history.

There was a thriving swordfishing industry here up until the forties and fifties. During swordfishing season, the streets of town would be alive with fishemen and those who came to see the catch. There were so many small boats here, you could walk from one side of the harbour to the other on the decks. That disappeared when the government put a ban on swordfish, as they said there was too much mercury in them. Another disaster! But that's the way it always was. Up one year, and down the next.

Sometimes, in winter, when they couldn't dock at North Sydney because of ice, big passenger boats would come in. So many people would come off looking for a place to spend the night that there weren't enough houses in town to hold them. The railroad station would be jammed full of people sleeping on the benches and all over the floor. Sometimes these people would be from the *Bruce*, a large passenger ship operating between Cape Breton and Newfoundland. They'd arrive at night and the train took them out in the morning. They would also need to eat, and the few stores in town would open up to accommodate them, no matter what the hour was. I've seen Huntington's store wide open and full of customers at three and four in the morning.

There was a lot of excitement here the night that the *Bruce* almost sank. She was heading for North Sydney, but the ice was real bad, and she was taking a terrible battering. The mate said to the captain, "We'll have to take her into Louisbourg." But the captain, a stubborn man, said, "This ship is supposed to go to North Sydney, and that's where she'll go." Drift ice is an awful thing. It can crush a ship if it gets it in its grip, or it can hold it there and never let it go. There've been many cases of passengers on a ship caught in ice being compelled to get off it and walk across the ice clampers to the Cape Breton shore. That's a very frightening thing to do in stormy weather. One false step and you could disappear forever. Anyway, the captain of the *Bruce* tried for hours to make it into North Sydney, but the storm was just getting worse. Finally, without admitting he was wrong, he turned around and brought her into Louisbourg, where there was no ice, and where he should have come in the first place. But you can imagine the terror that those poor passengers must have suffered before he came to his senses.

Louisbourg was always "the good port in a storm", always an alternate destination. Although we're only thirty miles from Sydney, that thirty miles was enough to make it inconvenient. When people get here, this *is* the end of the road, and they have to turn around and go back.

It's a funny thing in a way, and it's ironic, but the fortress is still the biggest thing that ever happened here. Even though it was gone for two hundred years, most people who come here today come because of the fortress, which was restored as an historic site and a tourist attraction. They did a tremendous job on restoring it. Everything is as authentic as it could possibly be. Unemployed coal miners were re-trained in skills of eighteenth-century artisans and tradesmen, so that when it was rebuilt, it was done exactly as it would have been originally. They searched out antique furniture, silver and china in France to match what had been there, and they even went to the same quarries for the stones. They found the original plans and worked from those to build it. Even the people who work there in the summer when it's open are trained to think and speak as those who lived there in the eighteenth century.

I think we've finally got something here now that isn't going to dry up and blow away as do so many other things in our economy. Isn't it ironic, though, that the newest thing we have is the thing that's been here the longest?

W. F. A. Turgeon A Province Is Born

The Canadian West was an irregular patchwork quilt of settlements in the years before Saskatchewan and Alberta became provinces. Manitoba had been a province since 1870, and British Columbia joined Confederation in 1871, but the prairie between these two provinces was still a part of the Northwest Territories and governed by a territorial legislature. The demand for provincial status grew as the prairies filled with immigrants and the West took on new importance. Politicians of the day used all the tricks in their bags to retain their power, and to gain increased power when provincial status was granted. For Saskatchewan and Alberta, those five years leading up to 1905 were the most exciting and exhilarating political years the West had ever experienced.

I was born in New Brunswick in 1875 and was educated in the law. Around the turn of the century, there was much excitement and talk about the future of western Canada, so, being young and adventurous, I decided to join the trek. I tried the area that eventually became Saskatchewan, although at that time it was part of the Northwest Territories. Frederick Haultain, who was later knighted, was the first and only premier of the Territories, and it was with him that I became involved in the exciting changes in those years leading up to 1905. After a great deal of planning and negotiation, it was decided that the land now known as Saskatchewan and Alberta should become provinces of Canada.

Now, Sir Frederick, whose politics were Conservative, had his own idea of how that should come about, and Walter Scott, who was head of the Liberal Party, had his ideas. To add to this, Sir Wilfrid Laurier, the prime minister in Ottawa, had his own plans, as did R. L. Borden, the federal Opposition leader.

Haultain had become a very powerful man during the sixteen years he ruled the Legislative Council of the Northwest Territories after it had been formed in 1889. He was a strong-minded man, accustomed to getting his own way, and he wholeheartedly opposed the idea of making all that land into two separate provinces. He thought it should be just one, and he fought hard for that.

Even among those who favoured the two-province idea, there was major disagreement. Some thought the line dividing Saskatchewan and Alberta should run east and west, instead of north and south as it now is. That would mean that all the wheat-growing area would be in the southern province, while the northern province would have all the mixed farming area. That made a certain amount of sense when you think of it. They also wanted the capital to be in North Battleford, where it had been up to the time of the Riel Rebellion in 1885.

There was some self-consideration in Haultain's one-province idea, as that would have left him exactly where he had been with his legislature sitting in the Saskatchewan part of that land mass. But with the two-provinces idea, and two capitals, where would he go himself? Anyway, when it became a certainty that there were to be two provinces, he chose to run in Alberta, where politics were hotter than in Saskatchewan. Haultain didn't believe in the party system. His governments in the Northwest Territories were always made up of coalitions of Liberals and Conservatives.

After settling the two-provinces idea, and the boundary lines running north and south, the Ottawa government declared that Edmonton would be the capital of Alberta while Regina would continue its role as a capital city, only it would be the capital of the new province of Saskatchewan. This was in 1905 and in the first elections held that year, Liberal Walter Scott became the first premier, and Rutherford, also a Liberal, became the first premier of Alberta. Haultain's coalition of Liberals and Conservatives, which he called the Provincial Rights Party, did not go anywhere.

I was appointed attorney general in that first government, although I still hadn't won a seat, which I would have to do to retain the office. The newspapers made a big thing of my youth. I was thirty, and they described me as "young, capable, and eloquent". I agreed with the "young" part only, as I had a lot to learn.

My first test was running for a seat in the by-election which had been called for Prince Albert that year. The Conservatives were determined that this "upstart Liberal", as they called me, was not going to win. R. L. Borden, the federal Conservative leader, came in from Ottawa and spoke on behalf of my opponent at meetings all over the riding, and just about every bigwig they had also came in against me to teach me a lesson. Borden gave a rousing speech in my riding the night before the election. I had challenged him to a debate, but he refused.

When the ballots were counted, the tally showed that I had lost by a margin of only one vote. Now here's where we come to a funny twist. In those days they had a system of voting with coloured pencils. One candidate would be assigned red, another green, another blue, and so on. The voters had to vote for their candidate with the proper pencil. There was no preparation of lists then: the voter simply came in, gave his name, and stated that he wanted to vote. If any of the scrutineers were doubtful as to whether or not he was entitled to vote, they would challenge him and his ballot was put in a separate box, and after the election, a date would be set to examine the votes that hadn't been counted. The challenged voters had to appear and justify their votes before the ballots were opened. Anyway, when that process was completed, there were enough votes in there for me to be declared the winner. That was the hardest election I ever went through to win.

During the campaign, a scandal broke which occurred when the government came into power during the original election. Some of the Liberal-appointed officials who had been appointed to tally votes in scattered outposts hadn't done their job too well, and, of course, Walter Scott's Liberals—and, by implication, me—were accused of corruption. Some deputy returning officers who were supposed to go up north, set up proper polls, and find the voters in this territory, decided it was just impossible, and they did all the voting themselves, filling in all kinds of names, such as Jim Codfish, Mike Whitefish, or Crayfish, and so on. I don't think they thought it would be taken very seriously, but it was, and became a major scandal for the Liberals in 1905. I can tell you, it didn't help me very much in my attempts to win that first by-election.

In those days, a candidate could run in two ridings at the same time. If he lost in one, he might win in the other. Sir Wilfrid Laurier ran in Quebec and Saskatchewan in the 1905 election and was elected in both. As he could only sit in one, the other would then have to be opened up in a by-election. Sir

Wilfrid chose to take the Quebec seat, so when the Saskatchewan one was declared vacant, I had my chance to run.

There were some very odd things indeed in politics back in those days. They could be best described as the horse-and-buggy days of politics, as that was literally the only way for a candidate to get around. The first time I had a car in a campaign was in the election of 1912. I ran in Humboldt that year. My organizer came one day to tell me he had bought me a little Ford car. "How much?" I asked, and he told me, "Two hundred dollars." I was a bit doubtful, but he said, "Give it a try. You'll get around a lot faster." Well, he was right. I got around faster, and to a lot more places, and I won the election. I sold the car for two hundred dollars, so all it cost me was a little bit for gas. They were noisy things, though, breaking down every thirty miles or so, and most people, including me, thought of them as a novelty. It wasn't long, though, before we knew they weren't just a passing fad, and that something had to be done to control them. There were all kinds of proposals. One was that no car should ever be allowed to go more than fifteen miles per hour. A great many felt that way about cars in 1912.

I remember a case where one poor fellow, a sewer worker, was killed by a car when he stuck his head up through a manhole. When the case went to the Supreme Court, one of the judges—who had never been in a car—said in his judgment: "The very idea of rushing down a public thoroughfare at the enormous rate of twelve miles per hour! No wonder people were killed!"

And the newspapers were always searching for something startling to write of. If you were to believe the press of 1912, Saskatchewan was on the verge of civil war. By this time, Alberta had a Conservative government, and they were out to kill the Liberals in Saskatchewan. They sent workers into our province disguised as Dominion Police. Their job during the 1912 election was patrolling the polls, telling voters that if they didn't vote Conservative, they would lose their homesteads and land. According to the papers, the Saskatchewan Liberals had formed a counter-police force of three hundred and sixty men called Calder's Cossacks to round up and chase these Tory invaders out of the province. The truth of the matter is that there was no such thing as these "special" forces. The whole story was an invention of someone's political imagination.

Demon rum was another big political football in those days. There was forever a temperance movement aimed at purveyors of booze. The hotels sold liquor by the drink, and it could be bought at shops by the bottle; and the temperance people wanted to get rid of both. In 1908 I introduced a bill that would provide for local option, allowing communities to decide by referendum which way they wanted to go. This bill passed, with the result that several areas of the province voted "dry", but the greater area remained "wet".

Events continued like this until the war in 1914, and austerity in all things became public policy. The temperance people came after us once again, demanding that the bars be abolished completely, which meant that if any liquor at all was to be available, it would have to be purchased through a system of government-operated stores.

Bar owners would defy the police with guns when they came to close them, and there was a lot of killing. The state legislature threw the prohibition measure out, and the governor stepped in and appointed men who were guaranteed prohibitionists to the Court of Appeal. As was to be expected, prohibition measures were in, with the government handling liquor sales, and the bars were closed.

It came to our attention that either North or South Carolina had put such a system in effect back in 1892, but it didn't come easily. We studied the Carolina records to find out how this system had worked while it was in force, and we found that it worked well and had not been abused, so we adopted a similar system, with the government taking over control of liquor sales. With some variations it's the same system that's in use today.

Another controversial question back then was votes for women. I remember the first woman elected to the legislature was a Mrs. Ramsland. It was inevitable that votes for women would, and should, come. It was as inevitable as our Canadian winters. Even after women got the vote, my opinion is that it never made the slightest difference. Women voted the way their husbands did, and whole families voted exactly the same way. All the women's vote did was double the number of votes.

One of our biggest problems came from the Doukhobors. When we made it mandatory for all children to attend public schools or else show that they were receiving a proper education, we prosecuted those who didn't comply. Many Doukhobors went to jail rather than give in. Naked Doukhobors were parading everywhere as a method of protest.

One day a group of them were in a naked parade from Kamsack on their way to Rosthern, where they had been told by someone they would find Christ. The people of Rosthern heard they were on their way, and they sent three men out on horses to meet them. One of these men, Archie McNabb, was quite a lively character. When they met all these naked people, Archie called out, "Where are you folks going?" He pretended that he didn't even notice they wore no clothing. "Oh," one of them replied, "we're going to Rosthern." "What are you going to do in Rosthern?" says Archie. "Jesus Christ is there, waiting for us, and we're going to join him," says one of them. "Oh no, no," says Archie. "You missed Him. He was there yesterday. He's down in Saskatoon today." The funny thing is that they believed him, and the whole lot just turned around and headed for Saskatoon. That Archie McNabb was a great man. Years later he was made lieutenant-governor of the province.

Another remarkable character was a half-breed named Gabriel Dumont. I got to know him in Duck Lake, when I first came west shortly after 1900. I would go there frequently on business, and I developed a respect for him. He was Riel's right-hand man in the 1885 Rebellion, and I recall him telling me, "If only Riel had let me have my way, we could have locked up Middleton's army and things would have turned out differently. But," he said, "Riel wanted a war without killing anybody." If you'll examine the history of that rebellion, you'll find that whenever Dumont led a battle, he always came out victorious. Historians now agree he was a military genius. He was a sharp-shooter too. He told me in a joking mood, "Sometimes I miss a man at a mile, but never at two miles." He was a marvellous old fellow.

The last time I saw him, he was getting on the train at Duck Lake and I was getting off. He was all dressed up like I'd never seen him before. I said, "Where are you going?" "Down to Regina, to see the Governor General of Canada," he says.

"You know, I've never declared peace, and this is as good a time as any." I don't know what transpired with the governor general, but he died when he came back. That was in 1906.

There were many great men who are now only names in history books. Sir Wilfrid Laurier, for example. He was a fine man, very imposing, tall and lean, and a tremendous speaker in English and French. He was a visionary, a statesman who could see far ahead into the future. I had many long talks with him and I admired his knack of getting rid of visitors. He'd tell a funny story, and while everybody was laughing, he'd stand up and begin moving people towards the door. They'd still be laughing before they realized they were outside and the meeting was over. When he spoke, you knew he was thinking of how his speech would be interpreted by others in fifty or one hundred years. He came into power in 1896, and was there till 1911, when the Conservatives took over under Borden and, later, Arthur Meighen.

Meighen, too, was a fine man—even though he was a Conservative. In fact, it was Arthur Meighen who made me a judge; not my own party, the Liberals. He was clever but had one drawback—his bitterness on the public platform. Outside the debating room, he was the finest, gentlest man in the world, but when he got up in the House of Commons, he was sarcastic and bitter. The result of this was that he didn't make any friends. I remember one old lady in Regina, who had always been a Liberal, but decided that she was going to vote Conservative. However, after hearing Meighen speak, she came out furious. "I'd never vote for a man who talked about Mr. King that way," she said—and she never did cast a Conservative vote.

I was part of the Saskatchewan government from the year the province was created until 1941, when I was asked by Mackenzie King to leave my post as Chief Justice of the province to take up a diplomatic career. In my opinion, King was a great statesman and a great politician, in contrast to Laurier, who was also a great statesman but not a politician.

This interview was recorded in 1963 when W. F. A. Turgeon was eighty-eight years old. He died in 1969 at the age of ninety-four.

Hartley Trussler The Cookery Was the Heart of the Camp

The northern section of Ontario is a vast land mass of more than three hundred thousand square miles into which the British Isles could be fitted twice—with enough room left over for the Maritime provinces. Northern Ontario was largely empty of people when this century began, but today there are large cities and towns, industries, and a stable population, owing mostly to the coming of the railroad and the mining and lumber companies that followed. Although the lumber barons like J. R. Booth had operated there for many years before, permanent settlements like North Bay, Sudbury, and Thunder Bay were opened up tremendously by the railroads, which provided year-round access to the south. Before that time, settlements were generally small and tended to move, as did the lumber camps when the supply of timber ran out. Hartley Trussler of North Bay was born in 1897 and spent many years working as a lumberjack in the Northern Ontario forests.

J. R. Booth's men cut lumber all over this area at a time when there were huge trees. They cut everything down, and then selected only the finest for the square timber they wanted. If there was a slight blemish like black-knot or butt-rot, these so-called imperfect trees were left there lying on the ground. Only the best were squared and driven down the South River to Lake Nipissing, and eventually shipped to England. There was an awful lot of waste, but, of course, one must remember that this was a time in our history when everybody thought that our forest resources were inexhaustible. My grandfather was a sawmiller who came along after Booth, and he saw great possibilities in these giant trees that had been left on the ground.

A big fire had burned everything around there except for these big trees, but aside from some charring, they were sound and they made perfect saw logs. Grandfather advised my dad and his brother to get in on this harvest, so they started a company, organized a bunch of lumberjacks, and got going.

Mother came along with her two babies, and did the cooking for the gang of men as they sawed lumber. I was just a youngster at the time, but I can remember huge planks of beautiful cork pine three and four inches thick and almost three feet wide from those waste trees. These charred monsters provided lumber for this mill for four or five years, but after that, he had to keep moving his camps to wherever the trees were.

The camps were always built of rough logs taken from the nearby forest, and they were always located beside a creek or lake so that there'd be a good water supply. The buildings were usually thirty or forty feet long and twenty feet wide, depending on the length of the available trees. The walls were about five feet high, and the roof was supported by a stout log ridge-pole with hand-hewn rafters, covered with inch lumber and tar paper. The logs were chinked with a split dry cedar and moss, and plastered with clay. When they were newly built, the fresh smell of the logs, the tar paper, the cedar-bough beds, along with the nice hot stove, gave you the most homey, comfortable feeling in the world.

There'd be one building for sleeping, one for cooking and dining, a little log cabin for the boss and the camp clerk, and a stable for the horses. In some of the bigger camps there was a night man who made his rounds of the buildings, keeping the stoves stoked and checking on the horses. He also cleaned the lanterns and was responsible for waking the men at 5:30 A.M., which was long before daylight in the winter. Breakfast would be at six, after which there'd be a walk of usually a mile to where they would work. Then it was a ten-hour day for them, from 7:00 A.M. until 5:00 P.M.

The noon lunch was prepared by the cook and packed in a couple of big wooden boxes, which would be carried or drawn on a hand sleigh out to the bush by the chore boy. He then had to shovel out a big circle from the snow, and make a huge fire in the centre, and cut cedar and spruce boughs to make seats on the snow around the fire. Then he'd heat up the big pot of beans of beef stew, boil the tea, and get the cakes and pies ready. The chore boy, who was generally the fool of the gang and the butt of jokes, got a hard time if everything wasn't ready at twelve o'clock sharp. At the same time, though, he was a very important person in any lumber camp.

The old-time camp was quite an institution—a self-contained community in which a lot of men lived together for seven months of the year, from October till May, with one break at Christmas and the New Year when just about everybody trekked out to civilization. For married men, it was the only chance to be with their families, but for the single men, it was usually a wild spree in the village hotels. Many lumberjacks did nothing during that week except drink, fight, and carouse. There was generally a sort of tournament to determine who was the best fighter, and quite often the loser, having lost face, didn't return to camp.

The cookery was really the heart of the camp, and a good cook was the most important person of the whole gang. A cook's reputation would become known far and wide, and men would try to find jobs in whichever camps had the best cook. Food was extremely important to these men, and each meal was a high point in their day. There'd be all kinds of roasts and different meats—vegetables, cakes, pies, and pastries, as much as a man could eat.

Most of the cooks were characters, and they weren't always men. The first one I knew was Mommy Lavigne, a big stout Irish woman with a heart as big as an ox, and the strength of a wrestler. She cooked and was the boss, while her meek little husband was the cookee—or "bull cook", as that job was often called. The cookee did all the slob jobs such as peeling and preparing vegetables, washing dishes, setting the table, and keeping ample supplies of food on the table. Woe betide him if the tables ran out of food while the men were eating. He would take the brunt of the men's grumbling, as the cook was the absolute boss of the dining room and one of the rules which was strictly enforced was that there was absolutely no talking during a meal.

Mommy Lavigne was as strict about enforcing this rule as any of the men cooks, and would throw a man bodily out of the building if he broke the silence. Some cooks would patrol the dining room casually swinging a meat cleaver to remind the diners that dire things could happen to any offenders.

Most cooks had a particular specialty they became famous for. Mommy Lavigne's was pancakes, which she made on top of her highly polished stove. Pius Keiswatter was a big Dutch cook whose specialty was pies and cakes. Billy Bogues was a small, trim man, always immaculate in a white uniform and long apron, which he changed after every meal. He was more of a chef than a cook, and made a real production of each meal. He made delicious plum puddings in the old-fashioned manner—boiled in individual bags. The most memorable cook for me was a little Englishman, with a gruff voice and a distinct Cockney accent. His specialty was called "Bully For All". It was a sort of casserole made of leftovers, and well-seasoned with sage and onions and baked in the oven. When asked for the recipe, he would say, "Just oddses and endses," but whatever it was, it was great!

Sunday was supposed to be a day of rest in lumber camps, but most men had personal chores to do. The clean ones washed their underwear in a big wooden tub provided. They mended their mitts and socks and patched their boots and moccasins. Some, however, wore their underwear for the whole season without washing them. They claimed they were warmer that way. Another chore, for the axe-men, was grinding the nicks out of their axes on hand-turned grindstones. It was a tedious job, but some of these men would grind all afternoon until their axes would be as sharp as razors. The family men wrote letters, and those with nothing to do played card games such as blackjack, pedro, and poker. There were no recreation facilities, and in those pre-radio days men didn't know what was happening in the rest of the world because very few newspapers made it to the camp. The lights were so dim that hardly any reading of any kind was done anyway.

The horses in camp were the pride and joy of the teamsters. On Sundays, every hair was curried and brushed; manes were trimmed and braided, as were their tails; and harness was oiled and brasses shined. Many of the teams were hired and driven by their owners, but the company teams were as well looked after as the privately owned. It was a real treat, listening to the bragging and bantering that went on amongst the teamsters about who had the best horses. Those were the days when horsepower was the only power, and the horses were almost as important as the men who drove them.

When spring came, and the camps shut down, the men just disappeared. But you could be sure that when fall came around again, you'd find those men back at camp somewhere; most likely in the ones with the best cooks.

Frederick B. Watt Great Bear—A Thing of Awesome Beauty

The great white North remained largely unexplored until well into this century. It was an uncharted wilderness, mysterious, frozen, and forbidding, and of no interest to homesteaders seeking good farmland on which they could raise their families. Much of the credit for opening up the North goes to the prospectors who sought to unlock the secrets of its mineral riches and the bush pilots who took them there. Frederick B. Watt relates some of his experiences in the North here and in his book, *Great Bear*.

When Gilbert LaBine made his big strike at Great Bear Lake in 1930, half the country was out of work, and the news spread across Canada like wildfire. Desperate men will do desperate things, and every unemployed man in the country dreamed about finding his own riches in the North. It didn't matter that some of them had never done anything more strenuous then push a pen in an office, or shovel the snow in the front of their homes. They all seemed to feel that if LaBine could do it, then why couldn't they?

Some of those who actually did go were the greenest of greenhorns. I know that as I was one of them. Up until the crash of the stock market, in 1929, everything in my twenty-eight-year-old life had been neat and orderly and successful. I was a newspaperman and a writer whose work was appearing in magazines all over North America. My wife, Ernestine, and I, along with our young son Erick, were living a comfortable life fuelled by the easy credit we took advantage of. For us the effects of the market crash were immediate and brutal. Nothing remained of the boom times, except the bills we owed.

We cashed insurance policies, sold furniture and other possessions, but still couldn't keep our heads above water. We moved from our smart apartment to an old frame house where the winter winds blew through cracks in the walls. We confined most of our living to the kitchen and huddled around the stove. The self-confidence which I had had so much of disappeared as fast as our money, and I was forced to face up to the fact that I couldn't even support my small family. For the following two years we lived on the edge of total poverty, selling a story here and another there, but never more than barely enough to keep the wolf from the door.

Occasionally I would be assigned to cover stories on the developing North and I'd fly in with one of the bush pilots. "Wop" May was one of them, and he talked his company into permitting me to fly with him to report on the first mail flight to Aklavik. Out of that came other northern stories about different prospectors and places for which I'd get paid three dollars a column by the *Edmonton Journal*. In the meantime, my love for the North was growing. I had been hearing about Great Bear Lake from the time that my parents, who were also newspaper people, settled in Edmonton in 1905, the year Alberta became a province. All sorts of people came to our home, and I would hear all these stories about the North, and especially Great Bear, from the mouths of those who had actually been there, trappers and hunters, prospectors and guides. So although it was all secondhand, Great Bear was no stranger to me.

Then my chance came. A man by the name of John Sydie formed a syndicate with some others to stake claims at Great Bear, and I was offered the job of going there with a prospector. This was late in 1931. When I told Sydie that I was no prospector, he said that I would be taught by the others. I would be paid in syndicate shares and there was a chance to make a lot of money. I could also sell newspaper stories which would be flown out by the bush pilots, who went back and forth with people and supplies. I was pretty excited about all of this because there was at least a chance to rise above the poverty level, but I was aware too that this would leave Ernestine and the baby alone.

When I put the proposition to her, she listened quietly without saying a word. When I had finished, she said, "If you want to know what I think, I think you should go. We'll get along all right, and perhaps some day the three of us can move into the Royal Suite at the Macdonald Hotel." We had a great laugh about that, but the result was that on February 16, 1932, prospector Ernie Beck and his new assistant, Frederick B. Watt, flew out of Edmonton, in a whirling blizzard, for Fort McMurray, in northern Alberta, the first step of our journey to Great Bear.

Over the months to come, we experienced the worst and the best of what nature had to offer. Great Bear Lake is a giant among the world's fresh-water seas. It is a thing of awesome beauty, and at the same time, as cold and pitiless as any place on earth. With my buddy, Ernie, we were to see it all.

The cold, and how to deal with it, was the first thing to conquer. In the darkness of our first night in a tent at Great Bear, we cut spruce boughs for beds, and banked the outside walls with snow for anchorage, and to reduce the floor draft. As we planned to make this our headquarters, we sorted our supplies and gear, deciding what could be left outside, and what we'd keep in. We set up our stove, lit a candle, and the tent began to look like home. Before we could settle down, though, one more problem had to be solved: we needed drinking water. Certainly there was plenty of it in the twelve thousand square miles of Great Bear, but the difficulty was that all of it was covered with a lid of ice several feet thick. Our only alternative was to melt snow. An enamelled water pail was placed on the stove and filled with snow. It was remarkable how much was required to provide even a cupful of water. When enough was melted and cooled to meet our immediate needs, I suggested it would be a good idea to continue the operation until we had enough water for the morning as well. Beck agreed and we melted half a pailful before calling it a night.

The first half-hour or so, lying in my bag, while the fire burned itself out, had me feeling wonderfully at peace with the world. The Arctic sleeping bag was snug, and the caribou hide between the down of the bag and the spruce-bough mattress was softer than my bed at home. At least, that was how it seemed in my weariness. It had been a long day, but the syndicate was now fully in business. I seemed to be lying on a luxurious pink cloud.

Very soon my cloud began to lose some of its fluffiness. Rocks and roots had been overlooked in the clearing of the campsite and the knobs and elbows of the hastily cut boughs jutted up everywhere. It was warm in the bag itself, but my head protruded, and I learned how quickly a fireless tent takes on the outside temperature. At minus thirty-five or minus forty degrees Fahrenheit, a nose or an ear responds to the frost with equal sensitivity on either side of an unheated canvas wall. I had kept the woollen toque I wore under my parka hood close at hand for such an eventuality and it protected the top of my head.

But there was no alternative to pulling my face, turtle-like, well into the bag. I had a claustrophobic first lesson in how to breathe while submerged. Somehow I dozed off. During the night I was startled awake by a deliberate cracking noise, quite close at hand. It had a metallic ring, and I immediately thought about the tins of food, stacked outside the tent.

The ghostly crackling continued. Every so often there was a pinging sound, like the ricochet of a tiny bullet. It was very distinct, in the otherwise silent night—and very close, but I was tired enough to go back to sleep in the middle of it. The mystery was solved in the morning. Our half-pail of water was frozen solid. On the surface of the ice was a litter of enamel flakes, the spent "bullets" of the ghostly fusillade in the night.

There were many lessons to be learned in the days and months ahead, and many of them learned the hard way. In the spring, we had travelled with a couple of other prospectors wiser than we in the ways of the North, Carl McKee and Charlie White. They allowed us to use what they had while we were with them, and that included the protection offered by their tent at night from flies and mosquitoes.

They had an excellent outfit built around a light and easily rigged tent with a sewn-in floor, and a sensible netting arrangement at the entrance. Within a few minutes of slipping our packs, this canvas shelter was available. The insects that had infiltrated it were eliminated by a few shots of repellent, after which perfect peace reigned inside. That refuge was only good for a few days, as McKee and White eventually went off in one direction while we set out the other way.

When our comrades shoved off, we had a sense of freedom and the satisfaction any prospector feels when he has a promising piece of ground to himself, although we regretted losing the use of the green, mosquito-proof tent. The terrain back of the rocky finger on which we landed was a clutter of pond-sized lakes, dismal swamps, and a forest of tangled undergrowth. There was a great deal of over-burden—ideal breeding ground for every vicious form of insect life. The bugs had made the most of it. To brave this jungle, we were equipped with one sleeping bag, and one fly-bar, both of which were dismally inadequate.

A fly-bar is a tent of sorts—a canvas roof with draped walls of netting, just big enough to be suspended over a single sleeper. It is supposed to be a secondary line of defence to guard its owner from the occasional infiltrator of the tent we didn't have.

It might have offered some protection for one man, but with two under it, the situation was hopeless. We lay with the tarp under us on a mattress of spruce boughs and uneven rock, the opened-out sleeping bags over us. The fringes of the netting lay loosely on top of the bag, offering numerous tunnels and gateways into our stronghold, and the enemy lost no time exploiting them.

Not every attacker got inside the bar. Great black sheets of bugs were plastered in almost unbroken ranks on the outside of the netting, keening with frustration, or possibly encouraging those who had penetrated our defences. In darkness the sight would have been bad enough; in the full light of arctic midnight, it was ghastly. Each time a few minutes of fitful slumber ended in feverish wakefulness, the first thing that met the eye was a field of bloated mosquitoes hanging like clusters of red grapes from the inner surface of the fly-bar's roof. On each awakening I could see that their numbers had risen. These were the storm troops who had taken all they could of Beck and Watt blood.

Earlier in the season, we had experimented with fly-dope brought from outside, and found it to be more trouble than it was worth, quickly running off with our perspiration, stinging our eyes, and making a general mess that was harder to take than any bites it prevented. We settled on using a large bandanna handkerchief drawn around the face and up under the hat brim, with only a slit open so we could see. It was a stifling arrangement in hot weather, but it did reduce the area of bare skin.

Beck wearied of taking this punishment, and lit a smudge. The utterly still air, however, caused the smoke to rise in a small, neat plume which failed to spread to where it would do any good. Standing over it was useless, too, as the smoke was so concentrated that it made us choke. We launched a blitz. The miniature grapes on the ceiling were bloodily crushed, even though they were too sated to do us further harm, and every active mosquito or blackfly we could locate inside our coffin-like sleeping space was individually hunted down and killed. There were a few minutes, then, in which we knew comparative peace, but only a few. Fresh legions crawled under our walls and the carnage resumed.

The final ordeal was caused by another bug species which up to this time had remained neutral. We felt movement inside our clothes. At first this was only mildly irritating, but when we scratched, the new enemy launched sharp assaults on tender portions which had previously escaped attack. The bites had authority. When we threw back the bag to seek out the new enemy, we discovered that the parachutists had been joined by ground troops... ants!

They had come primarily for the corpses of the flying bugs. Most of them were dragging away dead mosquitoes and flies, but the proximity of warm flesh had obviously been too much for the carnivorous instincts of some of them. Or perhaps they were just counter-attacking. Whatever their motive, they provided the climax to a night of utter misery. It was a relief to crawl out from the bloody hell beneath the fly-bar at 6 A.M. Much of our staking that day was in the swamps, and the flies continued to harass us, rising in clouds that at times stifled and blinded us.

Somehow, we managed to get our claim-staking done over the next few days; and it was with great relief that we climbed back in our skiff to make the voyage back to our base camp at Cameron Bay, leaving Contact Lake and the insect life behind. But that wasn't to be the end of it. At one mile-long portage, the flies had one more go at us. The experience of carrying the skiff over this portage was the worst I have ever known. When we reached the southwest arm of Echo Bay, the exposed part of each man's face—the band between hat brim and bandanna mask—was one great welt. Our eyes were sunk in puffed, red pockets, as though they had taken a physical beating. In my case at least, they were also inflamed by tears. Helpless and hand-tied under the skiff, I silently wept in an agony of exhausted nerves.

Our luck returned when we were crossing Echo Bay. The wind dropped, and Gossan Island broke the force of the heavy waves. At the end of the three-mile pull, the chimneys of Cameron Bay signalled dinnertime.

I didn't make my fortune in the North as I had hoped, but I

learned to love and respect that beautiful land. I treasure the friendships I built there, and regret the ones that were lost. As bushwhacked men, we said things to each other that time never completely heals. I regret that Beck and I were no longer friends when our time in the wilderness was finished.

When I returned to the outside later that year, my voyage of discovery was over, and my second child had been born. The Depression had deepened, and all the financial pressures I had dreaded at a distance were still there, hard and immediate. There was a period of three months in which my income totalled eighty-five dollars; but in time, this too passed, and I started earning my way again as a writer who could write about the North with the authority of firsthand experience.

Violet Wilson You Can Take a Girl Out of the West...

Settlement in the West in the early days of immigration was hard work and sweat with the possibility of better days many years in the future. Once established and over the initial shock of their new living conditions, most homesteaders generally accepted their lot and went to work. There was no time for frills and they didn't dare dream beyond anything but the basics for themselves or their children, who were an important and integral part of the working farm. The more children, the more hands to do the work that had to be done. For them, the one-room school provided all the education they would ever need. But in any society there are always some better off than others, and an important priority for the wealthier settlers in the new West was higher education and culture for their offspring, as Violet Wilson of Edmonton describes.

As you can probably imagine, the frontier schools of the West, didn't provide much for young people beyond the 3 Rs, and it was the practice of some of the better-off families to send their children back East to finish off their education and smooth off the rough edges. So when I was thirteen, in 1905, my father, who was a doctor in Edmonton, decided that it was time for me to learn some of the finer things in life. It didn't matter at all that I was happy where I was.

I was packed up and shipped off to Toronto to the Bishop Strachan boarding school, which was so traditionally English, it might as well have been in London, England. It was founded by the first Anglican Bishop of Upper Canada, and it was very much a church school at that time. Coming from the rough-and-tumble of Edmonton, which was a real frontier town, I was totally unprepared for what was ahead of me.

First of all, there seemed to be more religion than anything else. We had private devotions in our little cubicles every morning before breakfast, always under the eyes of governesses who kept checking to see that we were down on our knees. Then it was on to breakfast, where grace was said aloud, before and after meals. From there, we went to chapel for a service by a visiting chaplain before our classes began. During the day another chaplain gave us lessons in church history and scripture. In addition to that, we had regular classes on the Old Testament, and after supper, another long service in the chapel. To end our day, we had to get down on our knees again in our cubicles for more private devotions.

We weren't allowed make-up such as lipstick or powder, of course, but sometimes we'd sneak into the kitchen and steal some flour to take the shine off our noses. And, just to be rebellious, we'd sometimes crawl out on the roof for a smoke, although we didn't really like it. That was sheer bravado because smoking was not something that women did in public until after the First World War came along.

Once a week we'd have dancing classes in the school gymnasium and we'd be all dressed up in our best. Our teachers, who were all from England, would give us lessons on how to enter and leave a room, how to bow, and how to curtsy. They taught us the waltz, the two-step, the one-step, and a few square dances. Once a year the school had a dance, and the boys from nearby Upper Canada College would be invited. They would arrive wearing white kid gloves, all neat and clean in their best suits, and they'd have these little dance programs with tasselled pencils attached to them. The teachers would be seated all around the walls, keeping a sharp eye on everything, as if there was anything to keep an eye on. We didn't know a thing about boys because the only times we'd ever see them was in church.

Our clothes were something else, especially for me, a tomboy from the prairies. We were dressed in long skirts down to our ankles, and we wore shirtwaists with long sleeves and, under all of this, petticoats and bloomers. The bloomers were useful, though, for carrying in forbidden fruits such as candy. We'd fill up the bloomers and walk past the teachers with sweet innocent faces. That's the boring side of it.

There were advantages too. We went to events that we never would have seen in Edmonton. There were artists like Madame Schumann-Heinck, Nellie Melba, Enrico Caruso, and many others. I remember one time Yeats came to town to read his own poetry and the whole school was taken to hear him. He was such a romantic-looking figure with his long black cloak.

Then there were all the different theatre groups from England and New York. One time, I remember, there was an unforgettable performance of Shakespeare under the trees in one of the city parks. Another time I saw Pavlova dance.

As wonderful as these things were, there wasn't one moment of those five years that I wouldn't have preferred to be back home in the West. Everything there was new and exciting, and there was something happening all the time. Immigrants were coming from all over the world, and there was a feeling of freedom that I probably missed more than anything else while I was away at school. I was eighteen when I came back in 1910, and I resolved never to leave again, and I never did.

Dr. Margaret Arkinstall The North Gets Into Your Blood

In the years of the Great Depression people would go anywhere for a job, and they would do just about anything.
When the job market in southern Canada disappeared,
desperate men moved north where railroads were opening up new territory for the mining and lumbering industries. Many of those who had approached the North with
dread soon grew to love the rugged, beautiful country,
and when the Depression ended these men and women
stayed on—not because they had to, but because they
wanted to. Dr. Margaret Arkinstall has written about her
experiences in Hearst, Ontario, in *Pioneer Partners at St.
Paul's*.

When my husband, Bill, and I graduated in medicine in
1930, we both decided that the North was the place to go. He
had often said during our university years that he dreamed of
being up in the north country with the lumberjacks—not as a
doctor, but as one of them. He talked of the thrill of a new
country, the discovery of nature—seeing the forests of spruce
and poplar and birch—and knowing that you were part of it
all.

He realized his dream in April of 1931 when he boarded the
train for Hearst, a small railroad centre in Northern Ontario,
where he became a medical missionary. We were engaged to
be married, so the plan was that he should get established,
and then when we were married, we would work together;
which is exactly what we did. We married in September, and
after a short honeymoon we took the train for Hearst in
October.

It was still a pioneer community, flat as any prairie town,
which depended on the pulpwood companies and the railroads for survival, and there was a large transient population.
It was a young country with young families and very few old
people. There was no real road to the outside, and our one link
was the railroad. The train, a transcontinental, would pass
through at night, and it brought with it anyone and everyone
who might have business at Hearst. These were lumberjacks,

bootleggers—you name it. Many would spend the day shopping and banking before moving out on the next train, but the lumberjacks with their paycheques, earned after months in the woods, headed for the beer parlours or the bootlegger establishments.

There were several of these, and we were often called upon to patch up after the fights which inevitably took place. Those bootleg places not only supplied the men with liquor, they also often robbed them of their money when the men got drunk enough. One bootlegger establishment was "respectable", run by a Finnish woman. She supplied the men with liquor, but before they went to bed she demanded their wallets. In the morning she returned them, with all their money intact, except for the exact expenses they had incurred.

The hospital was small but good, and it was run by the Women's Missionary Society of the United Church. We found that a good deal of our hospital activity came from pulp cutters who had accidents in the woods that surrounded Hearst, but the maternity business ran a close second. It didn't take us long to realize that we were living in a real frontier town.

When one attempted to drive a car from Hearst to the outside, they were in for a real adventure. The road was clay, often mud, and there were no buildings or gas stations, and around the next corner you might come face to face with a bear, a deer, or a moose. All travellers, before departing through the forest, had to register with the authorities. At a place called Smooth Rock Falls, the road went straight through the pulp-mill yard. On our first trip, I thought we were lost, but no, we found that this was indeed part of the "highway".

When we came to cross the Groundhog River by ferry, it was late in the night and we ran into a thunderstorm and torrential rains. This was in 1933, and we had our year-old baby with us, and I was terrified lest we get stuck. The entrance to the ferry was a steep, very muddy, slippery hill. It was pitch dark and we could barely see the ferry, which was equipped with only a dim coal-oil lamp in the window. We managed to drive aboard, and as we did, the boat began to chug-chug, and we moved towards the other side. Once there, the chugging stopped and we drove off and proceeded to drive up yet another slippery hill to the highway. We never saw another human—either getting on the ferry, while we were aboard, or getting off. It was one of the most eerie experiences I've ever had.

Transportation in the north country was always a problem. Roads were not kept open in the winter, and we all put our cars up on blocks and left them that way until spring. We got around to our patients by horse and cutter, or by what was called a "speeder", which was a little motorized car that was lifted on and off the railroad tracks.

One of our dearest friends in the North, almost a part of our family circle, was a Scottish trapper named Doug Mitchell, a true pioneer. His house was set in the bush several miles from the railroad track, many miles from the nearest neighbour, absolutely isolated and very beautiful. The way to get to Doug's house was to take the train south of Hearst and get off at a telephone post that had a mile marker on it. Doug, of course, would know ahead that we were coming and would be waiting there with his canoe when we disembarked from the train.

We would load what we had brought, luggage, food, and so on, into the canoe. The first few miles we would travel a very narrow creek, so narrow that one could touch the trees on either side. After a few miles the creek opened up into a wide lake, Doug's lake. The canoe crossed this until we came to his cabin in the bush. It consisted of one very large room, but when Doug had ladies visiting, he hung blankets across the room to make a bedroom for them. He was very careful and particular to protect our privacy and spare us any embarrassment. Never did he take one woman to his house alone, always insisting on having at least two.

Sometimes it was impossible to land the canoe on dry land. In order to save his lady visitors from getting their feet wet, Doug, wearing his hip-high boots, would carry us one by one from the canoe to where there was good footing on the shore. He was tall and strong, and we felt perfectly safe in his arms.

We would spend our days canoeing along the lake, just enjoying the outdoors and the beauty of the surroundings. Doug remained a bachelor all his days. He loved the trapper's life. He knew that rare indeed would be the wife who would settle in this life-style, especially when he would be away for ten days at a time along his trapline. I suppose if he had found someone for whom he cared enough to marry, he would have had to decide between a wife and the life in the bush that he loved so much. Once he told us that he had been trying to decide whether to get a wife or a washing machine. He realized that he needed both but decided in favour of the washing machine—equally useful, and easier to get along with.

Medical practice in those days was in some ways different from what it is now. Since then many more laboratory tests for the diagnosis of illness have been discovered and perfected. We did have a laboratory at the hospital and were able to perform some tests, while others had to be sent away to Toronto. The same was true of X-ray results.

There was no blood bank with the various types labelled that we could call on at once when we needed to give a transfusion. For administering blood, we had to "type" the patient needing blood and then find a donor of the same type. We always had to start from scratch. We called first on relatives who would come to the hospital for testing. If we were not able to find the blood that matched, we had to try elsewhere, perhaps the hospital staff, perhaps friends. When we did discover a suitable donor, the patient lay on the operating table and the donor on a stretcher beside the patient. Then we withdrew the blood from the donor and gave it directly to the patient.

We stayed in Hearst until 1945 and we raised our family there. It was wonderful to be part of a growing community like that. The North gets into your blood and becomes very much a part of you. If I could do it all again, I would go back tomorrow. They were, without doubt, the happiest years of my life.

Gleneatha Green Hettrick They Had To Find the Sea

Between 1783 and 1785 a great wave of settlers moved into that part of the Maritimes that was to become New Brunswick. After the American War of Independence, many of those British subjects who wanted no part of the new United States of America made their way up to Canada, where they could still feel the comfort of living under the British Crown. While most of them flowed down through the St. John River Valley to settle along the way, one small group made its way to an island called Grand Manan in the Bay of Fundy. Today Grand Manan is populated almost entirely by descendants of those early loyalists, like Gleneatha Hettrick.

Our forefathers here were sea people—fishermen for the most part—from the New England states, and as they were making their way to Canada, they sometimes made mistakes as to where the actual border was. After all, there was no fence or anything of that nature, so a couple of times, when they thought they had travelled far enough and began to settle, they would find that they were still in the state of Maine. So they would be compelled to pull up stakes and move on until eventually they did cross the border. At this point, some just settled in the river valley, but that wasn't what the sea people wanted. They had to find the sea, and nothing else would do.

They kept pushing on until they came to the coast, where they spotted this island off in the distance—about eighteen miles from the coast. They decided that was the place for them, perfectly suited to the life-style they were accustomed to, a mixture of farming and fishing. Their group wasn't big, and the government did a head count of the population twenty years after their landing. There were just 121 people on Grand Manan in the year 1804.

My own ancestors were included in that number. Of course, you must remember that Loyalists still came across to Canada for quite a few years after that time. These are what are sometimes referred to as "late Loyalists" and they kept coming even after the War of 1812 was settled. Grand Manan got some, too, especially those who were fishermen, as it was easy to get to the fishing grounds in their small boats.

In the beginning, Moses Gearish led a group of seven families, who began to set down roots in Maine, thinking that they were in Canada. When they discovered they weren't, they moved on to St. Andrews, New Brunswick, and finding that not to their liking, they moved on till they came to Grand Manan. They settled along the shore of the island, the sea in front and their farmland in back, all along the shore down one side of the island, with a small bit of land, a big lot of sea.

Our island is just sixteen miles long and about eight miles wide, but we all live in that strip on one side, because the back part of Grand Manan is still what you might call wild country with very high cliffs that have a sheer drop to the sea below. Our population has never been more than 2,600, and ninety-nine per cent of them carry the blood of the original people. There's only fifteen miles of paved road, and that's along the strip where we live.

The result is a people who are terribly independent, and who can't bear working for anyone else. They love their boats and their gardens, and they've always been as self-sufficient as it's possible to be. Nearly every business on the island is privately owned, and practically everyone owns their home; and if they didn't actually build it themselves, chances are they had a hand in the building of it. They all take great pride in the appearance of their property, and despite the passage of two hundred years, most inhabitants of Grand Manan speak with a Yankee accent, the same accent their ancestors brought so long ago.

They lived in isolation at first, so there was no reason that their accents should or could change. The r is dropped from words, and a short a is substituted, so that "car", for example, becomes "ca". The g is almost always dropped from words such as "swimming", and very often an r appears where it doesn't belong, so that you get "warsh" for "wash", "idear" for "idea", and "Chicago" becomes "Chicargo". They'll even put an extra r on the name of our country, so that "Canada" becomes "Canadar". I don't have the accent myself now, as it was driven out of me when I became a school-teacher; however, even with watching for it, I seem to slip into

"Yankee" from time to time. Some people from the outside have a difficult time understanding my father, who is now in his eighties, and is to this day as Yankee in his speech as they come.

I think it's changing now with young people because of radio and TV, and also because of the great increase in travel these days. My grandmother was ninety-six years old when she died and she'd never been off the island. People long ago didn't even leave their village. Maybe once a year, in the village where I lived, people might get the horse and wagon and make their way to North Head only six miles away. You see, there was no reason to make the trip, as everything needed was in their own village. We barely knew the people in those other villages even though none of them were more than five or six miles away.

When I was in high school, we played a softball game with the school at Seal Cove a few miles up the road, and I can tell you, that was a big occasion. The movie theatre was in North Head, but those six miles might just as well have been a thousand. I never saw a movie until I was fourteen. It cost me ten cents to go up in the back of a truck and another ten cents for the ticket. But when boys came of age they found ways to travel those few miles, as they wanted to find girlfriends. It seems that they always wanted girls from farther away from home, and, of course, the boys from other villages came for girls here.

You might expect that we'd feel claustrophobic living like that, but no, it's the other way around. I don't believe a Grand Mananer is really comfortable unless he's back on his island. One of the problems, of course, is that there just isn't room here for a lot of people—not even for our own children. It seems that we educate them and then are compelled to send them away to earn their living in other parts. But many times they come back, and they come back when they retire. There's a definite pull to Grand Manan that makes us want to return to it.

We have very few of the problems that you'll find else-where—racial problems, for example. Just about everyone is of British descent from those original settlers. Then again, nearly everybody is related, and there seems to be a general contentment among people to keep things the way they are, which is nearly the same way they've been for two hundred years.

When the government offered Grand Manan a free ferry service, a referendum was held and it was turned down, because although we thought it would be nice to cross to the mainland without a fee, it just might encourage mainlanders to come over here in great numbers and ruin our island. I guess we're happy seeing things stay the way they are.

Asa Danard "Early Canadian History in Rhyme"

I've referred to the amazing memories some of our elders possess. Not long ago I was searching in libraries for a lengthy poem written around 1886 entitled simply "Early Canadian History in Rhyme". When I couldn't find it, I mentioned it on my radio program. The appeal produced not a printed copy, but the entire poem as recalled by Asa Danard. He has remembered it ever since he first memorized it as part of his school curriculum many years ago, a phenomenal feat.

The reader will notice that, as the poem was written in 1886, Alberta and Saskatchewan were not yet provinces of Canada. They joined Confederation in 1905; and Newfoundland joined in 1949.

John Cabot and his son Sebastian, fourteen ninety-seven, came
From the port of Bristol, England, in King Henry VII's name.
First they sighted Prima Vista which they called the new-found land
With its rocks and gloomy forests and its mighty banks of sand.
After that Prince Edward Island, Nova Scotia, and N.B.
Which the French, a few years later, called the land of Acadie.
From the seaport of St. Malo came Jacques Cartier to explore,
Found and named the Gulf St. Lawrence, fifteen hundred thirty-four.

One year later this bold sailor up the river took his way
Looking for a route to China and discovered Canada.
Where the mighty river narrows, Indians called the strait Kepec
To the village Stadacona, where is standing now Quebec.
What in English is a village, Indians call "Kanata";
Cartier thought they meant the country, so he called it Canada.

Next he went to Hochelaga, neatly built of logs and small
On a large and fertile island, which is now called Montreal.

Near the village stood a mountain, Royal Mount he called its
    name:
Long years after, sixteen forty-two, rose a city of the same.
Cartier also founded Charlesbourg Royal, fifteen hundred
    forty-one,
And the first attempt to settle the St. Lawrence was begun.
Henry Hudson crossed the ocean's wide expanse
And the French sent Verrazzano and he called the land New
    France.
Humphrey Gilbert sailed from London, fifteen hundred
    eighty-three,
Come to claim the land for England, but his ship was lost at
    sea.

So the French still held the country, sending rulers one by
    one,
But the Indians being hostile, little settlement was done.
Champlain founded Quebec City, sixteen eight, the first real
    gain,
There in thirty-two was buried, and his ashes still remain.
David Kirk, while Champlain governed, seized Quebec as
    England's due;
Here in twenty-nine he took it, gave it back in thirty-two.
Frenchman still succeeded Frenchman as the rulers of the
    land,
Immigration slowly followed, backward flowed, or seemed to
    stand.

Our Ontario, all a forest, at this time was little known
And where stand our swarming cities roamed the savages
    alone.
France and England, long unfriendly, at length came to
    blows
And before the war was ended, Canada engaged the foe.
First to rise and last to totter, old Quebec was last to fall,
Wolfe without led the English, French Montcalm within the
    walls.
England conquered, France was beaten, Wolfe and Montcalm
    both were slain.
Thus Canada came to England and will loyally remain.

Asa Danard

When Quebec and France surrendered on the Plains of
    Abraham,
British rule was instituted, storm subsided into calm.
France yielded up the country, part by part, to England's
    claim:
Some by cession, some by conquest, some by final treaty
    came,
Nova Scotia and New Brunswick, which Acadia had been
And by the Utrecht Treaty signed in seventeen-thirteen.
France confirmed this by another, seventeen forty-eight,
    Chapelle,
Both were known as Nova Scotia at the time of which I tell.

By a further final treaty, signed in Paris, sixty-three,
France renounced her claim forever to the land across the
    sea.
Save two islands near Newfoundland left to her by England's
    wish
Where her fishermen will gather, land to cure and dry their
    fish.

Over it one name extended, British North America,
And the names of "Upper" and "Lower" were unknown in
    Canada.
In seventeen seventy-six a portion railed at England's ruling
    race,
Thirteen colonies revolted, calling themselves United States.
These were eager that Canadians with their union should
    come in,
But they chose to stay with England and have ever loyal
    been.
After seven years of struggle, seventeen hundred
    eighty-three,
England yielded up the question, let the colonies go free.

But in those States there still resided many men to England
    true,
And these United Empire Loyalists soon to us for refuge
    flew.
For the States with cruel hatred, meaner spite was never
    found,
Seized their grain and cattle, burned their dwellings to the
    ground.

Thousands came to us for shelter. Proud is he who now can tell
That his father's father's father was a hunted U.E.L.

The British Commons, ninety-one, a bill had carried through
Known as the Constitutional Act, enforced in ninety-two.
It made two Canadas of one, an "Upper" and a "Lower",
And gave a parliament to each—there had been none before.
This system, representative, was popular, but a bill
That passed with it the Clergy Reserves was fraught with future ill:

For English clergy, in reserves, in stipends to be paid,
A seventh part of all the land of Upper Canada unsurveyed.
This led to furious future strife, for other churches claimed
The land belonged as much to them as to the clergy named.
Both Houses met in ninety-two, the capitals of the day
Were one, Quebec, and one, Newark, and one now called Niagara.
Next year Upper Canada led freedom's cause in abolishing slavery.
Ten years passed by, then Lower Canada did so in eighteen three.

The population eighteen four of Upper Canada was sixty thousand
(About a third of what Toronto is today!) [1886]

England claimed the right to search, made her intention known,
To search and take from Yankee ships deserters from her own,
And said that while she fought the French, 'twas not a friendly thing
For Yankee ships to trade with France, and aid and comfort bring.
So this brought war in 1812 and many men were slain
At Queenston Heights, at Crysler's Farm, Lacolle, and then at Lundy's Lane,
At Chippewa, at Stoney Creek, Fort Erie, and Chateauguay.
In eighteen fifteen at New Orleans, the Yankees won the day.

But in these ante-steamboat times, pre-telegraphic days,
Peace had been signed two weeks or more before this fight took place.

And now the war was over, gave people time to clear and
    build and sow,
To make good roads and dig canals and prosperously grow.
But frictions here and factions there caused many an anxious
    fear
While stormy times in politics grew worse from year to year.
From thirty-five to forty-nine throughout the whole extent
Of Canada, rebellion leagued with brooding discontent.

The French and English Lower Canada had quarrels by the
    score,
While the Family Compact, Upper Canada, caused full as
    many more.
At length Mackenzie, thirty-seven, our capital assailed,
But he was forced to flee for life when his rebellion failed.
Some Yankee sympathizers sought to aid the fallen chief
But England took the matter up in hopes to bring relief,
And eighteen forty passed a bill the union to restore;
It joined two Canadas as one, as they had been before.

Lord Sydenham, our governor, was killed by hunting fall,
In forty-four the parliament was moved to Montreal.
The malcontents mobbed Elgin there and caused him to
    resign,
And burned the House of Parliament in eighteen forty-nine.
Lord Elgin, at the Queen's request, still as our ruler stayed.
Toronto and Quebec by turns the capital was made.
At length the clergy lands were sold. Each municipal board
Received a share for public use, to spend, or loan, or hoard.

In fifty-eight, the capital took up the march again.
The Queen selected Ottawa—there may it long remain.
While times were hard and stormy times in politics still
    rougher ran,
The Yankee wars of sixty-one and Fenian raids began.
The Fenian hordes in sixty-six invaded Canada
But fled before our volunteers at Erie and Ridgeway.

George Brown, M.P., Toronto *Globe*, six years before had
    made
In parliament a motion that the Motherland be prayed
To join in one her provinces in North America.
Although it failed to carry then, it served to pave the way.

The Fenian hordes, old "rep. by pop.", the French and
    English feud
Now all contributed a share to move the multitude.

New Brunswick her troubles had, and Nova Scotia, too;
Confederate for self-defence seemed just the thing to do.
February sixty-seven, the twenty-eighth Confederation plan
Was passed in England. Loftier aims and broader life began.
This marks the close of period four and with it passed away
Old systems. Next July the first was Dominion Day.
July sixty-seven party strife was laid aside;
Four old provinces united and a new Dominion tried.

By the B.N.A. enactment, Canada was joined once more,
Nova Scotia and New Brunswick with these two made up the
    four.
Upper Canada rechristened, now Ontario became;
Lower Canada rejuvenated, in its ancient city's name.
House of Commons for the nation, federal laws to formulate;
Local houses in each province for affairs of lesser state.
Ottawa, the seat of power to confederate Canada;
Monck, Dominion Governor-General, July first, Dominion
    Day.

Thus we grew to be a nation; thus our banner was unfurled;
Thus we took a favoured station with the people of the
    world.
Riel raised an insurrection in the West in sixty-nine,
But was forced to flee for safety past the Yankee border line.
Eighteen seventy, Red River, to its interests alive,
With the name of Manitoba, joined the nation, number five.
British Columbia and Vancouver made a sixth in
    seventy-one;
Seventh came Prince Edward Island, seventy-three. The list
    was done.

Eighty-five, some Indian half-breeds in Manitoba grew afraid
That the government would seize their holdings, and an
    insurrection made.
Louis Riel became their leader, many volunteers were slain.
Riel was captured, executed, quietness returned again.
Eighty-six the C.P. Railway finished laying iron bands
From the rock-ribbed old Atlantic to Pacific's golden sands.

These have governed the Dominion in the name of England's
    queen:
Lisgar, Dufferin, the Marquis, Stanley, Aberdeen.

You who read the nation's progress from the records of the
    past,
Estimate our future greatness from the coming shadows cast.
We have lakes as broad as oceans, boundless forests, beds of
    coal,
Gold and silver, rolling rivers, Canada includes the whole—
Except a single province, Newfoundland, and she some
    future day
May claim confederation with the rest of Canada.
We have springs of healing waters, we have ever-daring rills
That circle in their journey, half a thousand happy hills.

Tell the oppressed of every nation, him who digs and him
    who delves,
If they cast their lot among us, we will make them like
    ourselves.
For the West will grow a garden and its brightness be
    unfurled
And its beauty as a byword with the people of the world.
While the East will build up shipping that will whiten every
    sea
And the boast of the Dominion shall be British liberty.